POOR MEN'S GUARDIANS

POOR MEN'S GUARDIANS

A Record of the Struggles for a Democratic
Newspaper Press, 1763–1973

by

Stanley Harrison

1974
LAWRENCE AND WISHART
London

ISBN 0 85315 301 9 (hardback)
ISBN 0 85315 308 6 (paperback)

Printed in Great Britain by
The Camelot Press Ltd., Southampton

Contents

Contents

Preface

No part of the condition of the British people lies under so deep a camouflage today as the mass media in general and the press in particular. The February 1974 election, in which press, radio and television appeared to many to be ruling the course of the poll and manipulating its outcome, raised the question of democratic representation and control in the media to front-rank political and social importance.

William Cobbett said, in a famous judgement of the state of the press during the Napoleonic wars, that it practised "that semblance of freedom by which men are most effectually enslaved". Today the semblance is cast in various guises over the whole field of mass communications, in which the daily and periodical journals of news and opinion were the first medium to develop.

The Times declared in a much-quoted editorial marking its 50,000th issue thirty years ago, that press freedom "is not a privilege of the newspapers but a fundamental liberty of the subject". Yet the press-owning millionaires still retain their despotic, irresponsible and morally obsolete power over hearts and minds.

This survey describes the struggles for press freedom, the conflict of definitions of freedom that marked it from the beginning, and the always tremendous stakes in the outcome of these struggles for the labour and progressive movement over a period of two centuries.

It will show that the liberty flag beneath which the Fleet Street baronage operates is a stolen one; and that the achievements of generations of working people's effort and sacrifice, heroic in many of its phases, require for their preservation and further advancement a more fundamentally democratic new deal in the ownership and control of the press. "Can you really run a democratic society," Mr. Tony Benn asked in 1970, "if the instruments of mass communication fail to allow people to talk to other people about their problems fairly and openly and without distortion?" Yet the modern labour movement at

official level has so far this century tamely accepted the command of
the press heights by its opponents. Little progress will be made in the
people's attempt to command the other heights of the economy and
of society—and no advances will be secure—until the power of the
Tory dictators of daily news and views is taken from them and
replaced by popular forms of ownership and management.

The screams of fear and anger with which Fleet Street greets the
smallest attempt to limit its archaic prerogative—whether by print
workers refusing to let it publish matter known to be false and slanderous or in the periodic outbursts of public criticism of its abuses of
power—clearly indicate the crucial nature of the issues involved. A
Committee on Communications has been investigating these matters
under the chairmanship of Mr. Benn since the 1973 Labour Party
Conference. It has in its hands a case requiring not piecemeal institutional reforms and legal "safeguards" against the abuse of a system,
but the scrapping of this system and its replacement by a genuine
democracy of the written and spoken word in all the media. To that
cause this book is dedicated.

STANLEY HARRISON
London
March, 1974

I

Birthright of a Briton?

> Princes and priests soon saw an enemy in the press. Type was in their opinion the most serious form that lead could take. . . . The rich classes— otherwise the conspiring classes—shut out as far as they could all knowledge of their doings, alleging that their object was to prevent the dissemination of "heresy and immorality".
>
> GEORGE JACOB HOLYOAKE

THE FIRST-BORN of the modern media began life not as an instrument of government but as a rebel. This is the story of that rebellion, its exploits and sacrifices and meaning for today. It starts in the coffee-house days of the "news-book" and ends amid the roar of the high-speed Fleet Street rotary presses. At the beginning, a newspaper "writer" communicates news and views by means of a simple craft process and at the end a vast industry using one of the most intensely social forms of production has replaced him.

Neither at the beginning nor at the end is the newspaper press placed neutrally apart from society—though at the end it endeavours by all means to wear that appearance, as do its younger companions among the media. Politics are about power, and the press is about politics, and its story interlocks at every point with the political and social changes; it is a saga of struggle against unjust laws, of assertion of the people's right to disobey them, of valour in the defence, and to a large degree, in the very creation of British democracy.

The potential of the printing press was early recognised. Church-and-state establishments fending off challenges to their supremacy saw in it a mortal danger from its first appearance. In Western Europe of the sixteenth century, the advent of the cheap new technology co-incided with the turmoil amid which the feudal order began to give way to capitalism. From the first, appearing on the scene as a slow extension of the manuscript production process, the press was kept under strict state and ecclesiastical control. During the complex to-and-fro of domestic and foreign forces that kept Tudor England perpetually on a political and military knife's edge, and throughout the seventeenth-century struggles that ended in the triumph of the landed oligarchy in 1688, succeeding authorities guarded jealously to themselves the right to oversee every expression of ideas through books, plays, poetry, political and theological tracts and scientific treatises. And under sharper scrutiny than all else came any attempt by private persons to conduct the always controversial activity of "telling it as it happened".

Every presumption to circulate *news* touched sovereignty—monarchical or republican, State or Church, Anglican or Presbyterian. For news interprets, and serves views and causes. Its circulation endangered the claim made by authority to define and fix the present no less than the past according to one doctrine or another, to establish authorised versions not only for Holy Writ but for the entire range of human experience and history. And so little had the real workings of social and economic forces begun to be understood that the authoritarian pattern persisted stubbornly on all sides and the belief in the possibility of enforcing it was slow to die.

The Tudor monarchs sought to keep full control by censorship and by forbidding presses to be set up except in the universities of Oxford and Cambridge and in London, where they could be more easily watched. The Privy Council, the Church, the London Corporation, and the Stationers Company all had the legal right to censor manuscripts. Even private letter-carrying services were suspect as possible sources of subversion, Elizabeth I and James I both essaying to stop them by royal prohibition. Earlier, an edict by Henry VIII had prohibited "certain books printed of newes of the prosperous successes of the King's Majesties arms in Scotland". It ordered them to be burnt, and imprisonment for anyone failing to do so. Not until late in the reign of James I (1603–25) was the first licence to print news issued, and this only for news from abroad, thought to be relatively harmless. In pace with the rising influence of the merchant and trading class, in the run-up to the Civil War, the appetite for news grew steadily. The first officially licensed weekly news-sheet, in appearance like a book title-page, and quarto-size, appeared in 1622. Ten years later, however, on a demarche from the Spanish Ambassador, the Court of Star Chamber of Charles I cancelled all licences. Not until after the Star

Chamber had been abolished in 1641, on the eve of the Civil War, did the first breakthrough for a degree of freedom of publication come. This was the period of the news-books, entitled Corantos, Diurnalls, Passages, Mercuries, Intelligencers, Posts, Spies and Scouts, which were well established by the time the Parliament men had Charles I executed. The Civil War produced a flood of pamphlets, petitions, and tracts. The ideas they carried to the artisans and apprentices of London, the soldiers of Cromwell's New Model Army, and all the Puritan factions, broke into new territory, extending to atheism and even to early notions of Communism.

"When I came to the Army, among Cromwell's soldiers", wrote one shocked Puritan divine, "I found a new face of things which I never dreamed of. I heard the plotting heads very hot upon that which intimated their intention to subvert both Church and State. . . . A few fiery self-conceited men among them kindled the rest and made all the noise and bustle, and carried about the Army as they pleased. . . . A great part of the mischief they did among the soldiers was by pamphlets which they abundantly dispersed. . . . And soldiers being usually dispersed in their quarters, they had such books to read when they had none to contradict them."

One of the best known of the champions of unlicensed printing, "Honest John" Lilburne, the Leveller leader and a doughty forebear of generations of fighters for press freedom to come, first struck the note of democratic defiance. On Star Chamber orders, he was pilloried, whipped through the London streets, and manacled hand and foot in prison for bringing in Puritan writings from Holland. When the mercantile and landed interests behind the revolution against Stuart despotism saw that this revolution was tending to enlarge the rights of the people and threaten those of private property they restored the censorship in 1643; Lilburne, between 1646 and 1657, when he died, was repeatedly sent to prison and once into exile for publishing sedition and malicious libel. For criticising the Earl of Manchester, he was haled before the Lords, fined £2,000, and sent to prison at their pleasure. The new authoritarians were denounced by the poet and left-republican Milton in words prophetic of the Stuart restoration to come:

"What should ye do then, should ye suppress all this flowery crop of knowledge and new light sprung up and yet springing daily in this city? Should ye set an oligarchy of twenty engrossers over it, to bring a famine upon your minds again, when we shall know nothing but what is measured to us by the bushel? Believe it, lords and commons! they who counsel ye to such suppressing do as good as bid ye suppress yourselves."

The warning was given in his pamphlet, *Areopagitica; or Speech for the Liberty of Unlicensed Printing*, written during the year in which the censorship was reimposed.

The Civil War, nevertheless, tore a wide breach in the whole conception of publishing as a closed preserve of authority. By 1648 six weekly news-books or papers were in circulation, with sales ranging from 1,000 to 3,000. Each appeared on a different day of the week, and *A Perfect Diurnall*, which appeared on Mondays, was seemingly the most popular. Rivalling it in influence from the summer of that year to the autumn of 1649 was *The Moderate*, edited by Gilbert Mabbott, chief censor during the Cromwellian army's first period of political dominance. Mabbott, the son of a Nottingham shoemaker, had been secretary to General Fairfax, and his sympathies were with the Levellers. His journal, which was the first that can be said to have belonged to a political party, owed its success to the Leveller agents who carried it far and wide to army camps and garrisons.

The Restoration in 1660 brought a special edict "For Restraining the Printing of New Books and Pamphlets of News without leave". Twelve judges ruled that it was criminal at common law to publish any public news, true or false, without the king's licence. A Surveyor of the Press, Sir Roger L'Estrange, was appointed, and under his regime the London printer John Twyn went to the gallows—and the still customary disembowelling and quartering—for publishing an unlicensed work of republican sentiment. Despite such excesses, however, Star Chamber powers over publishing could no more be permanently restored than could the old despotism; the controls were gradually eased as the working compromise reached between the Crown and the loose and shifting coalition of landed and mercantile interests that had made the Revolution settled down. The year 1695 brought the event which according to most schoolbook history marks the foundation of the free press, when the House of Commons allowed the licensing laws to lapse. The London daily newspaper, the provincial weekly, and the periodical of opinion—the three main departments of the press from that day to this—all established themselves in the four following decades. The first daily newspaper, the *Daily Courant*, appeared in

1702, followed by the *Post* (1719), the *Journal* (1720) and the *Advertiser* (1730).

The ending of the pre-censorship in 1695 drew a line under one of the keenest issues that had arisen out of the battles of the Revolution. It formed one item in that general settlement of 1688—called the Glorious Revolution by its beneficiaries—which fixed the main lines on which political power would be exercised for the next century and a half, secured the home base of the merchant capitalists, and turned the huge energies liberated by the Revolution into paths of world trade and empire.

The great glorifier of the not so glorious compromise of 1688, the Whig historian Macaulay, thought that the 1695 decision did "more for liberty and civilisation than the Great Charter or the Bill of Rights". A former editor of *The Times*, Henry Wickham Steed, pronounced in our century that "from that moment the freedom of the press was legally established in England, and with it a chance for the press worthily to discharge its functions. Experience of reaction under Charles II and James II had convinced a majority of the House of Commons that the dangers of freedom to print and to comment upon news could not outweigh the public advantages of such freedom. On the whole and despite some setbacks and lapses this conviction has governed English public life ever since."

In truth, the ending of pre-censorship marked not an end but a beginning. All the main battles—against legislation to make newspapers prohibitively dear, countless prosecutions for sedition, criminal libel and blasphemy, involving sentences of imprisonment and transportation totalling hundreds of years—still lay ahead. The Chartist, George Jacob Holyoake, recalled in his old age what really followed the 1695 decision. "The governing classes," he said, "were terrified at the apparition of the wilful little printing press." What he called "the Freed Press Terror", meaning the terror inspired in the upper orders, went on in his reckoning for 142 years after the Commons decision. "A free press was never a terror to the people—it was their hope. It was the governing classes who were under alarm."

In the reign of George III (1760–1820), Holyoake recalled,

"Every editor being assumed to be a criminally disposed person and naturally inclined to blasphemy and sedition had to enter into sureties. Every person possessing a printing-press or types for printing and every type-founder was ordered to give notice to the Clerk of the Peace. Every person selling type was ordered to give an account of all persons to whom they were sold. Every person who printed anything also had to keep a copy of the matter printed and write on it the name and abode of the person who employed him to print it. The printer was treated as an enemy of the State, and compelled to become an informer."

This attitude to a free press as incipient treason, and the wish to limit its circulation and influence, took legislative shape very quickly after the 1695 change in the Act that generations of democrats were to know and hate simply as the "Tenth of Anne". This Act of 1712 levied stamp duties on paper, newspapers, pamphlets and advertisements, as well as linens, silks, calicoes, and soap. News-sheets thereafter shuttled between publisher and Stamp Office, where each sheet was stamped by hand. By 1815 the stamp had risen to 4*d*. on newspapers, 15*d*. on almanacs, 3*s*. 6*d*. on any advertisement in any periodical and 3*s*. on each edition of pamphlets of up to 28 parts or books issued in periodical parts. Newspapers of one large folded sheet cost 7*d*., at a time when wages ranged from 9*s*. to 12*s*. for a labourer to 22*s*. to 27*s*. for a skilled London compositor. A newspaper priced in the same relation to wages in 1974 would cost well over £2 a copy.

If the stamp duty checked newspaper circulations, the libel laws provided the main curb on their contents. Most far-reaching was the law which made it a misdemeanor—involving an appearance before the magistrates—to publish anything that might in the opinion of the authorities lead to a breach of the peace. More serious was the common law on criminal libel. Any publication was a seditious libel if it tended to bring into hatred or contempt the King, the Government, or the constitution of the United Kingdom, or to excite His Majesty's subjects to attempt, otherwise than by lawful means, the alteration of any matter in Church or State by law established.

"It was thus criminal to point out any defects in the Constitution or any errors on the part of the Government, if disaffection might thereby be caused. It is uncertain whether the Press had any legal freedom whatever to criticise the authorities."*

Whether it was to have any such freedom was precisely the question over which the century's great set-piece battle involving the press was fought, in the famous "Wilkes and Liberty" agitation. The full signi-

* W. H. Wickwar, *The Struggles for the Freedom of the Press, 1819-1832*, pp. 26-27.

ficance of this battle cannot be grasped unless we first look briefly at
the governing establishment that emerged from the 1688 settlement,
the ruling set that the Chartist editor Bronterre O'Brien was later to
call the "mixed mongrel aristocracy of landowners and money-
mongers".

Sir Robert Walpole, leader of the Whig group, conducted Parliament and government for twenty years as a business, in which it was
said that the price of a seat in the House of Commons was better known
than the price of a horse.*

Successive Whig and Tory administrations presided over that
enormous process of wealth accumulation from many sources out of
which industrial capitalism and the factory system were born. Conducted under the flag of *defending* the sacred rights of property, it was
in reality a sustained war of conquest against the property and other
rights of the mass of the population. The Enclosure Acts that destroyed
small husbandry by appropriating millions of acres to the already
wealthy, the various measures that pauperised Ireland and depopu-
lated Scotland, the ever-more corrupt Parliament of pocket and rotten
boroughs, and the jobs-sale system in Army, Navy, Church and
administration formed the main content of politics at home. Abroad,
almost uninterrupted wars of conquest and loot in North America,
India and the West Indies, and above all the slave trade carrying
300,000 Africans a year over the Atlantic at an annual estimated
profit of £300,000 a year to Liverpool alone, contributed to the same
end.

Below these property-politics lay the motley "inferior sort of
people"—not yet a class conscious of its identity but a seething mass
constantly erupting in riots and commotions that kept the ruling
establishment in constant, uncomprehending dread. Its home was the
older urban centres, and above all the capital, to which all the dis-
possessed drifted, to fall into a sump of poverty, squalor and vice:

* The heart of the corruption lay in the borough representation in Parliament.
Some boroughs were owned by narrow councils of hereditary burgesses, others
by a lord or man of wealth, still others by two or more proprietors, and a further
large group by the Crown. Manchester, Leeds and other big towns had no
member. Totnes had 78 voters at the end of George III's reign, Bodmin 36,
Rye 14 and Winchelsea 7. The "accursed hill" of Old Sarum contained only a
thornbush. The county shire representatives were elected on a freeholder franchise embracing the gentry and larger farmers. Scotland was one shire and Wales
another, each returning two members.

cottagers ruined by enclosures of the common lands, cast-off soldiers and sailors, failed shopkeepers and small farmers, orphans, paupers and all manner of outcasts. They lived cheek-by-jowl with the merchants, war contractors, and stock jobbers, the landed wealthy in their town houses, the court and the Parliament. They linked up with the artisans and small masters, journeymen, labourers and apprentices to form the constantly swelling "mobility" or mob.

The "Freed Press Terror" that gripped the upper orders sprang from this situation; cheap news-sheets and sedition were bed-fellows. Prosecutions and stamp duty provided two curbs. A third was to take the fledgling press into the embrace of the system of corruption and patronage that controlled Parliament and the rest of public life. A combination of government subsidies—Walpole spent £50,000 on bribes to newspapers—and threats of prosecution kept the news press under uneasy control.

The Wilkes affair, which may be seen as a kind of dress rehearsal for later contests, involved most of the interests that were to fight over the press for the following century. They were the court and aristocracy, the middle class already aspiring to a share in power, and, as continual chorus to the action and occasional participant, the London "mob" and its counterparts in other cities and towns.

Over the eleven years of the Wilkes agitation a Radical movement that challenged both the older political parties of Whigs and Tories was born, and in its wake the outcast orders began to enter political life. The press question, around which the agitation principally turned, was raised to the top political importance which it was always to occupy afterwards.

The affair began at the heart of a first-class crisis of the administration. A king's party, built up in the first years of George III's reign by the extended and systematised sale of parliamentary seats and of paid offices of all kinds, turned the tables on the long-established Whig borough-monger gang when it pushed William Pitt the Elder out of office and replaced him with the Earl of Bute.

Whigs of every colour clung to a political pedigree derived from the "Good Old Cause" of the English Revolution, the popular anti-Catholic struggle to save England from "Popery and Wooden Shoes", the 1688 settlement, and their success in defeating the Jacobite movement which had tried in the first half of the eighteenth century to restore the Stuart monarchy with the aid of Catholic foreign powers.

Among the ousted Whig grandees little enough remained of the democratic ideas and egalitarian feelings (Puritan-style, under God) which the Revolution had generated and to which it owed its victory. But popular memories of the long fight for freedom remained strong and largely dictated the style and idiom in which the Whigs—and later the "king's men" too—thought best to present what "public image" they deemed it necessary to have.

As they saw the king's coup coming, some of the Whigs began to revive their public appeals to the liberty legend. In the City of London, their stronghold, there was vexation over what the City saw as the too soft terms on which the new government planned to conclude Britain's greatest war of the century with France and Spain over colonies. As early as March 1761, the Elder Pitt's chief supporter in the City, William Beckford, denounced in an election address the importance accorded to the "little pitiful borough", firing the City's first shot in the campaign for a reform of Parliament. Among the Whigs much nostalgia now began to be expressed for the great old days, and it was these fashionable new feelings which were vented in the opening number of the weekly newspaper *The North Briton*, launched by John Wilkes on June 6, 1762.

"The liberty of the press is the birthright of a BRITON, and is justly esteemed the firmest bulwark of the liberties of this country," the paper declared. The words were scarcely an accurate description of the real status of the press at that moment: rather they revived an ideal and raised a banner, beneath which John Wilkes assailed the upstart king's administration, employing all the scurrility normal both in Opposition and pro-administration news-sheets and pamphlets of the time. Lord Bute's Scottish nationality and his rumoured affair with the king's mother were two of his targets. The paper's name itself was chosen to deride Bute, who was giving sinecure posts to his Scottish friends and relations and places to many others, and was intended also as a retort to a government-run weekly paper, *The Briton*, edited by novelist Tobias Smollett.

John Wilkes, son of a wealthy distiller, a rake and libertine in the usual manner of the juvenile wealthy of his day, but also a talented orator and wit, was a political crony of Pitt and his group. The style of the campaign that he launched in *The North Briton* embarrassed many of the grand Whig aristocrats, including Pitt himself and his brother-in-law Earl Temple who had financed the journal. It proved too useful to them, however, both as a defender of their own record in office and as a goad in the side of the king's party, for it to be publicly disowned.

On April 19, 1763, the king's speech at the opening of Parliament commented on the peace terms then being discussed in Paris. Four days later appeared Wilkes' ever-celebrated *No. 45*. It opened with the proposition—still then controversial—that the king's speech had always been considered by Parliament and public as the speech of the minister. It regretted that "a prince of so many great and admirable qualities, whom England truly reveres, can be brought to give the sanction of his sacred name to the most odious measures and the most unjustifiable public declarations from a throne ever renowned for truth, honour and an unsullied virtue".

It was in vain, Wilkes said, for the king's speech to preach up the "spirit of concord and that obedience to the laws which is essential to good order". The government had sent the "spirit of discord" through the land. "I will prophesy that it will never be extinguished, but by the extinction of their power. . . . A nation as sensible as the English, will see that a *spirit of concord*, when they are oppressed, means a tame submission to injury, and that a *spirit of liberty* ought then to arrive, and I am sure ever will, in proportion to the weight of the grievance they feel."

To the government the words appeared as a heaven-sent chance to nail Wilkes for sedition and to smear the opposition leaders in whose interest he was acting. George Grenville, who had replaced Bute as head of the administration a fortnight before *No. 45* was published, summoned the Solicitor to the Treasury, Philip Carteret Webb,* to consultations on the following day. With the agreement of the law officers of the Crown, a general (naming no names) warrant was issued for the arrest of the authors, printers and publishers of "a seditious and treasonable paper, *The North Briton*".

Wilkes had been a member of the House for six years, sitting for the pocket borough of Aylesbury. The law officers decided that his immunity from arrest as an MP did not cover "the publication of a libel, being a breach of the peace". Four Messengers were despatched

* His twentieth-century successor in the post was employed by the Tory government in 1972 to save it from the consequences of a rash arrest of London dockers—"the Pentonville Five"—in the course of its attempt to enforce the anti-union Industrial Relations Act.

to take him into custody, and he was lodged in the Tower. On May 3 he was taken by coach to Westminster Hall, where a huge audience composed of supporters from the City cheered his speech declaring that the liberty of an Englishman "should not be sported away with impunity". He left court amid loud cries of "Liberty, liberty, Wilkes for ever". When he appeared again in court three days later, he made another ringing pronouncement: "My lords, the liberty of all peers and gentlemen and, what touches me more sensibly, that of all the middling and inferior set of people, who stand most in need of protection, is in my case this day to be finally decided upon a question of such importance as to determine at once whether English Liberty shall be a reality or a shadow." After legal argument, Chief Justice Pratt rejected the prosecution argument that a libel was an "actual breach of the peace", upheld Wilkes' immunity from arrest, and discharged him, to the accompaniment of another demonstration in court.

In the next round, Wilkes went over to the attack. At his prompting the four dozen printers, compositors, proof-readers and booksellers who had been seized under the general warrant sued for damages and were awarded sums ranging from £100 to £400. Wilkes himself, with a pending damages claim thought likely among his City friends to bring him £20,000, went off to Paris. In the two months he was away, the government primed a case intended to destroy him personally and end the support that he was still getting from some of the Whig notables.

The government obtained a proof-copy of part of an *Essay on Woman* which had been set up at a private press established by Wilkes before his departure. The House of Lords condemned it unanimously as a "most scandalous, obscene and impious libel" and reported the behaviour of the Member for Aylesbury to the Commons.

This assembly, by 273 votes to 111, had already declared *No. 45* to be "a false, scandalous and seditious libel" and ordered it to be burnt by the hangman at the Royal Exchange. But *No. 45* was not for burning. When the cold December day appointed for the ceremony came, several hundred people were waiting for the sheriffs at the entrance to Cornhill. They chased the fire party away, rescued *The North Briton* from the bonfire, and according to legend extinguished the flames by pissing on them.

In other respects, however, the heat was on for Wilkes. In mid-November he had been seriously wounded in a duel—suspected at the time to have been an arranged attempt to kill him—with a parliamentary opponent, Samuel Martin, MP. His backers were defaulting. Treasury spies shadowed his movements. On Christmas Eve he took the post-chaise to Dover and slipped across to France. Parliament expelled him on January 20 during his absence and a month later the Court of King's Bench found him guilty both on the *Essay on Woman* charge and on a charge of republishing *No. 45* at his private press. In November the court pronounced him an outlaw for failing to appear to a writ for his arrest.

Wilkes decided—he could do little else—to stay abroad, and the court party sighed with relief. The *Annual Register* declared that the "ruin of that unfortunate gentleman" was complete. But something that could not be buried had happened. That the *No. 45* affair was not forgotten was abundantly proved when its hero returned to London in February 1768 to make a still more nationally electrifying appearance on the political scene. On March 28 he was returned as MP for Middlesex in the general election, inflicting a defeat on the entire pocket-borough establishment. London erupted with joy and the tumultuous celebrations lasted for two days.

Organised supporters, including a 6,000-strong contingent of Spitalfields weavers, paraded the streets and forced every carriage to show either Wilkes' colours ("true blue") or chalk their vehicle with the slogan "Wilkes and Liberty" or "*No. 45*". The constables of London and Middlesex could not cope and the London train-bands would not turn out to face the people. Citizens were forced to light up their windows at night in celebration and every door from Temple Bar to Hyde Park Corner was reported to have been chalked with "*No. 45*". Horace Walpole, the diarist, recalled in his *Memoirs* that the Austrian Ambassador was dragged from his coach and had the magic number chalked on the soles of his boots. In the fashionable quarters there was an orgy of window smashing. Troops were placed in readiness, but the government did not dare use them; there were only six arrests and three convictions in the two days of celebration.

When Wilkes surrendered to the authorities to test the question of his outlawry, the Londoners stopped the coach that was taking him to prison and dragged it through Westminster and the City shouting "Wilkes and Liberty". On May 10 a huge crowd gathered in St. Georges' Fields expecting to see their leader freed on bail to attend the House of Commons; troops fired several volleys causing eleven deaths. Three of the military chased a demonstrator and, thinking they had found him, killed a farmer working in an outhouse. The massacre brought the government close to open battle with the populace, but it drew back from a conflict beyond its means. When Wilkes' outlawry came up in court on June 8, 1768, Lord Mansfield eased the tension by quashing the sentence on a technicality. Ten days later, however, the same judge sent Wilkes to prison for 22 months for his various misdemeanours.

Wilkes then asked Parliament to consider the question of privilege involved in the imprisonment of an MP. The answer of the House was to expel him again, on February 3, 1769, for an alleged slander on the Secretary of State in connection with the slaughter on May 10. Wilkes was thereupon re-elected by Middlesex three times in succession, on February 16, March 16, and April 13. The House re-expelled him within 24 hours on the first two occasions, and on the third resolved that the defeated government candidate, Henry Luttrell, has been duly elected. No demonstration so flagrant of the unrepresentative character of Parliament had previously been given. Defiance of the electors could scarcely go further. The affair was widely seen as a final intolerable provocation by the court and the borough-managers and it firmly launched the question of parliamentary reform as a public issue.

A cold draught from outside began to blow through the corridors of propertied privilege at Westminster. To shut it out, the Commons decided to stop the reporting in the press of its debates. This practice was technically illegal, but had long been tolerated. The debates were at this stage overwhelmingly the main source of news for the papers and the attempt to stop their publication aimed a body-blow at the press. In March 1771 the Commons summoned two printers to attend and explain their conduct after they had reported debates. Wilkes—who had been released from prison in the previous year and was now a City alderman—told them not to obey the summons, and when they were brought before him in his aldermanic capacity ruled that they were guilty of no offence known to the law and that proclamations by the House of Commons could not make an innocent act illegal. The enraged House sent Messengers to arrest the printers, but the Mansion House magistrates—Lord Mayor Crosby and Aldermen Wilkes and Oliver—promptly ordered the arrest of one of the Messengers. When the Commons then ordered the three City leaders to appear before it, Wilkes refused to attend except as Member for Middlesex. And it was then that the king threw in his hand, declaring that he would have "no more to do with that devil Wilkes". The House made a ludicrous attempt to save face by ordering the devil to appear before it in person on April 8—and immediately adjourning its proceedings until April 9.

The Commons motion to prevent the reporting of its debates said it was "a high indignity and a notorious breach of the privilege of this House for any news-writer . . . to presume to give any account of the debates". George III had demanded of his first minister, Lord North, that the "strange and lawless" publishing of the august assembly's proceedings should be stopped, but in such a way as to avoid exciting the minds of the vulgar.

One of the printers, writing in the *Middlesex Journal, or Chronicle of Liberty*, founded in 1769 to back Wilkes' parliamentary election campaign, had declared that the existing Parliament was "a mere emanation of the royal power made use of to scourge the people". Publication of debates, he urged, would enable the voters to "distinguish between the true patriot and the vile impostor".

The resolution that the printers be summoned to the bar of the House, there to kneel in repentance, was moved by George Onslow, MP, called "little cocking George" because of his attachment to cock-fighting. He complained that their journals had presented him sometimes as an idiot, sometimes as a villain, and sometimes as both. Onslow had certainly shown himself a thorough king's man and zealot for privilege. Once he had seized a milkman who was posting up in Bond Street a handbill reprint of Oliver Cromwell's speech dissolving the Long Parliament, and the Commons had sent the man to Newgate jail.

While the fate of Crosby and Oliver—who were also MPs—was debated, large crowds gathered daily outside the Commons, abusing the ministers, pelting some with filth from the gutter, dragging Lord North from his carriage—he barely escaped with his life—wrecking the carriage and seizing his hat, to be sold later in sixpenny fragments. Eventually the pair went to the Tower for six weeks, their chieftain Wilkes declaring that the parliamentary prostitutes had sent "the first magistrate of the greatest city in the universe to a garrisoned prison for his intrepidity in protecting the citizens under his care from ruffians". On May 8, 1771, Parliament rose for the summer recess and the MPs had to be set free. As they emerged, the Hon. Artillery Company fired a 21-gun salute on Tower Hill. Fifty-three City gentlemen escorted the heroes to the Mansion House in their carriages, to the pealing of bells, and London again celebrated far into the night with fireworks and toastings of "Crosby, Oliver, Wilkes, and Liberty of the Press".* Three years later Wilkes, by then Lord Mayor of London, was returned unopposed for Middlesex at a general election and quietly allowed to take his seat.

The epic of English liberty of which he was the centre raised the basic issues of freedom of the press and the respective rights of Parliament and people, and the questions merged with each other from his time onward. Underpinning Wilkes' public performance, with a subterranean rumour of battles to come, there stirred the early, half-blind movement towards political activity of the workers for wages. Wilkes drew his support scarcely at all from MPs, a good deal from merchant princes of the City, and a great deal more from large numbers of the middling and small tradesmen.† But in the streets the Wilkesite muscle power came overwhelmingly from the "lower orders of the people" including a significant number and variety of wage-workers. Watermen and merchant seamen, hatters and hat-dyers, tailors and glass-grinders and many more trades were involved in the struggle in one active fashion or another.

In the London of the seventeen-sixties and seventies, the workers as a separate interest—distinct from the suffering urban poor who had always existed—began to emerge into view. Years of distress caused by dear wheat and corn were marked by bitter trade disputes. The silk weavers of Spitalfields, in one of the city's main industries, rioted and clashed with their employers in 1767 over wages and conditions of work.

Such was the tension—in this quarter of the city that was a byword for poverty and distress and was for long to provide one of the bases of the working-class Radical movement in the capital—that orders were given for a "proper number of soldiers to be marched from the

---

* Reporting of debates continued without further hindrance. Not, however, until 1971, just 200 years after these dramatic events, was the Commons motion prohibiting it formally renounced by the House of Commons.

† G. Rude, in *Wilkes and Liberty*, has shown that the bulk of Wilkes' support in Middlesex came from the smaller freeholders (40s. to £10 a year) among the electors in this borough with the widest suffrage in the country.

Tower for the support and assistance of the magistrates when required of them".*

Partly through their own organisation and partly with the help of the Wilkesite Lord Mayor of London, the Spitalfields weavers in 1773 obtained an Act regulating their wages and conditions, which in bad times had been falling to as little as 10s. a week.

The coal-heavers of East London also made a brief appearance on the margin of the Parliament versus People engagement. When they attacked a public house owned by an employer they shouted "Wilkes and Liberty—and coal-heavers for ever". And demonstrators at the House of Lords in May 1768 accompanied their chants of "Wilkes and Liberty" with shouts of "It was as well to be hanged as starved". The press reported in April 1772 that "letters from almost every part of the Kingdom bring melancholy accounts of the distress of the poor and of their readiness to rise and do mischief".†

This was the menace that underlay all the Wilkes campaigns and helped to defeat the Crown and the MPs. Of his parliamentary Whig friends who were "playing the popular engines"—in a nice phrase used at the time—many were only lukewarm supporters from the start and most deserted him quickly as the affair threatened their privileges and drew the dreaded "mob" into the arena. In the country, however, the reform movement grew rapidly; a petition campaign in 1769–70 brought support for reform from the freeholders and freemen of some eighteen counties and a dozen boroughs. Sixty thousand electors signed petitions taken round the country by Wilkes' supporters on tours to speak at public meetings which were themselves an innovation. A section of the Whigs, too, began to press for reform. The Bill of Rights Society formed among Wilkes' supporters, and the persistent campaigning of the Yorkshire reformer Major John Cartwright, launched the cause in organised form. In his pamphlet *Take Your Choice*, published in 1776, Major Cartwright argued the case for annual parliaments, equal electoral districts, payment of members and adult manhood suffrage. In 1776 Wilkes introduced a Reform Bill. From Wilkes' day on, the movement to democratise the constitution and the defence of freedom of press and speech proceeded always as a twin cause. Radicalism—the name under which its various trends came to be known—developed in a complex fashion. It involved both the industrialising bourgeoisie, at odds with oligarchs of both the Whig

* Rude, op. cit., p. 39.   † Rude, op. cit., p. 188.

and the Tory brand, various elements of the "middling people" in town and country, the long-established class of artisans, small masters and journeymen in the old towns, and the operatives in the new factory towns.

In the years between Wilkes and the French Revolution of 1789 the middle class gave the movement its leaders and set the tone, drawing many workers along with it. The upheaval in France, bringing democratic ideas and demands that were a hundred-fold magnification of those that had inspired England's seventeenth-century Revolution, disrupted the movement stemming from the Wilkes agitation: it alienated the middle class from Radicalism and caused the propertied of every rank and kind to make common cause against revolutionary France and the lower orders in Britain fired by the French example.

A lengthy break in the "respectable" Radical tradition occurred. It was this break that helped later Whig and Liberal parliamentary radicals to present the Wilkes years as a rogue episode that merely ruffled the smooth waters of Westminster, and to minimise the importance of the repeated rude intrusions of the common people into the closed preserve of government. Historians anxious to write down the part played by direct action outside the House and to place the centre of gravity of politics firmly within the successive "structures" of the two-party system in Parliament have often followed this tradition. But the eleven years of turmoil over Wilkes were no sideshow. Certainly, the working population, and labouring London in particular, never saw them in that light, but always as their own cause: they gave new meaning to the old liberty legend and prepared the way for a kind of commotion quite different from the typical eighteenth-century rioting over a dozen diverse *symptoms* of social and economic distress. From the Wilkes days onward a militant wing of the parliamentary reform movement and of every Radical cause existed continuously. Its activities were inextricably linked with the formation of the working class and its political movements. With the French Revolution, the wars against Napoleon and their aftermath, came struggles around Wilkes' "Birthright of a Briton" that laid the real foundations for press freedom.

2

Hog's Wash and Botany Bay

Two things the jury must attend to which require no proof. First that the British constitution is the best that ever was since the creation of the world, and it is not possible to make it better. The next is that there was a spirit of sedition in the country last winter which made every good man uneasy. . . . Yet Mr Muir had at that time gone among the ignorant country people making them forget their work, and told them that a Reform was absolutely necessary for preserving their liberty, which if it were not for him they would never have thought was in danger. . . . Mr Muir might have known that no attention could be paid to such a rabble [of ignorant weavers]. What right had they to representation? A government in every country should be just like a corporation and in this country it is made up of landed interests who alone have a right to be represented.

> LORD BRAXFIELD, judge at the trial of the Scottish reformer Thomas Muir, sent for fourteen years to the penal colony of Botany Bay in 1792.

A GREATER EVENT than the English Revolution whose ideas were stirring again in the seventeen-seventies and eighties burst on Britain as these years ended. In no country of Europe did the upheaval in France have more immediate, deep and long-lasting consequences. The democratic press commenced in this cauldron.

Quite rapidly, too, it acquired a working-class tone. The explosion of advanced ideas that accompanied the storming of the Bastille and overthrow of the feudal order in France coincided in Britain—as nowhere else—with the most critical years of a capitalist industrialisation that brought a savage transformation of life for working people. The French cult of man—"liberty, equality and fraternity"—struck with the force of revelation England's lower orders who felt themselves at bay against the advancing reign of property in all its guises. It formed the ideas of those whom Holyoake called the "men of thought and action" on the popular side, and coloured the ideas of almost two generations before the workers developed in Chartism their first independent political movement on a national scale. In

Britain the earliest militants on the labour side were Jacobins before they were Socialists, revolutionaries before they were trade unionists. Ranged against them stood a ruling coalition headed by the multi-acred aristocracy and the early war-contractor and factory-owning capitalists, and bonded together by a shared fear of the people. This coalition was at war with France for over a quarter of a century, apart from a brief interval in 1801–3. In France and most of Europe in these years, the Revolution destroyed or undermined numerous obsolete feudal institutions, while the wars impoverished the economies and delayed industrialisation. The counter-revolution of the monarchical *ancien regime* arrived in force only in the baggage-trains of the armies that defeated Napoleon. In Britain, however, counter-revolution was on a war footing with both revolutionary France and its sympathisers in England, Scotland and Ireland from within a very few years after 1789.

The first response of the democratic nation in England to the miracle of liberty in France was a conviction that it would usher in the happiness of mankind. Wordsworth's salute to "France standing at the top of golden hours, / And human nature seeming born again. / . . . Bliss was it in that dawn to be alive, / But to be young was very heaven", is remembered as the most glowing expression of this hope, but it pervaded the minds of the entire "class of 1789" in British politics, literature and art. The belief fused immediately with the native English reform movement.

In Parliament a progressive group of the Whigs, born out of the Wilkes agitation and the movement of support for the American War of Independence, at first saw France's 1789 as a re-enactment of England's seventeenth-century struggles. Outside Parliament, middle-class enthusiasts joined the Society for Constitutional Information, a dining club of friends of parliamentary reform which had existed since 1780, and was revived two years after the French Revolution by Horne Tooke, a one-time lieutenant of Wilkes. Others rallied to the Friends of the People, a new foundation of similar political complexion. But it was the men who had appeared mainly on the side-lines in the Wilkes battles, the artisans and small masters, who responded to the Revolution with forms of action that rapidly placed the respectable liberty-diners in the shade. Eight working men met at London's Bell Tavern in January 1792 and set up the London Corresponding Society. The subscription was a penny a week (the Constitutional Society's was five guineas), the society reached a membership of 3,000 by the year's end, and Sheffield, Norwich, Nottingham and other towns where skilled trades had a long tradition of association rapidly developed similar societies. It was at this working men's end of Radicalism that there now began to flow the stream of news-pamphlets and news-sheets, handbills and embryonic newspapers that was to grow into a torrent over the next half-century. The flow originated mainly in centres where artisan communities offered the booksellers a ready audience—with *Hog's Wash*, *The Tribune* and *The Moral and Political Magazine*, associated with the Corresponding Society in London, *The Patriot* and *The Sheffield Iris* in Sheffield, *The Cabinet* in Norwich, *The Cambridge Intelligencer* and several more. In Britain the rebel press and the democratic movement were born at one birth.

The Corresponding Society and its associated bodies were suppressed in a very few years—but not before they had served as a school for the writers and sellers of the Radical press who are the ancestry, in an unbroken tradition, of the modern labour, trade union and progressive movement.

The weavers and watchmakers, carpenters and shoemakers, compositors and cabinet makers of the society campaigned for universal suffrage and annual parliaments, and their main activities were pamphleteering and public meetings. The government, preparing for war on France, where the Jacobin left wing of the Revolution was in the ascendant, struck back hard. Late in 1792 a campaign of prosecutions against printers, publishers and sellers of seditious literature was set on foot; in 1792-3 there were as many state trials for sedition as there had been in the preceding century.

Early in 1792 the Scottish Jacobins held a convention in Edinburgh. It was for reading to this assembly an address from the United Irishmen—already then preparing for their revolt in 1798—and for recommending the works of Tom Paine, that the leading Scottish reformer Thomas Muir was transported to Botany Bay. In May 1793 seven leading members of the LCS and six of the Constitutional Society were arrested. The LCS leader, Thomas Hardy, shoemaker, the first to be sent for trial, was acquitted by a Middlesex jury* and the govern-

---

* In the preceding year Charles James Fox's Libel Act had given juries important new powers. Previously they had only been able to decide on certain questions of fact. The Act placed with them the decision on whether a libel had actually been committed. Almost every libel case affecting the press became a political battle in consequence of this enactment.

ment case collapsed. But this was the highwater mark. Afterwards the LCS began to lose influence—rapidly when France headed towards the Napoleonic autocracy and Wordsworth's "blissful dawn" turned sour for most of the early admirers of the French example.

In July 1797, amid panic over naval mutinies at Spithead and the Nore, an Act was passed completely prohibiting "all corresponding societies of any city, town or place". It effectively barred the road to any organisation of a *national* party for reform. Two years later the working men's efforts to organise in defence of wages received a heavy blow when Parliament rushed through the Combination Acts making trade unions illegal.

In the decade that it took the government to get the better of English Jacobinism, the advocacy not merely of parliamentary reform but of any change whatsoever—as Lord Braxfield's judgement in the Muir case* and hundreds more by magistrates throughout the country made clear—became a criminal act. The people, in words used by the Bishop of Rochester, had "nothing to do with the laws but to obey them".

This proposition echoed crudely the main idea expressed in *Reflections on the French Revolution* published by the turncoat Whig reformer Edmund Burke in 1792. This book, which tried to place the constitution beyond the impious reach of the populace, provided the propertied classes with a new political bible. Burke presented the constitution as part of a complex natural order with which "the swinish multitude" must not be permitted to meddle. The famous phrase provoked the freeborn Englishman to long-lasting rage which was expressed in tracts and periodicals with titles like *Hog's Wash*, *Pig's Meat* and *Mast and Acorns*, and was kept burning for decades by Radicals of every hue. A 1793 *Address to the Hon. Edmund Burke from the Swinish Multitude* said: "Whilst ye are . . . gorging yourselves at troughs filled with the daintiest wash; we, with our numerous train of *porkers*, are employed, from the rising to the setting sun, to obtain the means of subsistence by picking up a few acorns."†

Hog's Wash (1793–4), later called *Politics for the People*, was published

---

* When another of the accused at the Scottish reformers' trial pointed out to the learned judge that Jesus Christ, too, was a reformer Braxfield chuckled from the bench: "Muckle he made o' that: he was hanget."

† Quoted by E. P. Thompson, *The Making of the English Working Class*, p. 98, as an example of the unending popular ripostes to Burke's "epochal indiscretion".

by the intrepid Daniel Isaac Easton, whom the government found the
most incorrigible of all the political booksellers. In this first year of
the war, it kept up a withering fire on "the war of combined kings
against the people of France . . . a war of the most *diabolical* kind". It
pledged itself to keep up the struggle for parliamentary reform
"though we follow our brethren in the same glorious cause to BOTANY
BAY". By 1812 Eaton had been prosecuted seven times and served
three years of imprisonment for his printing activities.

Burke's *Reflections* also elicited a reply which provided the workers
at the outset of their activity as a class with a weapon, an education,
and a morale. Tom Paine's world-shaker, *The Rights of Man*, sold
200,000 copies in three years. Although it was banned almost at once,
cheap editions continued to be sold after the author had declared that
he wished to make no profit from the work and anyone who chose to
ask for leave to reprint it would be given permission to so so. One and
a half million copies had probably been sold by 1809, including sales in
Europe and a vast circulation in Ireland. No single work in all the
years up to the *Communist Manifesto* published in 1848 was to have so
pervading an influence. At Hardy's trial, the prosecution claimed that
"every cutler in Sheffield" had a copy. The work went into every
town and village, often to take its place as an authority for belief and
action besides the Bible and Bunyan's *Pilgrim's Progress*. It had a particularly enormous progeny in the periodical press.

Born in Thetford in Norfolk in 1737 of a Quaker family, Tom
Paine emigrated to America shortly before the English colonies rose
in revolt. As publicist and soldier he took a leading part in that struggle;
his pamphlet *Common Sense* contained the first open demand that
independence should be the aim of the colonists and he is credited with
having made the first draft of the American Declaration of Independence. He returned to England two years before the French
Revolution and the first part of *The Rights of Man* appeared in 1791,
followed by the second part a year later. To Burke's hymn to the
English Constitution, Paine retorted that there was no such thing,
but only a kind of "Political Popery". "Government by precedent,
without any regard for the principle of the precedent is one of the
vilest systems that can be set up." All governments, except the revolutionary regimes in France and America, were based on conquest and
superstition. And "as revolutions have begun . . . it is natural to expect
that other revolutions will follow . . . they may be considered as the

Order of the Day". Paine covered kings, lords and bishops with ridicule and contempt. He declared: "All hereditary government is in its nature tyranny.... To inherit a government is to inherit the people as though they were flocks and herds."

To Burke's argument that the settlement of 1688 had established the form of the Constitution for ever, binding successive ages, he replied that the rulers of that day might as well have passed an Act to enable themselves to live for ever. He went further than the contempt for the aristocracy, which had existed since Puritan times and, indeed, in still living popular legend, traced all its crimes back to the original sin of the Norman Conquest which had enslaved the people's free Anglo-Saxon forbears. Paine conveyed, too, the new feeling that revolution had its own momentum that could not be resisted. In the second part of his book he outlined some of the changes that a representative system of government might make: cuts in military and government expenditure; a graduated income tax out of which the plight of the poor would be eased; family allowances; old age pensions as a matter of right; marriage and maternity benefits; and a humane system of caring for society's outcasts to replace the hated Poor Laws. The scheme, in the second part's celebrated fifth chapter, has been called the first sketch for a Labour programme of government. Going beyond the devastating criticism of monarchical governments whose objects were "trade, plunder and revenue" and whose methods were human butchery, it envisaged a coming victory for the victims of this system. Paine contrasted this emerging hope with the negative prospects held out by all earlier revolutions, which "had nothing in them that interested the bulk of mankind. They extended only to a change of persons and measures but not of principles, and rose or fell among the common transactions of the moment." Neither philosopher nor economist, he evolved no theory of social development, still less of Socialism. But he stormed Burke's property Bastille. He gave hope to the oppressed poor and made them combative. As he was awaiting trial for sedition in 1792 he declared: "When the rich plunder the poor of his rights, it becomes an example to the poor to plunder the rich of his property."

For this trial, which was to be before a special jury hand-picked by the Crown, Paine did not wait. At the urging of friends, he took the Wilkes road to Dover and France. At the trial in his absence, *The Rights of Man* was condemned as a seditious libel and Paine was sentenced to outlawry for his absence without leave from the court. He left behind him a democratic movement very different from the old chorus in the country to the Whig oppositionists and City people, burgesses and the middling gentry of the shires who had led the early reform movements.

The Combination Acts forced the various associations of workers underground, with the prohibited political Radicals as their fellow-travellers along clandestine paths. Forming or joining any kind of union of trades was a political act, and a dangerous one. The two movements that emerged were the machine-breaking Luddite riots that swept many parts of the country in 1811–13, and the preaching of insurrection that went on continuously from the nineties to the forties of the following century. "The country is mined below our feet" Tory novelist Walter Scott told Tory poet Robert Southey in 1812. He was writing in the middle of the Luddite disturbances and of a strong trade unionist effort in Scotland. Certainly, the "underground" of the Nottinghamshire knitting frame workers, the West Yorkshire cloth "croppers" and other skilled workers gave cause for panic to the rulers who had tried to root out by legislation the beginnings of working-class organisation.

The croppers issued an appeal over the name of "General Ludd" to all croppers, weavers and the public at large saying: "Come let us follow the Noble Example of the brave Citizens of Paris who in sight of 30,000 tyrant Redcoats brought a Tyrant to the ground. . . . "*

These were the years when, as the Hammonds say at the start of their famous account of the life of the artisans in those days, "the history of England . . . reads like a history of civil war".† In this war an armoury of new weapons was developed on each side. The Tory government headed by the younger Pitt, locked in combat with Napoleon's Europe, felt its rear quaking. It built 155 barracks during the French wars, so that the troops should not catch the Jacobin infection in civilian billets. Mercenaries from Hesse and Hanover were brought over in large numbers to be used if need be against the population as they had earlier been used against the American rebels. Informers, already employed in the Wilkes battles, came into systematic use. "Church and King" rioters, often paid from government funds,

* Quoted from A. L. Morton and George Tate, *The British Labour Movement, 1770–1920*, p. 37.

† J. L. and Barbara Hammond, *The Skilled Labourer.*

attacked Radical notables. Habeas Corpus was suspended in 1794 and the suspension was not lifted for ten years.

Strengthened defences on the other side included the secret oath-taking societies—sometimes associated with machine breaking and arson—that were the answer to the Combination Acts. After Parliament had nipped working-class organisation in the bud by passing the Corresponding Societies Act, the scattered reformers largely followed their various self-taught lines of thought and action according to the Paine gospel, and many and bitter were the divisions within their proud and angry ranks. It was in the local union societies—any national organisation would have been inconceivable—that a sort of unity began to be created, and then only in struggles against employers.

For the skilled working men the wars brought a sharp rise in money wages—from 22s. a week in 1793 to 36s. a week in 1813—though this never caught up with a soaring cost of living. Machinery and the factory system had not yet developed widely enough to devalue their precious old skills in shipbuilding, metal working, handloom weaving and a hundred other crafts. In the occupations employing still the great majority of people, those of agriculture, it was a very different story. Wheat prices rose from an average 26s. 2d. in 1786–90 to 94s. 3d. in 1811–15 and touched over 126s. in the famine year of 1812. Wages rose by far less—probably by no more than an average 4s. or 5s. on the going rate of about 8s. 6d. when the wars began. Landed gentry and large farmers made fortunes as millions more acres were enclosed and rents rocketed; a growing surplus population in the countryside became paupers.

This was the reason why the first application of Paine's ideas to make a social stir came not in urban industry but in agriculture. *Pig's Meat*, a periodical published three years after the French war began by Thomas Spence—the diminutive, querulous and indomitable schoolmaster from Newcastle who called himself the "unfee'd Advocate of the disinherited seed of Adam"—reflected the deep rural distress and bitterness. Spence had thought out a plan for the nationalisation of all land as early as 1775. He advocated that the parishes should recover the land taken by usurping landlords, in particular through enclosures, and rent it in small lots. When he came to London in December 1792 with missionary zeal for this cause, he was arrested almost at once for selling *The Rights of Man*, and to the end of his life in 1814, he eked out a living as a seller of illegal tracts between long spells of imprisonment.

B

Around Spence there grew up a circle that may have been planning revolt as early as 1794, and that certainly founded a tradition of insurrectionary teaching: his ideas were to be interwoven with much working-class Radical politics and publishing well into Chartist days. From his agrarian Communist outlook many ideas in advance of his time developed. One of his tracts bore the fully explanatory title, in the manner of the pamphleteers of the day, *The Rights of Infants: or, the Imprescriptible RIGHT OF MOTHERS to such share of the Elements as is sufficient to enable them to suckle and bring up their young.* Another, espousing the right of the common people to divorce, demanded: "What signifies Reforms of Government or Redress of Public Grievances if people cannot have their domestic grievances redressed?"

A follower of Spence, Thomas Evans, who was one of the last secretaries of the London Corresponding Society, said in a tract entitled *Christian Policy the Salvation of the Empire*, that all the land, waters, mines, homes and property "must return to the people . . . and be administered in partnership like that of the church". He went on: "First, settle the property, the national domains, of the people, on a fair and just basis, and that one settlement will do for all . . . and produce a real radical reform in everything; all attempts to reform without this are but so many approaches to actual ruin . . . that will not disturb the relative classes of society."

It was, however, another LCS member, the lecturer and journalist John Thelwall, who was the first really to unite in one person the news-pamphleteer and the Radical politician. Thelwall, silk mercer's son, poet and friend of many of the leading intellectuals of the 1789 generation, took Hardy's place at the head of the corresponding societies movement after the shoemaker's arrest. He fought on, with tenacity and caution, through the worst repressive years. In 1793-5 he struggled with the London authorities—a scarcely less closed corporation of privilege than Parliament itself—for the right to give lectures and hold debates. After being driven from hall to hall, he eventually secured rooms at Beaufort Buildings which served both as a lecture centre and as headquarters for the hard-pressed LCS in 1794 and 1795. His twice-weekly lectures appeared in his weekly, *The Tribune*, which also carried commentaries on the news of the day. Spies and informers usually attended his lectures—to be treated on at least one occasion to a lecture by Thelwall on the Tory government's spy system. After one of the large open-air meetings held by the LCS, some of the organisers repaired for supper to Soho's Compton Street. With them, drinking porter and proposing toasts, was a spy who afterwards swore that the company toasted "the lamp-iron in Parliament Street" and that Thelwall, as he blew the head off a pot of porter, said: "So should all tyrants be served."*

Mobs of sailors and dragoons attacked Thelwall on his speaking tours in the north and in Derbyshire. He continued them, however, until the invasion scare of 1797 created an atmosphere of intimidation which put an end to the hospitality which he had enjoyed from sympathisers among artisans, shopkeepers, dissenting ministers and schoolmasters.

Many a Radical working man of days to come took his first fire from Thelwall's *Tribune* or from hearing his lectures. With Paine as a starting point, Thelwall pioneered much of the later working-class thinking on economic and social matters. Writing even before the Combination Acts, he denounced the already severe legal curbs on efforts to form trade unions. These, he said, penalised "the poor journeymen who associated together . . . while the rich manufacturers, the contractors, the monopolists . . . may associate as they please". He urged in his pamphlet *The Rights of Nature* that without working twelve or fourteen hours a day from six to sixty every man, woman and child had "a sacred and inviolable claim . . . to some comfort and enjoyment . . . to some tolerable leisure . . . and some means of, or such information as may lead to an understanding of their *rights*".†

His ideal of a society of smallholders, small traders and artisans who would be protected from the worst oppressions of large accumulated capital foreshadowed both the Co-operative ideas of Robert Owen and aspirations widely current among the early Chartists.

He tried, also, to prove that according to both "natural law" and old precedent, the working day should not exceed eight hours. And, perhaps most importantly, he spelt out the internationalism taught both by Tom Paine's life as a revolutionist and his assault on kingship and priestcraft as a *common* enemy of the people. In his lectures he denounced the suppression of Poland's independence in its partitioning in 1795 between Russia, Austria and Prussia. He stood up bravely to the hysteria in Britain over the Robespierre Terror in France. The

---

* P. A. Brown, *The French Revolution in English History*, p. 138.
† Thompson, op. cit., p. 175.

excesses in France, he said in *The Tribune* (April 25, 1795), did not flow from the new doctrines of the Revolution but from "the old leaven of revenge, corruption and suspicion which was generated by the systematic cruelties of the old despotism".

In *The Rights of Nature* he wrote (I, pp. 21–24) that "monopoly and the hideous accumulation of capital in a few hands . . . carry in their own enormity the seeds of cure", and then produced the following insight, extraordinary for his early day, into the future development of society under the impact of the factory system:

> "Whatever presses men together . . . though it may generate some vices, is favourable to the diffusion of knowledge and ultimately promotive of human liberty. Hence every large workshop and manufactory is a sort of political society, which no act of parliament can silence and no magistrate disperse."

Thelwall's lecturing, pamphleteering and press activities gave a foretaste of the great expansion of Radical journalism that was to come after the long war. This development could not occur until the authorities' attitude that advocacy of parliamentary reform was tantamount to treason had been worn down. The beginning of a break came during the 1802 peace, when the reform movement resumed under more cautious middle-class auspices. At the general election Sir Francis Burdett, a reforming Whig and friend of Horne Tooke, ousted the sitting member for Middlesex. Napoleon's acceptance of a crown as Emperor of the French at this time took the wind out of English Jacobin sails and dreams of revolution in England faded. The emphasis shifted back to the cause of parliamentary reform. A new chapter opened in which a journalistic star of the first magnitude advanced from Tom Paine's challenge to property in its oligarchic eighteenth century guise to a marvellous championship of human rights against the inhuman industrial system that grew from it in the following century. With William Cobbett the democratic press came of age.

3

Trumpeters of Freedom

Whatever the pride of rank, of riches or of scholarship may have induced some men to believe, or to affect to believe, the real strength and resources of a country ever have sprung and ever must spring from the labour of its people.... Without the Journeymen and the labourers none of them could exist; without the assistance of their hands, the country would be a wilderness, hardly worth the notice of an invader.

WILLIAM COBBETT, *Address to the Journeymen and Labourers,* 1816.

THE FATHER FIGURE for all the Radicals during a whole long generation, William Cobbett was born in the year that No. 45 of the *North Briton* was published. He came of small farmer parentage in the Surrey village of Farnham, and before the war with France had been successively farmer's boy, gardener, lawyer's clerk and soldier in the British Army in Canada. He bought his discharge when he returned from Canada in 1791 and tried to get his officers courtmartialled for their peculations in the colony, which he had observed at close quarters in his rank of sergeant-major. This brave but hopeless tilting against one department of the regime of aristocratic property placed him in some personal danger and he fled in the following year to France, where he foresaw the outbreak of war and quickly moved on to America. There he made a reputation as a pamphleteering heavy gun on the Tory side, and this put him at odds with the pro-French sympathies of the majority of the newly independent American people and involved him in several libel actions. It was partly to escape these that he came home in 1800.

His reputation as an anti-Jacobin had preceded him and he was promptly offered the editorship of a Tory government newspaper. This he refused, but it was with the help of the Secretary at War, Windham that two years later he founded *Cobbett's Weekly Political Register*. The paper continued to support the war against France, even

after the brief Peace of Amiens (1802–3) which all England welcomed
with illuminations, and its office was wrecked by a mob in retaliation
for its bellicose editorials.

Two years later the famous conversion of Cobbett into the scourge
of privileged power began. He took the first step during a by-election
in Wilkes' old constituency of Middlesex. The Government mounted a
great effort, with all the customary bribery and corruption, to push
the leader of the reform movement in the Commons, Sir Frances
Burdett, out of the seat. But its smear campaign against Burdett as an
alleged pro-Jacobin failed: he was elected with a majority of one. On
the following day, the Sheriff reversed the decision on a technicality.
At this point Cobbett changed sides in disgust. In the *Political Register*
of September 1 he declared that the danger now was despotism at
home, supported by a bought press, in the interests of a mob of
"court-sycophants, parasites, pensioners, bribed-senators, directors,
contractors, jobbers, hireling lords, and ministers of state." Cobbett's
aim was still uncertain, with its characteristic blend of patriotic sentiment and anger at the plight to which freeborn Britons had been
reduced. Quite rapidly however, he took up more clearly committed
positions. In 1806 a by-election was held in Westminster, where some
20,000 people qualified as electors on a householder test and many
better-off artisans and even some journeymen had the vote. Elections
at Middlesex and Westminster had been since Wilkes' day the nearest
that England came to a democratic test of opinion on national questions. In 1806 the Whig and Tory interests—now in coalition in the
"Ministry of all the Talents"—planned to conduct the election as a
safe two-sided affair excluding the parliamentary reformers. At the
last moment, however, the reformers found a candidate in James
Paull, a Perth tailor's son recently returned home enriched from India.
Paull had been trying to secure the impeachment of Governor-General
Wellesley for "acts of wanton aggression and tyranny" during his
rule in India. The whole force of the borough faction, Cobbett wrote
later, stood united against Paull. In the campaign, Cobbett's journal
addressed four letters to the electors, appealing in particular to the
journeymen and artisans to demonstrate their independence. Their
response was to organise support in the trade clubs of the city, and to
join the parish committees that were set up to canvass for the democratic challenger. Paull lost the contest, but he was only 300 votes
behind the Whig winner Richard Brindley Sheridan, and the reform

side with justice claimed a moral victory. In the general election that followed, the reformers carried both Westminster seats.

The *Political Register* became steadily more Radical as the war against France went on. It denounced in particular the methods of financing the war by inflating prices, the issue of paper money and the reckless piling up of the National Debt. During the war years, this increased almost four-fold to the prodigious total of £860 million, equal to one-third of the country's total capital wealth, and imposed an annual burden of interest charges of about £45 per head of the population.

Cobbett believed that real power was being handed over by the administration of the younger Pitt to stock jobbers and a whole tribe of new rich filling their coffers with profits from war contracts. After he had bought his own farm at Botley in Hampshire, he began to see and feel the distress of the agricultural workers at close quarters and his journal took on a deeper tone of social protest. In 1810 he was imprisoned for two years on seditious libel charges for publishing an article denouncing the flogging of English militia men at Ely under the eyes of the German mercenaries who garrisoned some parts of the country. He was also fined £1,000, had to find sureties of £3,000 himself and two other sureties of £1,000 each. The affair nearly ruined him and he was beset by money troubles for the rest of his life.

We meet at this point a figure who is to become very familiar—that of the editor in prison, but still working and sustained by his public. Cobbett recorded later* that while he was in Newgate he "wrote and published 364 Essays and Letters upon political subjects". He was visited "by persons from 197 cities and towns, many of them as a sort of deputies from Societies or Clubs". When he came out, 600 people attended a London celebration dinner at which Sir Francis Burdett presided and similar dinners and parties in his honour were held all over the country. On his way home to Hampshire he was received at Alton with the ringing of the church bells, and after a dinner at Winchester he was "drawn from more than the distance of a mile into Botley by the people".

For long afterwards the editor-politician, hewing his own rough-cut way through the baffling complexities of the age, was to be one of

* "English Liberty of the Press—As illustrated in the Prosecution and Punishment of William Cobbett", *Political Register*, July 25, 1812.

the two main types of public man thrown up by the Radical movement. The other type, who made his appearance somewhat later than Cobbett and his many emulators, was the master-orator capable of commanding the vast open-air meetings that for the next thirty years were to be the most extensive organised form taken by the working class in its formative period. His day arrived when the years of deep social distress after the war, setting hundreds of thousands of working people in movement, brought the first of the long series of confrontations out of which today's labour and trade union movement was born.

No trade unions had yet appeared overtly. Their absence made the Radical privateers of press and platform, and the meetings in taverns to hear a reading of Cobbett's or Sherwin's *Register* or Wooler's *Black Dwarf*, all the more important; such occasions provided the main centres for popular politics, discussion and expressions of solidarity. The Combination Acts could not stamp out trade unions but they delayed their growth. One of the most notorious of the persecutions under this legislation was conducted by Cobbett's most detested adversary, *The Times*, which pursued a strongly anti-union policy now and throughout the century. In 1810 its compositors went on strike after the proprietor, John Walter II, had refused to grant an increase of wages from 42s. to 48s. a week that had been agreed by the other newspaper owners. He had the twenty-eight strikers prosecuted under the Acts. Nineteen were sent to jail by the hated judge Sir John ("Bloody Black Jack") Silvester. One of the men died in prison and the affair created a scandal never forgotten among the London skilled artisans who were to lead the campaign which led to the repeal of the Acts fourteen years later.

The Times, which had been founded in 1785, began life as a government-subsidised sheet like most of the journals of the day. Its founder, John Walter I, received £300 a year from the Treasury to supplement the revenue from advertisements which was the paper's principal means of support. Under his son, who became sole manager of the journal in 1803, it embarked on the course which was to give it an at first unique image of independence from control by government. The paper turned away from the ministerial hand-outs which were the main source of the very small amount of news that the patronage sheets carried, and developed its own news-getting organisation. And it established a pre-eminent position in the advertisement field, which grew apace with the commercial and industrial progress. Lord Stanhope's invention of an iron press in 1800, allowing a large broadsheet (36 × 23½ inches) to be printed, and in 1817 the installation of the steam-powered Koenig printing machine provided the means for a large expansion of *The Times*, which increased its production from a daily 2,000 copies in 1800 to some 7,000 at the end of the wars. Politically, the journal began to see itself thus early as the consensus voice of basic ruling-class interests—"ever strong upon the stronger side" in the piercing description given by the Whig *Edinburgh Review*.

The war ended three years after the squire extraordinary of Botley was drawn home in triumph by his people. The victors of Waterloo did not merely celebrate the end of the war and victory over the French; they set out to consolidate and extend their victory over the people at home. Measures immediately taken benefited the rich and injured the poor. They included the repeal of the income tax which had been introduced as a wartime measure, and higher taxes on the necessities of daily life. A 100 per cent tax on tea by itself contributed between £3 million and £4 million to an annual budget of about £55 million, and similar amounts were collected on sugar, tobacco and beer. A simultaneous fall in prices, which had doubled during the war, raised the real value of the fixed interest paid on the swollen National Debt. When wheat prices fell to just over 65s. a quarter in 1815 Parliament passed the first Corn Law, behind a ring of troops warding off angry crowds; the law forbade the import of corn until the price had reached 80s. a quarter, with the aim of maintaining farm rents at their inflated wartime levels. Unemployment, increased by the demobilisation of 300,000 soldiers and sailors, made its first massive nationwide appearance. Exports, after a brief postwar boom in 1815, fell from £51 million to £42 million in 1816 and 1817, to £35 million in 1819. And in 1821 came a crowning injustice—the restoration of the Gold Standard, which raised still further the value of money and the wealth of holders of the National Debt.

In this year, riots and great assemblies of starving people occurred in many parts. In Spitalfields, 45,000 people were estimated to be in want of food and trying to get into workhouses. This was the year in which Cobbett wrote his historic *Address to the Journeymen and Labourers* in a calculated act of double defiance: the address ushered the prohibited lower orders on to the political stage; and it was published at a price within their reach. It was the first of a series of pamphlets,

published unstamped at twopence, after Cobbett had found a loop-
hole in the stamp regulations. Each pamphlet in the "Twopenny
Trash" series was a reprint of the leading article from the stamped
Political Register, which sold at 7½d. By the end of the year, the weekly
sale was 60,000 copies, many times the circulation of any contemporary
newspaper, and the address itself may have sold as many as 200,000
copies.

Overflowing with a remarkable solidarity of feeling with the
labouring people, the address poured scorn on the hypocritical alarm
in ruling quarters about the burden of high poor rates caused by hard
times. It went on:

> "But not a single man complains of the immense sums taken away to sup-
> port the sinecure Placemen who do nothing for their money. . . . There are
> several individual placemen the profits of each of which would maintain *a
> thousand families*. . . . The unfortunate journeymen and labourers and their
> families have a *right* they have a *just claim* to relief from the purses of the rich.
> For, there can exist no riches and no resources which they, by their labour,
> have not *assisted to create*. But, I should be glad to know how the sinecure
> placemen and lady pensioners have assisted to create food and raiment, or
> the means of producing them. The labourer who is out of work, or ill,
> today, may be able to work, and set to work tomorrow. While those place-
> men and pensioners never can work; or, at least, it is clear that they never
> *intend* to do it."

The only true remedy was a reformed Parliament—"we must have
that first or we shall have nothing good"—the address concluded.
After 42,000 copies had been sold by the end of November, Cobbett
exclaimed: "*Let Corruption rub that out if she can.*" His blast on the
democratic trumpet resounded throughout the land and made him
a marked man with the government as well as a popular hero. At this
time, Samuel Bamford recalled in his *Passages from the Life of a Radical*,
Cobbett's writings "suddenly became of great authority; they were
read on nearly every cottage hearth in the manufacturing districts of
South Lancashire, in those of Leicester, Derby and Nottingham; also
in many of the Scottish manufacturing towns. . . . He directed his
readers to the true cause of their sufferings—misgovernment; and to
its proper corrective—parliamentary reform."

Two years afterwards, defence counsel for Jeremiah Brandreth, the
leader of an abortive uprising in Derby engineered by the government
spy Oliver, pleaded that the prisoner had been deluded by Cobbett's

Address, which he described as "one of the most malignant and diabolical publications ever issued from the English press".

Cobbett's crime was that he saw the "journeymen and labourers"
not in the conventional way as a brute mass, but as countrymen with
rights equal to his own. More than that, he opened up some dangerous
insights into what the future held for these millions still outside the
pale of civilised society.

In a letter published on January 27, 1820, to the Bishop of Llandaff
—who had claimed that the "vulgar" could not comprehend argument—Cobbett wrote:

"The people do not, I assure your Lordship, at all relish simple little tables.
Neither do they delight in declamatory language, their minds have, within
the last ten years undergone a very great revolution. . . . Give me leave to
say . . . that these classes are, to my certain knowledge, at this time more
enlightened than the other classes of the community. . . . They see further
into the future than the Parliament and the Ministers. There is no advantage
attending their pursuits of knowledge—they have no particular interest to
answer; and therefore their judgment is unclouded by prejudice and selfishness."

That the submerged class now breaking surface should have found
its first champion in the yeomanly William Cobbett need cause no
surprise, for it was as a destroyer of established popular rights and
elements of security that the new money power made its first impact
on the people's lives. Cobbett expressed a widespread baffled rage
which had built up since Wilkes' day and reached a peak as the wars
ended. The majority of the people, facing the front formed by the
despotic oligarchy and gentry and the millocracy of Lancashire and
Yorkshire spawning the hideous new factory towns, despaired of
ever understanding the new forces in their lives. Their enemy appeared
to them as the two-headed monster that Cobbett called simply "THE
THING".

On the one hand, it meant the accumulating evils of the old system:
boroughmongers, hordes of hangers-on in Church and State, absentee
parsons holding several livings, army officers stealing the soldiers'
rations, children being appointed to well-paid sinecures, jail keepers
battening on their prisoners, the vast extension of the criminal laws,
especially the new Game Laws, and the sheer hatred for the poor that
was engulfing Cobbett's imagined England of benevolent squires,
contented labourers, and artisans paid fair money for their work.

On the other hand, THE THING meant the war-making banker and mercantile class that was mortgaging the country with huge issues of paper money and a mounting National Debt. It meant the manufacturers' new doctrine of Political Economy, according to which machine production was conferring benefits on the industrious classes despite all appearances to the contrary; it meant the savage persecution of suspected opponents of the propertied classes, the factories and their slavery and, as the symbol of the abomination that had arrived, the daily growing capital itself, the "Great Wen", centre of all the influences bringing distress and ruin. But although the twin evil might defy explanation, it appeared self-evident, and was common ground to Cobbett and his generation, that only through a democratic reform of Parliament might it be cured.

This demand formed the common postwar platform of all the Radicals and all their papers and pamphlets. At the time of Cobbett's *Address*, the reform movement was in the midst of its first peacetime upsurge. Disturbances set off by unemployment and the passing of the Corn Law were spreading out from London to the north and the Midlands. In the capital, three immense popular gatherings at Spa Fields ended on December 2, 1816 in a riot which the government claimed was an attempt at armed insurrection. The ministers, the magistrates and the Tory papers whipped up hysteria to a height unknown since the nineties, with the intention to blacken the protesters as Jacobins, scare the middle-class reformers who were at the head of the movement, and prepare to settle accounts by force.

In January 1817, after a missile had been thrown through the glass window of the Prince Regent's coach on his way to the opening of Parliament, the government rushed through the Gagging Acts, which banned meetings of over fifty people, and again suspended Habeas Corpus. From the Home Office went out a circular urging magistrates to arrest everyone even suspected of spreading seditious libel. Believing that the clampdown was aimed at himself, Cobbett left for America in March. In this year the government, already subsidising most of the daily press, started a scurrilous counter-war on the people's papers. The order went out from Lord Sidmouth in 1817 to "write down" Cobbett, and a flood of little pamphlets appeared. They were advertised with a placarding campaign which according to the intended victim must have cost at least 2,000 guineas; but the advertisements were pulled down, or effaced, the hour they were put up, and the same treatment repeatedly given to new placards, "as one wave succeeds another in the sea", according to Cobbett's account. Eight numbers of the *Anti-Cobbett*, some of them written by the Minister, George Canning, ran from February 15 to April 5, 1817. Other subsidised papers included the *White Dwarf* which ran for twenty-two numbers up to April 1818. The paper fizzled out after its editor Gibbon Merle had threatened to publish his confidential correspondence with the Home Office. In Islington, London, one W. H. Shadgett launched *Shadgett's Review of Cobbett, Wooler, Sherwin and Other Democratical and Infidel Writers*. Its purpose was to provide "an antidote to their dangerous and destructive doctrines", but it failed after seventy-eight numbers. A public appeal for funds to rescue it met with a poor response and Shadgett, after being jailed for debt, emigrated to Canada. At this time, the *Spectator* recalled many years later, sedition was "universal and organic". It added that the cause was "teaching people to read and neglecting their well-being, or to put it another way, one that rose from the incompatibility of democratic newspapers, which the government could not suppress, with near-starvation wages".

Cobbett's departure left an immediately felt gap. The reform movement had no central organisation and any attempt to create one would have breached the Corresponding Societies Act. The part played by leaders with a personal following won either through the Radical press or as speakers at the mass gatherings that followed each other in many parts of the country was consequently a crucial one. The chief of these leaders in the two fields were Cobbett and "Orator" Henry Hunt, whose mesmeric power over crowds was not matched by any clear knowledge of what to do with it. Now and for a long time after, highly individualistic and often vain and egocentric personalities set the tone of the Radical movement and gave it such overall leadership as it had.

Cobbett, like many another, prided himself on his lone status. He described himself in this year as "a sort of self-dependent politician" not enlisted under the banner of one party or one minister, and the pro-Radical essayist and critic William Hazlitt said that Cobbett had become "a kind of fourth estate in the politics of the country". The alarm aroused by the departure of this one-man institution for America found a typical reflection in the columns of the *Black Dwarf* the celebrated weekly launched in this year by Thomas Jonathan Wooler, a printer's apprentice who came from Yorkshire to London to start a printing business of his own.

The *Dwarf*, which reached a circulation of 12,000 copies a week in the early part of its exciting seven-year life, had the backing of the reform movement's indefatigable senior politician Major Cartwright. On April 9 it launched—with "unfeigned regret"—an attack on "the grand trumpeter of freedom" for having deserted his country and demanded to know how this "traitor" could still dare to call himself a general. More significant than the bitterness, however, is Wooler's consternation at the defection of the head of the cause. He assured him, that the people would not have allowed "a hair of his head to be injured without ample retaliation" if he had remained in the country. Just four weeks later, however, the *Black Dwarf* itself appeared with the headline ARREST OF THE EDITOR, to announce that Wooler had been charged with criminal libel in connection with an article on the Right of Petition.

Of the Radical journals that now served the mass audience which Cobbett had created, neither the *Black Dwarf*, William Hone's *Reformists' Register* nor *Sherwin's Political Register*, the three principal new contenders, achieved an influence comparable to that of the *Register*, whose publication Cobbett shortly resumed from his two-year exile. Together, however, they spurred the postwar build-up of the reform movement. The small-shop industry of the Radical press, providing a livelihood for the editors, local agents, booksellers, and hawkers was effectively the organiser of this movement. The Radical papers, moulded by the privateer politics of their publishers and editors, were not yet too sharply differentiated in their contents and general policy. The *Black Dwarf*, with its connections with the old "constitutional" wing of the movement, consistently opposed all the talk now again spurting up about the need to resort to arms. It was strong for organising on the model of the Hampden Clubs which had been started by reformers in the Whig tradition in 1812 and had revived the reform of Parliament as a matter for public meetings and discussion.

The paper appeared first in quarto size, unstamped, with eight and sometimes ten pages, and later in 32-page pamphlet format, when its price was 4*d*. Its first issue (Wednesday, January 29, 1817) declared that the real freedom of Englishmen lay in their power and their will to uphold their liberties, not through the Constitution which was simply the "recorded merits of our ancestors", but by deeds. It warned, in an issue just before Habeas Corpus was suspended, that "the higher orders think the best mode is to *destroy* the Constitution altogether and then their cause can run no further risk". And after the suspension, it declared that Britain's liberties had been "delivered into the hands of an administration which we shall never cease to brand as the most decided enemies of Britain". This was also the number in which the *Black Dwarf* upbraided Cobbett for saying that clubs of all sorts were of mischievous tendency. It called this theory "a libel on the common sense of mankind". It was not a matter of right or policy but of *sheer necessity* that "good men should associate when the bad combine to injure them. Our enemies are *clubbed* in every direction around us. Do military clubs, and naval clubs and clubs of boroughmongers do no good to the cause of corruption? Are not all associations clubs; and is it not quite evident that the *associated* powers of a number are more likely to produce an effect than the individual exertions of twice or three times the number? . . . For heaven's sake, sir, do not thus betray us into the hands of our enemies by advice that can only produce mischief."

The question of clubs, of political organisation, was to be a bone of contention right through the eighteen-twenties and thirties. Involved in it were the social and economic questions on which the working-class and middle-class wings of Radicalism were more and more to part company. In these early years, while no journal took up any clear position on what was becoming known as the "social question", this question was pressing enough to be discussed in one or two of them. Two in particular made some attempt to explain the reason for the fearful distress. One was *Sherwin's Political Register*, later to become the celebrated *Republican* of ex-tinsmith Richard Carlile. The other was the lively *Gorgon* (1818–19), edited by John Wade, a former journeyman woolsorter, which dealt extensively with trade union matters. To these Wade gave an informed attention of which Cobbett, who saw the factory workers merely as pitiable victims, would have been incapable. The paper was connected with the London trades on the one hand and with Francis Place, the Westminster moderate reformer, on the other. Place, who served for many years as a kind of link man between the London artisans and the handful of reformers inside Parliament, wrote articles in the *Gorgon* in the autumn of 1818 on the conditions of workers in his own former trade of tailoring as well as in print and other trades. Although Wade was under the influence of middle-class reformers and the Political Economy school that sought to provide a "scientific" justification for the total freedom of action demanded by the manufacturers, he did some pilot work in looking into social conditions and published the results. Now and again this also led to some pioneer thinking about the workers' real position in society. Defending Manchester cotton-spinners who were on strike, *The Gorgon* said that it no longer believed as it formerly had that the "prosperity of masters and workmen was simultaneous and inseparable". It went on:

> "We have no hesitation in saying that the cause of the deterioration in the circumstances of workmen generally, and the different degrees of deterioration among different classes of journeymen, depends entirely on the degree of perfection that prevails among them, which the law has pronounced a crime—namely, COMBINATION. The circumstances of the workmen do not in the least depend on the prosperity or profits of the masters, but on the power of the workmen to *command*—nay to *extort* a high price for their labour" (November 21, 1818).

In the issue of August 8, 1818, Wade compared the "industrious orders" to the soil, out of which everything is evolved and produced. The other orders he likened to the trees, tares, weeds and vegetables drawing their nutriment from the soil. When humanity reached "greater perfectibility", the industrious classes alone ought to exist. "The other classes have mostly originated in our vices and ignorance . . . having no employment, their name and office will cease in the social state."

Groping foresights such as this were, however, exceptional at this time, when Cobbett was setting the tone. Only later, when disagreements had grown between the working men and a whole band of Whig and middle-class reformers trying to take the working class in tow, did questions of this kind begin to be raised consistently in the Radical press.

In the first few years after the war, the face of the early capitalists and manufacturers as a separate class remained partly masked by their alliance with the ruling Tory oligarchy based on land owning. Political tyranny, either in the shape in which Tom Paine had denounced it, or as Cobbett's "Old Corruption", appeared to Radical working men to be their principal foe, Opposition to the Tory tyranny extended far and wide through the old society shaken to its roots.

This was also the reason for the profound isolation in which the postwar rulers stood, not solely from the dreaded multitude, but also from the great majority of the intellectual and creative men. To an extent greater than before or since, almost all the leading spirits of the age took the Radical side. William Blake and Lord Byron, Robert Burns, John Keats and Percy Bysshe Shelley, Godwin and Mary Wollstonecroft Shelley, and in their younger and effective days Coleridge, Wordsworth and Southey, all paid allegiance to hopes and ideas stemming from the French Revolution. This Radical intelligentsia stood shoulder to shoulder with the common people, sharing and partly forming their aspirations. The most casual perusal of the Radical press up to its great Chartist days will show how keenly its writers valued this alliance, and with what scorn they condemned deserters to the Tory side.* No account of the democratic press in its beginnings can omit to give at least a passing salute to these allies among writers and artists. They included the man who was both the most stubborn defender to his days' end of the vision of Liberty, Equality and Fraternity that had appeared over France for all his generation, and a journalist of great eloquence and penetration—William Hazlitt.

"Better than any other Englishman of his time," Michael Foot has written, "he captured the flow of Rousseau's inspiration which had overturned the Bastille in France, saw 'the prospect of human happiness and glory ascending like the steps of Jacob's ladder in a bright and never-ending succession', watched that Revolution spread not hope but panic among Britain's rulers, protested with all his powers against the horrors of the Holy Alliance, and fought the evil doctrine at home that hunger was disloyalty and the dream of English liberty something that Pitt or Castlereagh could mutilate as they wished with their spies, their *agents provocateurs*, their Combination Acts, their corrupt judges and packed juries."†

The journal with which Hazlitt was particularly associated was the sharp-eyed *Examiner*, founded in 1808 and edited by John Hunt‡ which carried the inscription below its title-piece: "Paper and print 3½d., Taxes on Knowledge 3½d., price 7d." Hazlitt's *The Spirit of the*

* We find the *Black Dwarf* on January 7, 1824, promising, for example, to deal with "Sir Walter Scott who has begun to *pervert history* with his *novels* and to serve the despotism which he loves".

† *Tribune*, September 19, 1947.

‡ Not the orator. The brother of critic and essayist Leigh Hunt.

Age and *Political Essays* remain to this day a merciless verdict. If they have been partly forgotten it is because bourgeois historians have endeavoured to bury the memory of Hazlitt the democrat under his own achievements as essayist and literary man, as they were to try later to bury William Morris the Communist under his work as artist and writer.

Every brand of Radical idea current since 1789 and many picked up from earlier English popular struggles found expression in the teeming little postwar papers. In the Jacobin tradition, which had never been broken, there appeared numerous journals in the insurrectionary vein. Many began and ended quickly, often lasting for only a few weeks, changing their names, and occasionally known only through odd copies sent to the Home Office by angry magistrates demanding a government prosecution. One of the best known was the *Medusa: or Penny Politician*, issued by Thomas Davison, bookseller of Smithfield. Its motto was "let's die like men and not be sold like slaves", and it promised to spread political knowledge "unto every village, hamlet and workshop in the kingdom" (December 11, 1819). It threatened its enemies with summary justice and editorialised on the "need to blow up the present system". Robert Shorter's *Theological Comet or Free-Thinking Englishman* belonged to the same stream.

In the two years after Cobbett's flight, the government fomented and itself became the victim of a mounting dread that an attempt to "blow up the system" was imminent. On the Continent, the Holy Alliance of the restored monarchies was savaging the democratic movements. In Britain the government in which the execrated lords Castlereagh, Eldon and Sidmouth were the leading ministers saw itself as one sector of this counter-revolution of hereditary monarchy and aristocratic property and privilege—and it had a quarter of a century of counter-revolutionary experience at home on which to draw. Above all else, it feared that the long-established reform movement would fuse with the masses of people thrown into almost uninterrupted commotion by the economic crisis. Military force offered no immediate solution. So the government's first step was to attack freedom of meeting and the press and to intensify the use of spies and *agents provocateurs*.

The campaign, which began with the Gagging Acts after Spa Fields, backfired almost at once. In March 1817 the Crown lost its treason case against the Spa Fields prisoners, after the activities of the spy John Castles had been thoroughly exposed in court. In June, a moderate reform weekly, the *Leeds Mercury*, uncovered the provocations of the spy Oliver, in a scoop that seriously embarrassed the government and its whole campaign. Enormous meetings continued to be held in spite of intimidation.

The organisers of an all-Lancashire rally to demand parliamentary reform called for August 16 had been alerted by the Spa Fields persecutions to the authorities' eagerness to find plots real or invented. They took thorough precautions to ensure that the meeting was peaceful. The contingents of 60,000 to 100,000 men, women and children marched to the rally in faultless order with their bands and banners. Then as Orator Hunt began to speak, the Manchester Yeomanry, with a troop of hussars in reserve, was launched at the packed throng with drawn sabres. In ten minutes eleven people lay dead and over 400 wounded. The murderous, calculated blow was struck not at one of the long-familiar gatherings for riot, not at plotters dreaming of a British 1789, not at a starving mob or a desperate drilling with pikes on the moors, but at a disciplined and orderly demonstration by the working population of one of the main centres of the new industrialism. The rally, Samuel Bamford recalled later, "presented a spectacle such as had never before been witnessed in England", in its well marshalled unity and order. Yet the end was the massacre for which the working-class Radical *Manchester Observer* coined the name Peterloo, in derision of Wellington, victor of Waterloo and the most maniacal anti-Jacobin in the government ranks.

One representative of the Radical press who was on the spot to record the event was Richard Carlile of Sherwin's *Register*. In the confusion on the platform at the moment of Hunt's arrest, he slipped away and took the first mail coach to London to tell the story in his paper. His weekly placard for the next issue appeared on the streets announcing:

"Horrid massacres at Manchester.—A letter from Mr Carlile (who was on the hustings . . .) to Lord Sidmouth on the conduct of the magisterial and yeomanry assassins at Manchester on Monday last. A call upon his Lordship to bring these murderers to the bar of public justice—Case of a poor woman whose infant was drenched in its mother's blood!—Description of the meeting.—The attack, and the conduct of the People—If the executive power denies justice to the inhabitants of Manchester, the People have but one resource left; the duty of the People will then be to go armed to public meetings.'

The discipline and good order of the demonstration reported by Carlile and every other witness alarmed the authorities most of all. Several other meetings that summer—in Stockport, Birmingham, London and Leeds—demonstrated the workers' growing organisation and appeared to the Home Office to confirm its worst fears. No previous event in the movement for parliamentary democracy had made so profound an impact on the working men and their families. *The Times* estimated that when Orator Hunt—in an interval between the massacre and his trial—made a triumphal entry into London, 300,000 people turned out to welcome him.

Peterloo caused a crop of new twopenny weeklies to appear. They included the *London Alfred or People's Recorder* which began with an account of the "Manchester butcheries", and the *Democratic Recorder and Reformers' Guide*. This declared that if ever it was the duty of Britons to resort to the use of arms to recover their freedom and cry vengeance upon the heads of their tyrants it was now. Another, the *Cap of Liberty* issued by Thomas Davison, said that it would point out to its readers the moment "when arms must instantaneously be taken up or else their liberties as immediately laid down". In the provinces, Boston had its *True Briton* and Dudley its *2d Patriot*, whose motto was: "God Armeth the Patriot". According to a police report this sheet was written by a person long known "as a very active agent in the formation of Union Societies". In Glasgow, a Unitarian Minister, Gilbert Macleod, sold 1,000 copies a week of his *Spirit of the Union* at threepence. Later he was charged with sedition and transported to New South Wales, where he died shortly after his arrival.

The journal on the Radical side which probably came closest at this time to functioning primarily as a newspaper was the weekly *Manchester Observer* which had a working-class readership of about 3,000. After Peterloo, this journal—described in one report to the Home Office as an organ designed to inflame the minds of the lower classes—raised its circulation to about 4,000 copies and in the autumn was publishing the story of the massacre in fourteen weekly parts at twopence each.

The *Manchester Observer* held its own in news coverage with the five other Manchester weekly newspapers—four Tory, and one reforming. The great eye embodied in its title-piece formed a striking symbol in the post-Peterloo days of the new political involvement of the workers as a class, for which August 16, 1819, was seen at the time to mark the real beginning and has been accepted as such by the labour movement ever since. But the paper lacked financial backing and suffered from a shortage of advertisements, which filled only one of its twenty-four columns. Prosecutions rained down on the editor, James Wroe, and appeal after appeal was made in the paper for funds to conduct his defence. Wroe was jailed for one year and his successor sentenced to the same after he had protested against an attack made by soldiers who injured a dozen Radicals in a public house. Two months before a group of cotton manufacturers launched the *Manchester Guardian* as a four-page weekly newspaper, the *Manchester Observer* foundered under the weight of the prosecutions and its financial troubles.

This persecution on the Peterloo home ground was one small part of a sustained attempt after 1819 to shut the mouth of the Radical press for good. In the teeth of facts that rapidly became known all over the country, the government and its press trumpeted their conviction that a threat of revolution had been averted at Peterloo by the prompt action of the magistrates and the yeomanry. The Home Secretary, Lord Sidmouth, and the Prince Regent congratulated them both and Eldon, the Lord Chancellor, opined that the meeting itself was an act of treason that presented the country with a "shocking choice between military government and anarchy". A plan was entertained for some time to prosecute Carlile for treason, on account of his London street placard and the report of the massacre in *Sherwin's Political Register* to which it referred. But it was decided to proceed first with numerous charges of blasphemy that were pending against him.

Far from bringing the murderers to the bar as Carlile's placard had demanded, the authorities prosecuted Hunt, Carlile and a wide range of pro-reform personalities, extending to Major Cartwright and to Sir Francis Burdett, the moderate leader of the cause in Parliament. On December 30, the Six Acts were rushed through. They threw the whole book of repression at the reform camp, by extending the already stiff powers given to the government in earlier legislation to search for arms, control meetings, and prosecute on seditious libel charges. The fourth Act, around which the press freedom issue turned for the next dozen years, tightened the definition of criminal libel and imposed a new tax of 4*d*. on all publications, like Cobbett's twopenny *Register*, that were sold at less than sixpence. It also tightened the definition of a newspaper. Radical papers were forced either to pay the newspaper stamp and sell at 7*d.*, or appear as monthly pamphlets, selling at a price no lower than sixpence. Carlile's *Republican* and Cobbett's *Register* turned pamphlet and doubled their price. Davison's *Cap of Liberty* and *Medusa* were combined and enlarged and sold for sixpence until the end of 1826.

Five weeks before the Six Acts were passed, the Prince Regent had called in his speech from the throne for the "utmost vigilance and exertion to check the dissemination of the doctrines of treason and impiety and to impress upon the minds of all classes of His Majesty's subjects that it is from the cultivation of the principles of religion and from a just subordination to lawful authority that we can alone expect continuance of that Divine favour and protection which have hitherto been so signally experienced in this Kingdom". The Vice-Chancellor, Lord Eldon, said the press had become the "most malignant and formidable enemy to the Constitution to which it owed its freedom". There was now "scarcely a village in the Kingdom that had not its little shop in which nothing was sold but blasphemy and sedition". Another peer, Lord Lifford (December 27, 1819) said that if sedition was allowed to go on, the seditious tracts "would write down any Government on earth". Lord Sidmouth said a conspiracy to subvert the Constitution was well known to exist and the press was "one of the principal means adopted for the accomplishment of this end".

The sedition cry, throughout the war years and for long afterwards, was the Tory government's chief weapon. Writing from America in his *Register* (October 25, 1817) Cobbett said that "as there *were no treasons*, treasons would be made and traitors would be *hired*", and exclaimed "What? Was the country too *quiet* for them?" In the following May, in a letter answering charges that he had inspired the Derby uprising, he said: "There was not a man . . . who did not know that the discontent was created by the tyrannical Bills and that it was worked into a rising by OLIVER." In a passage expressing the popular wrath he went on: ". . . the Derby men knew very well that according to law as well as to reason, *Resistance of Oppression* is a RIGHT, and not a CRIME. They *might* be wrong, as to whether oppression did, or did not, exist; but in their *doctrine* they were perfectly right. Their measures, too, were efficient, had they not been betrayed. Even here their humanity was the cause of their defeat. OLIVER was suspected, and so strongly that a rope, as I have been assured, was ready prepared for his neck; and, he would have carried intelligence to the Devil at once instead of to Lord Sidmouth, if justice had not spoke and said: 'He may be innocent. It is better to run any risk, than put an innocent man to death.'"

As the Six Acts were going through Parliament, a final throw on the insurrection hope was in contemplation among those who had tried several times to stage an English version of France's July 14. Amid the shock waves from Peterloo, there were men, among the shoemakers who had supported the London Corresponding Society, the Spital-fields weavers, the survivors of the United Irishmen movement of 1798, and in the areas where Luddism had been strong, who were ready to support such an enterprise if somebody would organise it. Someone did—Lord Sidmouth. The Cato Street conspiracy of 1820 involved Arthur Thistlewood, a veteran Republican who had been active in Jacobin plottings since the nineties, and several other followers of Thomas Spence and his land nationalisation programme. The plot was controlled through all its stages by Lord Sidmouth's spy Edwards, who wrote the script and even supplied many of the proper-ties. The Cabinet was to be assassinated at dinner, and a provisional government set up. Edwards planted swords, pikes, guns, pistols, powder and shot at Cato Street and in the lodgings of various con-spirators, as was proved at the trial. Thistlewood said in the dock that his own motives had been concern for his starving country and anger over Peterloo. He and the other leaders of the conspiracy were hanged. His friends later presented an indictment against Edwards for high treason and conspiracy, and the Grand Jury at the Old Bailey found it a "true Bill". But Edwards was never found.

The victims of Lord Sidmouth's plot were long seen as martyrs and their motive as a desire to avenge Peterloo. T. J. Wooler, the "per-severing Pigmy" as he later called himself, drew himself to his con-siderable full height to comment on the sentences. The real conspirators were the government ministers, he charged, and went on:

"These poor, friendless and destitute beings must pay the forfeit which the law demands, for plotting against the ministers; but the latter may plot against the *people* with perfect impunity. They may sanction the destruction of the people without being called before any tribunal. The *intentions* of the desperadoes now before the public are sufficient to convict *them*; while the *deeds* of others attract no judicial inquiry. Of the blood *actually spilt* at Manchester is taken no account; while the severest reckoning is enacted for that which it is asserted was intended to be shed in London. Might not men, so ignorant as these, have easily concluded that they had as much right to shed blood as the yeomanry of Manchester? Might they not have believed that what was approved, at Manchester, was divested of all criminality? War was there levied against the *peace* and honour of the king! An act of treason was committed against his unoffending subjects! Yet *no inquiry* was permitted. No responsibility followed! The agents were *thanked*—the prompters of the mischief *rewarded*!" (April 26, 1820.)

Eloquently did the *Dwarf* incarnate the people's anger.

After Cato Street the emphasis in working-class Radical politics shifted still more decisively away from Jacobin dreams and towards the advocacy of parliamentary reform as the key that would open all doors. In the aftermath of Peterloo, the press which had done so much to shape the postwar democratic wave faced a threat to its existence. The years 1819–21 brought 120 prosecutions for seditious and blasphemous libels, ending in numerous jailings. But the Tory attempt to extinguish the dissident papers of all trends was defeated; the Radicals launched one of the greatest counter-attacks in the whole press freedom story and it ended in the first major victory for this cause since Wilkes.

4

Knowledge is Power

An unexampled profusion of slanderous, seditious and blasphemous publications . . . inveterately hostile to public and private virtue and favourable
only to whatever tends to degrade and debase mankind. Nothing would so
much improve and elevate the Press itself as their suppression.

*Constitutional Society for Opposing the Progress of Disloyal
and Seditious Principles, 1820*

The printing press has become the UNIVERSAL MONARCH and the Republic of
Letters will go on to abolish all minor monarchies, and give freedom to the
whole human race by making it as one nation and one family.

Richard Carlile, *Republican*, July 11, 1832

A DEMOCRATIC PRESS is a living affair created by its writers and
readers. The journals of the Cobbett springtime already possessed this
general character. No journal up to Peterloo, however, was in any but
the loosest affiliation to outside bodies. The daring life-style of the
Radical publisher and editor, as a small entrepreneur of protest living
in continual danger and spending much time in prison, was not to
change greatly for many years; indeed, the worst tribulations of what
Paine called "the times that try men's souls" lay ahead for Radical
pressmen. Their links with their readers, however, began to change in
three ways during the twenties.

In the first place the battle changed, on the legal side, from a
generals' war into a soldiers' war, in which the "Constitutional
Society" quoted at the head of this chapter was routed. Secondly,
there emerged Radical journals which directly represented the views
of the "journeymen and labourers", and promoted the emergence of
the "general unionism" which was the first ancestor of the modern
trade union movement. And thirdly, the Radical journals began to
debate the problems facing the working men as a class—the Political
Economy propaganda of the factory masters, the various hopes of
escape from this anti-human doctrine, including ideas of Co-operative

production and exchange, and the shape of the future, as working men began to feel themselves capable of moulding it.

Such in broad outline is the progression reflected in the Radical press scene from Peterloo to the late eighteen-thirties when Chartism, the world's first massive political movement of the working class as an independent force, made its challenge. Humped up across the middle of these years lies the great divide of the Reform Bill of 1832—a near-insurrection in which the new industrial masters won a share in state power, and the working people, although they had borne the heat and burden of the day, won nothing.

The struggle for legal press freedom had begun in spirited offensive style two years before the Manchester massacre and it involved the whole field of publishing. Great peals of laughter marked the first round of the campaign in which so many tears were to be shed. On December 18, 1817, the bookseller William Hone, who had belonged to the London Corresponding Society in the seventeen-nineties, was brought to trial for selling parodies on the Catechism, the Litany and the Athanasian Creed, which Carlile had published. The audience in the Guildhall roared with merriment when the Attorney General started reading to the jury Hone's "horrible blasphemies". Then Hone, who had done his homework while in prison awaiting trial, produced numerous examples proving that parodies of the Church liturgy had been an accepted form of amusement in polite society for many years, and that George Canning, a member of the Cabinet, was famous for his parodies, one at least of which treated with disrespect the Anglican prayer book. The jury found Hone not guilty, amid the rapturous applause that so often greeted popular verdicts in the endless trials involving freedom of speech and publication. Two more efforts to convict Hone, before a second and third jury, ended in the same result, and the prosecution had to be abandoned.

Tinplate worker Richard Carlile had been inspired at the age of twenty, as he wrote, "with an ambition to get my living by the pen, as more respectable and less laborious than working fourteen, sixteen and eighteen hours per day for a very humble living", and moved to London from his native Ashburton in Devon. He wrote in his memoirs: "I shared in the general distress of 1816, and it was this that opened my eyes. Having my attention drawn to politics, I began to read everything I could get at upon the subject with avidity, and I soon saw what was the importance of a Free Press. . . . " To this cause he devoted

himself with a single mind. He was a propagandist and pedlar for the
liberty papers before he ever edited one; while he was on short time
in 1817 he borrowed 20s. from his employer, bought 100 copies of
Wooler's *Black Dwarf* and resolved to "try his fortune at giving them
a more extensive circulation in London". He placed them in twenty
shops in and around the capital, walking sometimes thirty miles a day
for a profit of eighteen pence. In the next year, his spirit of aggression
caused even veterans in the Radical camp to tremble for him. Against
their advice he published in 1817 and 1818 one after another the
writings of the forbidden Paine—*Common Sense, The Rights of Man*
and *The Age of Reason*. The first two appeared serially in Sherwin's
Register and the third as a book at half a guinea. By the time he stood
on the Peterloo platform there were eight indictments against him
awaiting trial.

When he appeared in the Guildhall on October 12, 1819, charged
with blasphemy, Carlile succeeded in reading the whole of *The Age of
Reason* into the record, and tried to call leaders of every church from
the Archbishop of Canterbury to the Chief Rabbi to prove that nobody
could say exactly what the word religion meant. The judge told the
jury that if they considered that the work published was calculated to
deprive men of their religion—"even temporarily, as had happened in
France"—they must find the prisoner guilty. On this and another
blasphemy charge the jury so found him, and he was sent to prison for
three years, fined £1,500 and ordered to find securities in £2,000 to be
of good behaviour for life. The savage sentence received a heroic answer.

After the prosecution of his Peterloo issue of Sherwin's *Register*,
Carlile had changed the paper's name to the *Republican*. This he did
partly because Sherwin had severed his connection with the journal,
and partly because Cobbett had returned from America and was about
to reissue his better known *Register*. The entire stock of Carlile's shop
in Fleet Street—the Temple of Reason as he called it in good Paine
style—was confiscated under a distraint order to pay his fines. Early
in the following year, however, his wife reopened business with the
report of his trial, including the whole of Paine's hitherto unprintable
work. A shopman called Davidson, Mrs. Carlile and Jane Carlile, his
sister, were successively indicted and imprisoned each for two years,
bringing the entire family into jail.

The main persecution was conducted not directly by the government but by a kind of private Inquisition of the propertied and pious

directed by several prosecuting societies well supplied with funds. Carlile believed that enough volunteers and enough money to wear down the societies could be collected. From all over Britain, when he made his appeal, volunteers flowed to the shop in Fleet Street, and funds came in at the rate of £500 a week. The *Republican* reappeared and a flood of works considered seditious or blasphemous issued from the shop. They included Shelley's *Queen Mab* and *Necessity of Atheism*, Byron's *Cain*, Southey's early Jacobinical work, *Wat Tyler*, which he was anxious to forget, and—an example of the thoroughness of Carlile's campaign—an article written by the Utilitarian philosopher Jeremy Bentham thirty-one years earlier in 1792 and never previously published.

By May 1823, when the prosecuting societies' funds were running low, every prosecuted book was being openly sold in Fleet Street. The Treasury Solicitor stepped in and arrested eleven people who had been shopmen or vendors. He was answered by an issue of the *Republican* which took the form of a mock proclamation, headed with the royal arms upside down, and gave notice "that all persons who will present themselves [at 84 Fleet Street] to sell books in the said shop, free of cost of getting there, are desired immediately to forward their name and they may be regularly called upon, so as to prevent the stoppage of sale in the said shop". It was most distinctly to be understood, the proclamation added, that "a love of propagating the principles, and a sacrifice of liberty to that end, as far as it may be required, AND NOT FOR GAIN, must be the motive to call forth such volunteers".

The Whig *Morning Chronicle* had expressed the opinion that the new prosecutions would "break up *that* concern . . . we can hardly conceive that mere attachment to any set of principles without any hope of gain or advantage will induce men (in any number) to expose themselves to an imprisonment of three years." It forecast that the shop in Fleet Street would close down "as a matter of course". To this prophecy Carlile's magnificent reply came in the *Republican* of July 2, 1824, describing the forecast as a "sample of the drivelling to which the proprietors and editors are forced to preserve their readers . . . THE SHOP IN FLEET STREET WILL NOT BE CLOSED AS A MATTER OF COURSE, nor closed at all."

Early in this year Carlile had finished his sentence—and been at once imprisoned again for debt. But the main fight was won, as the *Black Dwarf* at once recognised. It wrote:

"The law only authorises his detention as a debtor. . . . On the great question he has conquered. . . . The judges are tired of hearing the prosecutions of his agents. A new shop has been opened in Fleet Street. Every publication which has been prosecuted is sold openly without any contrivance or evasion. . . . The battle is won, though he has been taken prisoner."*

"The contrivances" of Carlile's shopmen were many and devious. The most famous was the "invisible" shopman; instead of a counter, the shop used a partition in the middle of which an indicator could be pointed to the names of works arranged around a dial. Customers turned the finger to the book they needed, put their money in a slot, and the book dropped to them along a chute. This stopped informers seeing who was serving them and going to court to swear away a shopman's liberty.

The chief of the prosecuting societies, the "Constitutional", spent £30,000 in less than five years and was bankrupt by the end of 1823. Shortly afterwards, the "Vice Society" (Society for the Suppression of Vice, Blasphemy and Profaneness) also collapsed for want of funds. Carlile took them all on, with rancour and glee.

"I take the opportunity", he wrote in the *Republican*, "of repeating my thanks to the Vice Society for the extensive circulation they are again giving my publications. I hear from London that the prosecution of Mrs Carlile produces just the same effect as my prosecution did—it quadruples the sales of all her publications. I will convince the members of this Society before seven years have passed away that they have been arrant fools to themselves as well as knaves to me. . . . A prosecution becomes the grand impetus for reading a particular book, and in the language of Paine I say again: May every good book be prosecuted."

Briefly, the government itself stepped in. It made a final attempt to subdue the rebellion when it had eight of Carlile's shopmen sent to prison for periods ranging from six months to three years in 1825. But by now, partly because the post-Peterloo panic had subsided, public sympathy had veered toward the irrepressible publisher. The

* The *Dwarf's* own struggle, however, was near its end. For seven years it had loosed its democratic barbs in the form of despatches to the "Yellow Bonze" in Japan, describing the peculiar customs of the English nation. Early in 1824 it was apologising to its readers for not having carried out its original plans for a good literary and theatrical coverage, and blamed the "resistless tide" of political subjects. Its last number on November 1—published at 3d. because it was only half the usual size—reported the funeral of its supporter Major Cartwright—"this friend and patron of the human race".

trials made "good copy" and were reported at great length in most of the daily newspapers. Carlile himself was freed unconditionally, and his fines were remitted, on November 25. Here is how he himself savoured his victory in a *Republican* article:

> "My long confinement was, in fact, a sort of penal representation for the whole. I confess that I have touched extremes that many thought imprudent, and which I would only see to be useful with a view of habiting the Government and people to all extremes of discussion so as to remove all ideas of impropriety from the media which were most useful. If I find that I have done this I shall become a most happy man; if not, I have the same disposition unimpaired with which I began my present career—a disposition to suffer fines, imprisonment or banishment, rather than that any man shall hold the power and exercise the audacity to say, and to act upon it, that ANY KIND OF DISCUSSION IS IMPROPER AND PUBLICLY INJURIOUS."*

There spoke the Painite individualist, the last of the great "Old Jacks". For Carlile, reason itself shone from the works of Paine, which he called "a standard for anything worthy of being called Radical Reform". He despised clubs, saw no need for political organisation, had little sense of belonging to a class. He saw the press—which he described as a "multiplication of mind"—as the only form of organisation that was necessary. He believed that once Paine's ideas were understood "everything that is necessary to put them in practice will suggest itself . . . let each do his duty, and that openly, without reference to what his neighbour does".

His boast was just, but yet it told only half the story. There was an obvious discord between such doctrinaire individualism and the close-knit rallying of hundreds of working men and women which he called forth to the freedom cause. This was the point in the press story at which working-class readers and supporters of the first journals

---

* Years later, his "disposition unimpaired" had further opportunity to prove itself. In January 1831 he was indicted for comments on the "uprising" of the agricultural labourers in the southern counties of the previous year. He told the "insurgent agricultural labourers" (November 27, 1830) that even if they were proved to have been incendiaries they had "more just and moral cause for it than any king or faction, that ever made war, had for making war". The comments appeared in his journal the *Prompter*, one of the first of the periodicals that appeared without a stamp to defy the law. They cost him, with some other offences, a further two years and eight months of imprisonment, bringing his total personal losses in the struggle to £10,000 worth of confiscated stock, £3,000 in confiscated bail, and nine and a half years' loss of liberty.

which they saw as their own first intervened in a decisive manner to defend a liberty which had been maintained only precariously and in the aftermath of Peterloo was in danger of extinction.

When the *Republican* reappeared, Carlile appealed (January 4, 1822) for the formation of "a phalanx around myself such as shall be strong enough to support me whilst I put into practice the common right of Free Discussion". That the phalanx rising to his appeal from all England numbered many from among the artisans, labourers and factory workers the records leave little doubt. Carlile's agents in 1824, for instance, included James Mann, a cropper at Leeds; Holmes, a shoemaker at Sheffield; Penny, a Huddersfield weaver; Barling, a shoemaker at Salisbury, Roberts, a singer in Dorchester, and Joseph Swann, the Macclesfield hatter, most stubborn of all vendors.*

At the Fleet Street shop, friends sat in the evenings to receive subscriptions. People came forward, complete strangers to Carlile, and he entrusted his business to them. He corresponded tirelessly from prison with sympathisers in London, Birmingham, Leeds, Stamford and other towns. Outside, little groups would meet to celebrate his birthday and drink his health. He supplied his shopmen and newspaper vendors with written defences ready to read in court. Hawkers of his paper, to avoid prosecution, sold straws instead and then "gave" the journal to customers. All this constituted the strength of "General Carlile's Corps"—the 150 volunteer shopmen and vendors who together with their officer served over 200 years of imprisonment in the battle.

Shopkeepers and newsvendors who handled journals were also publishers in the eyes of the law. The vendors who obtained a modest living from the Radical papers† were the particular object of government anger and attention. Six men were brought before the Bow Street, London, magistrate in September 1819, charged with imputing the crime of murder to the magistrates. Their offence: *selling* the issue of Friday, September 3 which contained an open letter to the Prince Regent "on his thanking the magisterial and yeomanry assassins for murders committed by them on the 16th of August last". All were bailed by Carlile. One of them, Robert Shorter of the *Theological*

---

* Patricia Hollis, *The Pauper Press*, p. 112.

† Cobbett said that by selling 300 or 400 *Political Registers* a week a man could support a small family. One vendor had made £3 15s. by selling 1,800 copies, he said.

Comet, exclaimed in his paper's next issue (September 11): "Well! And what if it *do* impute the crime of murder to the Manchester Bloodhounds. Are they not deserving of it?" In May 1820 all were sentenced to prison, three of them for six weeks and three for a month, and obliged to give recognisances for good behaviour for three years. Carlile write: "We have pretty good proof that the Attorney General does not altogether want the authors, he knows that the authors remain authors after committed to prison; but the vendor who has a large family is sure to be ruined and reduced to misery."

Joseph Swann was jailed for two and a half years for selling pamphlets (blasphemous and seditious libel) and attending a meeting after Peterloo to advocate parliamentary reform (seditious conspiracy). The magistrate who sentenced him was himself a "Manchester bloodhound"—he had been a commander of the Cheshire yeomanry on August 16. During Swann's imprisonment in Chester Castle, his wife—also detained for a short while—lived with her four children on parish relief, supplemented by some help from Cobbett and Carlile. He was still in jail when the execrated Tory Foreign Secretary Lord Castlereagh committed suicide, an event provoking an outburst of popular exultation. And it was to Swann that his "faithful Friend, and most obedient servant Wm Cobbett" addressed a letter in the *Political Register* informing him: "MR. SWANN, CASTLEREAGH HAS CUT HIS THROAT, AND IS DEAD! Let that sound reach you in the depth of your dungeon. Of all the victims, you have suffered most" (August 17, 1822).

Then there was also the Dorset carter Richard Hassell, who left his village at the age of twenty-two and visited Carlile in prison to "ask the truth about the old religion", as he told the jailer. Hassell volunteered to join the "corps" two years later, and at his subsequent trial defended himself in highly original style, in a speech widely reported in all the press. In Newgate prison, to which he was sent for two years, he established the *Newgate Magazine* and taught himself French and mathematics. He wrote regularly for the *Republican* and on his release on June 1, 1826, worked for Carlile as printer and translator.

In Exeter a cripple vendor of Radical journals was jailed until he could find £300 in bail and sureties. Then he was sent to prison—six months for sedition and nine for blasphemy—and ordered to be kept there until he could find £200 security for good conduct. The mayor of the town bought his stock-in-trade and had it burnt. The cripple's crime: selling Hone's Parody on the Lord's prayer.* In some provincial districts at this time, magistrates and gentry indeed appeared intent on putting the clock back to the days when Prynne lost his ears for unlicensed publishing in 1637 and was branded SL ("Seditious Libeller") on both cheeks. Shropshire magistrates in 1817 had men flogged at the whipping post as vagrants for selling Cobbett's works. In this year when Habeas Corpus was suspended, and for several years afterwards, more than a whiff of Charles I and the Court of Star Chamber with which he enforced his censorship was in the air. Some of the Tory rulers nurtured the clear hope of extirpating all liberty of press and printing—in the full spirit of the Holy Alliance against democracy on the Continent of which Castlereagh was a principal architect. And in the early twenties the most persistent confrontation occurred not in Parliament, not in large clashes between demonstrators and the state authority in arms, still less in strike actions, but over the widest field of struggle for freedom of the press. The *Morning Chronicle* put the matter this way: "Misgovernment must destroy the Press, or the Press will destroy misgovernment" (September 3, 1822).

Carlile's victorious emergence from prison in 1825 marked the conclusion of one phase of the legal battle. It engaged the sympathies of the middle-class reformers whose resentment of restrictions by the predominant landed interests was by this year already overcoming their fear of the people. It was under the influence of the Carlile agitation that advanced Whigs like James Mill and his son John Stuart Mill had already written—the first in the *Encyclopaedia Britannica* and the second in the *Morning Chronicle*—articles hymning the virtues of a free press.

Carlile's triumph prepared the way for the still more fundamental contest that lay ahead: a frontal assault on the "Taxes on Knowledge", the Battle of the Unstamped, in which the material burden on press finances and circulations would be challenged. In Carlile's rugged personality the classical old Prynne type recurred, although the mental armour had changed from Puritan theology to the anti-clericalism of

---

* "Our Lord who art in the Treasury, Whatsoever be thy name. Thy power be prolonged, thy will be done throughout the empire, as it is in each session. Give us our usual sops, and forgive us our occasional absences on divisions, as we promise not to forgive them that divide against us. Turn us not out of our places; but keep us in the House of Commons, the land of Pensions and Plenty; and deliver us from the People. Amen."

c

Paine. Carlile formed a bridge between the traditional one-man-band style of fight, all defiance, and obsessed with liberty as an individual right, and a new kind of struggle for more substantial freedoms, in which the workers found and formed themselves as a class.

The two modes overlapped in the Carlile story. It was he who founded in 1830 the Rotunda debating club in the Blackfriars Road, where London workers of all trades first met to debate their future. He started the club to hold lectures on atheism, which he reported in his journal the *Prompter*, but in the middle of the following year the National Union of the Working Classes and Others became the tenant of the Rotunda during Carlile's last imprisonment. From jail he wrote expressing regret that this body intended to *organise* the next round in the struggle. "I have nothing to do with any association", he wrote and insistently warned, as Cobbett had warned, against political clubs.

It was precisely from the growth of "association", however, that the next wave took its energy. Before its events can be described, we have to look at this development which transformed the manner of conducting Radical newspapers and their content.

Such was the solidity of the postwar Tory reaction that it was nine years before the first breach was made in the fortress of repression. In 1824–5 a campaign by joint committees of trade societies, assisted by skilfull manœuvres involving the handful of parliamentary Radicals, and stage-managed by Francis Place, obtained the repeal of the Combination Acts.* The explosion of militancy that followed the repeal astonished everyone; a wave of demands and strikes for higher wages involving cotton spinners in Manchester, cutlers in Sheffield, seamen on the Tyne and Wear, and the London shipwrights revealed that trade unions, developing under a number of guises dictated by the conditions of illegality, had made big advances. The *Sheffield Mercury* wrote that "almost the whole body of mechanics in the kingdom are combined in the general resolution to impose terms on their employers".

The repeal also provided the first open view of the links between organised workers and Radical politics and press. John Gast, a mighty man of the London river, is the personality who emerges most clearly. For twenty-eight years Bristol-born Gast had been a leading hand in a Deptford shipyard where, as he said later, he had helped to build

---

* A. L. Morton and George Tate, *The British Labour Movement, 1780–1920*, gives a useful short analysis of this complex happening.

"twenty to thirty sail of men of war . . . exclusive of merchant ships". He had been at the centre of several attempts to organise the dock-yards and of the Philanthropic Society, or Philanthropic Hercules, of 1818 which aimed to link up nationally the various friendly societies and embryonic trade unions into a *Trades Union*. The society's founda-tion articles were published in John Wade's *Gorgon*. John Gast was influential in all the committees of the London trades in the early twenties and it was he who, on behalf of The Committee of the Useful Classes, welcomed Orator Hunt to London on his release from prison in 1822.

The shipyard men were in the thick of a country-wide fight that started over the Combination Acts in 1825 when the employers, hard hit by strikes, lobbied successfully for a new Act that left strikers and unions formally legal but hedged their legality with severe restrictions on union rights in practice. In this year the trade unionist circles around Gast, organised in the Metropolitan Trades Committee, launched their own journal, the stamped *Trades Newspaper*, and on it inscribed the motto "They helped every one his neighbour". This was the first paper owned by trade unions. The London skilled workers, among whom relatively high wages were paid in good times, were receptive in the twenties to Political Economy doctrines such as the alleged common interest of master and man in the expansion of production through unrestricted competition, and to the theory of "Parson" Malthus that unemployment was an insoluble problem arising from the "surplus" of population.

Out of the class battle of 1825 over the Combination Act, however, new ideas arose and were reflected in the new journal. Its first number attacked Francis Place for subscribing to the Malthus theories. If the Political Economists were to be believed, Gast wrote, "the working classes have only to consider how they can most effectually restrict their numbers, in order to arrive at a complete solution of all their difficulties . . . Malthus & Co. . . . would reduce the whole matter to a question between the Mechanics and their sweethearts and wives [rather than] a question between the employed and their employees —between the Mechanic and the corn-grower and monopolist—be-tween the tax-payer and the tax-inflictor."

Later in the same year the *Trades Newspaper* published instalments of a famous pioneer work by Thomas Hodgskin, one of the first Radical writers to set out to equip the workers with their own theory of society and guide to action. The full title of his pamphlet, *Labour Defended against the Claims of Capital: or The Unproductiveness of Capital with Reference to the Present Combinations amongst Journeymen*, points straight to the topicality which the instalments must have had for skilled workers already suffering from the economic depression beginning in that year.

Hodgskin, a retired naval officer, was a founder of the London Mechanics Institution (later Birkbeck College) and one of his colleagues there was J. C. Robertson, first editor of the *Trades Newspaper*. Hodgskin belonged to that group of early thinkers along socialist lines whose work later drew from Marx the tribute that the theorists of the English factory workers "were the first to throw down the gauntlet to the theory of capital". Among the journal's readers in the London trades there would have been many in the hard times of 1825 who recognised from their experience the truth of Hodgskin's indignant declaration that the masters had not only appropriated the produce of the labourer but had succeeded at the same time in persuading him that they were his benefactors.

Efforts to form a national trade union organisation increased and class solidarity ideas grew stronger. The *Trades Newspaper* reported each stage of a strike by Bradford wool-combers in the summer of 1825 and gave details of the support sent by workers in many parts of the country. In its September 11 issue it declared: "It is all the workers of England against a few masters at Bradford."

Other journals born from this feeling were associated with John Doherty, leader of the Lancashire cotton workers, a man of formidable ability and a prototype of the great race of pioneers combining socialism and devotion to trade unionism. The Webbs in their history of trade unionism called Doherty "one of the acutest thinkers and stoutest leaders among the workmen of his time". Borne at Larne in County Antrim in 1799, he was at work in a cotton mill by the age of ten and rose to prominence among the Manchester cotton spinners in the 1825 campaign to repeal the Combination Acts. After a bitter six-month strike by the cotton-spinners in 1829 had ended in defeat, Doherty started the first national trade union—the National Association for the Protection of Labour—with the weekly *United Trades Co-operative Journal* as its organ. This ran into trouble with the Commissioner of Stamps for carrying news and comments on the news. Suppressed in July 1830 it re-emerged as the *Voice of the People* (stamped, price 7d.). The paper was launched after a subscription list, said by the treasurer, Francis Place, to have extended "from Birmingham to the Clyde", had raised £3,000 and possibly £5,000. Appearing first in January 1831 the paper carried full reports of the meetings of the association in Manchester and Nottingham and of the questions of the day most closely interesting all Radical politicians. In its founding programme it declared: "Labour is the source of wealth; the working men are the support of the middle and upper classes; they are the nerves and soul of the process of production, and therefore of the nation." The address of the association "to the Workmen of the United Kingdom" began:

> "Fellow Worker—The fearful change, which the workings of the last few years have produced in the condition of every class of labourer, summons you to a serious investigation of the cause. . . . Your power as regards the operations of society is omnipotent. . . . You are the great lever by which everything is effected . . . let British operatives once become firm and united and their unanimous voice of complaint will command respect."

Within two years the association, and some other organisations loosely affiliated to it, claimed a combined membership of 100,000 —miners, potters, blacksmiths and millwrights, as well as Doherty's textile workers. The association was quickly ruined, however, by what Doherty called a "spirit of jealousy and faction". Two other journals conducted by Doherty later, the *Poor Man's Advocate* and the *Herald of the Rights of Industry*, also devoted themselves to forging the "great lever" of a united trade union movement, as well as the agitation for factory reform and the long fight to win the Ten Hours Bill.

The third influence that began to shape the working-class Radical press in the late twenties—Doherty's journals reflected it strongly— was the conception that the working people could slip out from under the iron heel of the new masters by developing a Co-operative system of production and exchange employing their own labour and means. This hope, and associated dreams of a happy future based on brotherly affection, stemming from the work of the philanthropist and Utopian spell-binder Robert Owen, provided by far the strongest common platform of the papers written for workers, after the solutions offered by Paine and Cobbett had failed.

Robert Owen, starting with his model cotton mill at New Lanark and other experiments in practical benevolence, progressed in his thinking to the elaboration of a plan to build a new society piecemeal. Reason would dictate the course that the change should take, and it would bypass the horrors of large-scale capitalist industrialism. In 1820 an Owenite society was formed in London, with its own periodical, the *Economist*. This journal said (August 11, 1821) that Co-operation had no levelling tendency—its aim was to "elevate all" and the whole wealth of the new system would be "newly produced". A correspondent wrote (October 13, 1821) that the workers "if they will but exert themselves *manfully* have no need to solicit the smallest assistance from any other class, but have within themselves . . . superabundant resources". The journal was run by the founder of the Co-operative and Economical Society, George Mudie, as an adjunct to his lecturing, and called itself a "periodical paper explanatory of the new system of society projected by Robert Own Esq.". It lasted for fourteen months. Later Mudie edited the *Political Economist and Universal Philanthropist* (1825), the *Advocate of the Working Classes* (1836–7) and the *Gazette* of the Exchange Bazaars. In 1824 the London Co-operative Society was established with the object of forming a community based on mutual co-operation and restoring "the whole produce of labour to the labourer". It declared that "only through progress in moral and political sciences could man come to see that competition and private accumulation or excessive inequality could never produce happiness". The society resolved to "renounce all the evils of trafficking or mere commerce, likewise profit, which implies living on the labour of others, all our exchanges being proposed to be for fair equivalents, representing equal labour, and destined for immediate or gradual consumption, and not for accumulation to command the labour of others".

In the same year the London journeymen printers with whom the *Gazette* was connected set up a committee to investigate a Co-operative scheme of production. It produced estimates of the cost of living of 250 families and showed that if Co-operative production were started these families could save nearly £8,000 a year. If foreign countries would not take British machinery in exchange for their agricultural produce, it argued,

"we trust that agricultural customers will spring up at home and that we shall 'ere long find the means to divide among ourselves, by a fair exchange of produce, all the goods and provisions that our domestic industry and ingenuity can create, and indeed so to open, renovate and enlarge the home market as to render it much more valuable to all the interests of the State, to the labourer, the farmer, the manufacturer, the merchant and the land-owner. . . . Let us but be placed together in contiguous dwellings, and with the command of a small portion of the land, for which we will pay the usual rental, and we shall soon show our legislators what we are capable of doing for ourselves for our children and for all" (*Economist*, 1829, No. 3).

The printers' project failed because the funds to set it going could not be obtained.

By 1826 the movement had its central organ in the *Co-operative Magazine*, which ran for four years. It reported at length the discussions of meetings of the London Co-operators, and the questions debated in its columns included the moral and physical evils arising from the competitive system of producing and distributing wealth, the reasons for the universal poverty of the producing classes, the value of combination—could it raise wage rates?—and whether surplus population was the reason for the country's troubles. By the end of the decade one variant or another of the Owenite outlook coloured the ideas of most of the leading people in the working-class and trade union movement. By 1832 about 500 Co-operative Societies had been established with some 20,000 members. This was the beginning of a movement that brought Utopian Socialist ideas to workers far and wide, through millions of tracts, the activities of Co-operative "missionaries" like William Thompson, who gave as many as 1,450 lectures a year, and press articles.

It was to be long, however, before any clear lines of debate took shape. In the field of ideas, the Radical papers made no sharply critical break with any part of their past: the ideas of Paine and Spence, the moral and patriotic passion of Cobbett (which the Reform Bill crisis brilliantly revived), and a variety of class-conscious attitudes growing up under the roomy mantle of Owenism co-existed in a wide stream of anger and protest, extending into Chartist days and beyond. "The minds of thinking men", declared the rules of a Co-operative Society formed in Rippenden in 1832, "are lost in a labyrinth of suggestions what plan to adopt in order to better, if possible, their conditions".

The new class indeed faced a superhuman task in breaking through to self-knowledge. Mercilessly long hours of labour, the dead hand of a tradition denying education to the "lower orders", the pit of distress and starvation into which it was so easy to fall, combined to make this road long and painful.

To appreciate the obstacles with which the Rippenden Co-operators' labyrinth was littered, and the difficulties facing "thinking men" among the working population, as well as to take the measure of the challenge that confronted Radical and early Socialist journalism, it will be useful to look over to the other side of the great fence that separated the workers from the world of the propertied classes, to look into the minds of magistrates and MPs, the government press, the societies prosecuting sedition and blasphemy and, after their collapse, the host of Whiggish and middle-class bodies devoted to "improving" the thinking, morals and character of the teeming new urban millions.

We see at the beginning a situation of near-total non-communication between the two sides. Not only the right to think about social and political matters, but the most elementary tools of knowledge with which to do so—apart from a minimal knowledge of reading and counting—were denied to laborious man as a matter of policy and the hereditary right to govern of the landed gentleman. The policy was defended to the last gasp. The main assault of the early Radicals was directed against this citadel of arrogance. Their journals, especially those most clearly in the Paine tradition, placed this task on a level with parliamentary reform itself and some even above it. Carlile appeared to believe that loud enough blasts on the trumpet of popular enlightenment would cause the citadel walls to tumble.

"Let us then endeavour to progress in knowledge, since knowledge is demonstrably proved to be power," he declared (*Republican*, October 4, 1820). "It is the power of knowledge that checks the crimes of cabinets and courts; it is the power of knowledge that must put a stop to bloody wars and the direful effects of devastating armies."

Of this knowledge, the free press was the principal arm, he declared. The Radical papers practised this belief, giving many workers their first education, not merely in home politics, but over a wide field of knowledge of the world and history as well as mathematics and science. Cobbett had good reason for the pride he expressed in a farewell address (*Political Register*, January 6, 1820) to the last issue of "TWOPENNY TRASH, dear little twopenny trash".

"Thou hast acted thy part in the great drama. Ten thousand wagon loads of volumes that fill the libraries and booksellers' shops have never caused a thousandth part of the thinking nor a millionth part of the stir that thou hast caused. . . . And thou hast created more pleasure and more hopes in the breasts of honest men than ever were before created by tongue or pen since England was England."

The Constitutional Society averred in its prospectus that the Radical papers flooding the country—"without excepting even the day of sacred rest"—were beyond doubt criminal since they consisted of the "most false and inflammatory statements respecting public institutions and public men . . . and offer direct incitements to violence and crime". Seven hundred persons, including the Duke of Wellington, nearly 40 MPs and over 100 clergy, subscribed to the society.

Its press voice, the ministerial *New Times*, answering people who objected that there had always been libels in England and they had done the country no serious harm, produced this "conclusive answer": the libels of former times were "only read by the higher classes, which possessed the means of detecting their falsehood—those of the present are extensively read by the lower orders, who are *destitute* of all means of arriving at the truth". Former libels were only intended to drive a ministry from office—the object of the present one was to "dethrone the King and overthrow the Constitution". (The society's treasurer, Sir John Sewell, had a solid interest in opposing the reformers—he was said to hold sinecures to the value of £1,500 a year.) This was the institution that William Hone called "The Bridge Street Gang", and John Hunt's *Examiner* "this canting crew". A party of ignorance, engaged in an extensive conspiracy against every form of education for the people, was in the saddle.

One of the very few Whigs to dissent from the chorus of hate, in a Commons debate on the Gagging Acts, was the great lawyer Lord Erskine, who caused deep anger on the Tory benches when he expressed his disagreement with "the principle and opinion that the safety of the State and the happiness of the multitude in the laborious conditions of life may be best secured by their being kept in ignorance of political controversies and opinions". In a debate on March 26, 1823, on the "Vice Society", Secretary of State Robert Peel defended the imprisonment of Carlile's sister, which had caused much indignation. The law of the country, he declared, made it a crime "to make any attempt to deprive the lower classes of their belief in the consolations of religion, and while the law remained unrepealed he should think himself wanting in his duty if he shrank from applying it and enforcing it".

The writer of a pamphlet published in 1831 entitled *Suggestions Respecting the Political Education of the Lower Orders* demanded a counter-attack on Cobbett and Carlile. He wanted to see well-written pamphlets for the lower orders in which they "would be led first to doubt, and then to desert the principles of their self-elected leaders". With the influence they acquired they would "at length be enabled to instil into the minds of their pupils, in a gradual and almost imperceptible manner, any principles and doctrines they desired".

This early anticipation of some of the twentieth-century press lords' attacks on trade union independence and daily brainwashing of their readers never got off the ground. One curt answer, as good now as then, was given in the *Poor Man's Guardian* (April 14, 1832) commenting on the soothing syrup being provided by the newly-founded *Chambers Journal*. The choice, it said, was between "knowledge calculated to make you free" and "the namby-pamby stuff published expressly to stultify the minds of the working people and make them the spiritless and unresisting victims of a system of plunder and oppression".

This is our first meeting with the celebrated paper which first served the workers as an all-round fighting weapon, involved in their trade union activities, and committed to their independent political aspirations and self-awareness as a class. It spoke to and for readers much advanced from the Peterloo days in their thinking. By now the journals of Paine, Cobbett, Wooler and Carlile, who fought in their various ways for the Rights of Man, were giving way to a press proclaiming the rights of the working class. A link-up with the trade union movement and with Socialist and Co-operative thinking had begun. And the single banner of Radicalism, beneath which middle-class and working-class campaigners for the reform of Parliament had served side by side for half a century, would be taken into battle for the last time—in the Reform Bill crisis. In the decade after that momentous event it would be rent in twain.

5

The Great Unstamped

Of all the taxes levied (or attempted to be levied) upon the poor man, the most odious and the most inexcusable is the tax upon political knowledge.

You may have "*religious* knowledge" and all sorts of romantic and idle stories "dirt cheap" but if you wish to know anything about the pickpocket machinery which robs the poor man of eight shillings out of every thirteen which he spends; then the Aristocrats say "You shall know nothing about our black art, our dirty works and our swindling schemes, unless you pay us fourpence for a red mark which we put upon the paper". . . . But the *Poor Man's Guardian* . . . if properly supported by the working classes will shew them not only that "knowledge is power" but that power in their hands shall produce knowledge. . . . Finally let every man do his utmost to oppose the three most besotting peculiarities of Englishmen, viz. gin-drinking, boxing-matches, and a veneration for titles.

Letter from a FRIEND TO LIBERTY, *Poor Man's Guardian*, August 20, 1831

THE CHANGES in working-class Radical thinking took place within a general advance of the movement for parliamentary reform, accelerated by the economic crisis of 1825. The postwar ice-cap over politics at the top began to crack, as it came under pressure from the new wealthy of trade and industry. Unrepresented in Parliament, hampered by the Corn Laws, by a tax system favouring landed wealth, and by numerous curbs on industrial expansion and trade, and resentful of jobbery and incompetence in administration, these interests now demanded a share in power corresponding to their growing economic strength.

The Tory government headed by Lord Liverpool which had been in office since 1812 first split, about 1822, into a diehard party and a group trying concessions to the new men, and about 1827 into warring factions, some of which crossed to the Whig side. THE THING, Cobbett's single front of privileged property, corruption, mercantile banks and the factory masters, broke into two pieces. After 1827 came a five-year period of unstable cabinets, followed by long years of shifting new alignments among the traditional aristocratic rulers and the representatives of property as capital, to lead eventually to the Victorian two-party power game in which Whigs, restyling themselves Liberals, and the Tories, trying to bury the odium of their past by calling themselves Conservatives, took turns at superintending the full development of capitalist society.

In the run-up to the big battle of 1832, reform changed at the parliamentary level from a minority to a majority cause. From right to left it comprised a Whig aristocratic group which aimed both to minimise change and consolidate its grip on office with middle-class support; a more advanced group whose leaders were Lords Brougham and Durham, with the *Edinburgh Review* as their press voice; and, more directly connected with the merchants and manufacturers and professional classes, the "Philosophic Radicals" basing themselves on the teachings of Jeremy Bentham, who were theoretically for manhood suffrage but considered it impracticable. All the working-class reformers took their main stand on manhood suffrage, but to the left or Cobbett and Hunt, the main proponents, there now existed a big front of Owenites and trade unionists interlaced with revolutionary trends in the tradition of Paine and Spence. The Rotunda was its general headquarters.

In these years a powerful reinforcement arrived in this camp from Ireland. It was to form one of the big influences in Radical politics and journalism throughout the century. The election of Daniel O'Connell, leader of the Irish Catholic peasantry's revolt, as MP for Clare in 1828 produced a situation in England's first colony where the choice for the government lay between making concessions and making war. The Catholic Emancipation Act in the following year saved British rule, but in the disarray that it caused in the Tory ranks the Whigs came to power—and a narrow opening for the reform campaigners appeared. From then on a body of Irish Catholics sat in the Commons at Westminster. Already tens of thousands of Irish immigrants were established both in London and the new factory areas where they provided an extreme left of Radicalism, fertile in orators, journalists and trade union militants. The National Union of the Working Classes espoused their demand for the repeal of the Act of Union of 1801* scarcely less vigorously than it worked for the parliamentary reform.

* Abolished Ireland's separate parliament and united the colony with England, Scotland and Wales, after the defeat of the revolt by Wolfe Tone and his United Irishmen in 1798.

The year 1830 brought the foundation of the famous Birmingham Political Union and of similar unions in other towns, to form together a kind of ad hoc extra-parliamentary party of middle-class and working-class Radicals joining forces to win reform. In the same year revolutions in France and Belgium caused a stir of hope among the lower orders; and among their allies higher up the social scale the fact that these revolutions did not lead to the tumbrils quieted some of the old fears. On November 15, the Duke of Wellington resigned and a Whig Cabinet headed by Lord Grey replaced the Tories. Its first act was to suppress the movement of starving agricultural labourers in the southern counties, sometimes known as England's last agrarian revolt. The courts had nineteen men hanged and 481 transported for machine-breaking and arson. As the Tories had done in 1817, the Whigs tried now to silence Cobbett; but he was triumphantly acquitted on a charge of incitement brought in one of the dirtiest of the court persecutions of those days.*

In March Lord Grey brought in a reform Bill. It proposed to abolish some of the rotten boroughs, give representation to some previously unrepresented towns, like Manchester, Leeds and Sheffield, and extended the franchise in the boroughs to the £10 householder—which excluded almost all workers—and to the better-off farmers in the counties. The Bill passed its second reading in the Commons by one vote. Defeated in committee, Grey called a general election, at which he won an increased majority. But when the Commons again passed the Bill, the House of Lords rejected it. In the eight-month crisis that followed the country came to the brink of insurrection. The contest mounted into a confrontation of democracy and aristocracy in which sight was partly lost, on the popular wing of the Radicals, of the Bill's limitations. When the Lords tried to kill it by amendments in Committee the central watchword on the reform side became: "The Bill, the whole Bill, and nothing but the Bill."

On June 7, 1832, the Bill became law after Lord Grey had threatened to create enough new peers to force it through the House of Lords. The real lever that he used, however, was the prospect of revolution

---

* Cobbett defied the government's intimidated witnesses—"the miscreants and base wretches" who had imputed to him responsibility for the risings of the labourers and the fires. He went on, though, to cry that if he were possessed of the power, sitting in London, to cause such destruction, and if he deemed it right to render evil for evil—"I should be *fully justified in exercising that power*".

if the Bill were not passed. Earlier he had defined his aim with brutal clarity in a speech in the Commons on November 31, 1831: "There is no one more decided against annual parliaments, universal suffrage, and the ballot, than I am. My object is not to favour but to put an end to such hopes and projects."

During, and even more after, the great battle, the two streams of Radicalism began clearly to go their separate ways. The first voice amid the din to be heard denouncing the Bill loud and clear was that of the *Poor Man's Guardian*. The paper first appeared, more or less daily, under its original title *Penny Papers for the People*, on October 1, 1830, six weeks before the Bill was introduced. Its publisher, Henry Hetherington, who had been one of the staunchest of Carlile's shopmen, nailed colours to his mast that were to remain there until the journal ceased publication five stormy years later. An opening editorial article in good round Paine style declared:

"It is the cause of the *rabble* we advocate, the poor, the suffering, the industrious, the productive classes. . . . We will teach this rabble their power —we will teach them that they are your master, instead of being your slaves."

In July 1831 the paper appeared in a form that was itself a challenge. It carried not the little red spot of the stamp duty, but in its place a black design of a printing press and the slogan "Knowledge is Power". The words "Published in Defiance of the Law, to try the Power of Right against Might" were printed below. The paper declared itself to be "established contrary to law" and said that it would "contain (in the words of the prohibitory Act, here in italics) *news, intelligence, occurrences and remarks and observations thereon tending* decidedly *to excite hatred and contempt of the government and constitution of the tyranny of this country as by law established, and also vilify the abuses of religion.*"
Hetherington wrote:

"Defiance is our only remedy; we cannot be a slave in all; we submit to much—for it is impossible to be wholly consistent—but we will try the power of Right against Might; we will begin by protesting and upholding this grand bulwark of all our liberties—the Freedom of the Press—the Press, too, of the ignorant and the Poor. We have taken upon ourselves its protection, and we will never abandon our post: we will die rather."

The twelfth issue (September 24) addressed this message to the "Self-elected, self-authorised, and self-legislating hereditary Society, self-called House of Peers":

"We, the Poor Man's Guardian, proclaim that we represent the working, productive, and useful but *poor* classes, who constitute a very great majority of the population of Great Britain. We proclaim that some hundreds of thousands of the poor have elected us the GUARDIAN of their *rights* and *liberties*."

The style was in the Paine tradition, but the message went well beyond Paine. From the outset the paper was closely associated with the National Union of the Working Classes and Others, founded early in the same year. This was the new title taken by the Metropolitan Trades Union under the influence of the Reform Bill excitements and the growth of the Political Unions in which working-class and middle-class reformers worked together. The title reflected a conviction that, as an April resolution of the organisation said, "the working classes must obtain their rights as *men* before they could obtain them as *workmen*". The *Guardian* (March 3) summarised the advanced Radical programme of this body, whose development can be followed in its columns. Earlier, Hetherington had written a prospectus for the Metropolitan Trades Union defining its two aims as the winning of universal suffrage and trade unionist and Co-operative measures. The prospectus was sent to 150 working men's clubs in London, and it was the consequent rapid growth in the organisation's numbers that made necessary the move to Carlile's larger premises at the Rotunda, which held 1,000 people.

By May 25, when meetings were held to debate the constitution which Hetherington and the London working men's leader William Lovett had drawn up for the National Union, fears already growing in connection with the current switch of middle-class opinion to Radicalism were already clearly apparent. A motion was proposed that "no member of the Union shall be elected on the Committee who is not a producer, or who does not earn his living by labour". The Owenite Socialists, who rejected this approach, proved stronger on this occasion and the motion was defeated, but the debate on the underlying question of whether workers could gain anything from what middle-class Radicals said would be their "virtual representation" in the new parliament went on throughout the crisis.

A month earlier, on April 29, the paper had published a letter, the first of several addressed to "the Working People of England", from an anonymous handloom weaver who had been ruined by the advent of machinery. It declared the Reform Bill to be *worse* than the old franchise. He wrote:

"People who live by plunder will always tell you to be submissive to thieves. To talk of *representation*, in any shape, being of any use to the people is sheer nonsense, unless the people have a House of working men, and represent themselves. Those who make the laws now, and are intended, by the reform bill, to make them in the future all live by profits of some sort or another. They will, therefore, no matter who elect them, or how often they are elected, always make the laws to raise profits and keep down the price of labour. Representation, therefore, by a different body of people to those who are represented, or whose interests are opposed to theirs, is a mockery, and those who persuade the people to the contrary are either idiots or cheats. . . . "

This audacious thinker went on to say that the people should stop arguing about "electing a legislative in the present shape" and "contend night and day, every moment of their lives, for a legislature of their own, or one made up of themselves". He also assailed the Owenite delusion:

"Co-operation is of no use, unless the people would get the raw materials without going to the land-stealer, then dispense with the use of money, and live by bartering their manufactures with each other. No one could then get either rent, tax, or profit out of them, but as they cannot do this, Co-operation has little or no effect than that of feeding the rich and starving those who can scarcely live. . . . As soon as it becomes generally understood that Co-operators can live a shilling a week cheaper than before, their employers will reduce their wages to that amount; and thus will their employers reap all the advantages of their co-operation. . . . "

In November (19 and 26) the anonymous correspondent was describing, as an example of the sort of men who would form the new House of Commons two candidates already named by "the profit-men or middlemen, for our town". "One of them everybody knows, and therefore I shall say nothing about him; the other, I am informed, is a Cockney of the name of Young, a shipbuilder who possesses as much information *as my loom*. . . . It is but common justice that the people who make the goods should have the sole privilege of making the laws."

As the struggle neared its end in March 1832, he recalled in another letter how he had uniformly told the workers that the Bill would do them "an incalculable deal of harm". Attacking one of the main planks of the middle-class Radicals, he wrote that the evils under which working men laboured were not produced by taxation. "I have shown you that the whole expense of the government, from the King to the common soldier, does not amount to more than one halfpenny a day upon each individual in the two kingdoms; and that the abolition of the whole government would relieve you to the amount of only that one halfpenny a day."

The papers that served such views, unlike earlier Radical journals, gave news in the government definition of the word, as they reported and commented on each stage in the Reform Bill struggle. They also belonged to the workers' movement in a more direct and organised way than previously. Doherty's *Voice of the People* reported (June 18, 1831) that "almost every large town has its *Trades Herald, Workman's Advocate, Workers' Guardian* or some other equally zealous and useful publication, all strenuously advocating the necessity of duly rewarding labour, and of improvement in the condition of the working classes".

Whenever Hetherington was out of prison in 1831–3 he visited the north and Midlands to found both branches of the National Union and agencies for the *Poor Man's Guardian*. Lovett said that the journal was the "principal reporter" of National Union meetings and for this reason "held first place in the estimation of its members". And its sales, which reached 16,000 during the Reform Bill crisis fell to below 5,000 after the collapse of the National Union in 1834. At its peak circulation, some two-thirds of the copies went to the provinces where many of the retail agents whom Hetherington recruited on his tours combined the selling of the unstamped papers with their own trades. Twenty-five of his forty provincial agents went to prison.

Hetherington's paper and most of the other working-class Radical journals gave much prominence to the idea of winning power by a month's general strike, advanced early in 1832. The project was put forward in a pamphlet, *Grand National Holiday and Congress of the Productive Classes*, by William Benbow, a printer, publisher and coffee-house owner who had served at least two sentences of imprisonment for seditious activities. A general strike, he said, was necessary, because "we are oppressed in the fullest sense of the word; we have been deprived of everything; we have no property, no wealth, and our labour is of no use to us, since what it produces goes into the hands of others. . . . " It proposed that "committees of management of the working classes . . . be forthwith formed in every city, town, village and parish", to put into execution a plan to "establish the happiness of the *immense* majority of the human race, of that *far largest* portion called *the working classes*".

The passage of the Reform Bill, after the popular upheaval that forced it through, inevitably engendered hopes that, as Cobbett thought, real democratic advances might be built upon this success. On July 21, 1832, in the run-up to the general election for the re-formed Parliament, the *Poor Man's Guardian* published a list of pledges that candidates should be asked to give. One of them was to support "an effectual reform" of Parliament including manhood suffrage and vote by ballot. Others were to abolish the taxes on knowledge and to repeal the Corn Laws and "all the taxes pressing upon the necessaries and comforts of the labouring man". But the character of what the paper had called on April 11 this "wicked, tyrannous, dishonest and diabolical measure" was so clear—and the new Parliament followed it so quickly with diabolical legislation—that the initial half-hopes entertained by many working men soon flickered out.

By October 25 the *Guardian* was giving its own clear verdict:

> "The promoters of the Reform Bill projected it, not with a view to subvert, or even remodel, our aristocratic institutions, but to consolidate them by a reinforcement of sub-aristocracy from the middle-classes. . . . The only difference between Whigs and the Tories is this—the Whigs would give the shadow to preserve the substance."

A year earlier, on October 1, 1831, the paper had already taken a derisive view of the Whigs' employment of the revolution spectre to coerce Tory opposition. It said that "a violent revolution is not only beyond the means of those who threaten it, but it is to them their greatest object of alarm, for they know that such a revolution can only be effected by the poor and despised millions, who if excited to the step, might use it for their own advantages."

The struggle of the *Guardian* and its companions of the Great Un-stamped fused two causes. The first was the most decisive challenge yet to the taxation curbs on the press, in which Hetherington and his rivals and emulators and their vendors bore the brunt. The second was the mental effort through which the editors of these papers gave the workers an identity as a class and the beginnings of an independent working-class social and political theory. Of these men, who laid the foundation for Chartism, the most influential was James Bronterre O'Brien, who became editor of the *Guardian* in November 1832, after a period as editor of the *Midlands Representative* in Birmingham, general headquarters of the reform movement in its broadest form. The son of an Irish wine merchant, and a graduate of Trinity College, Dublin, O'Brien came to London in 1829 to study, as he said, "Law and Radical Reform". Ten years later, his compatriot and the overall chieftain of Chartism, Feargus O'Connor, called him "the schoolmaster of public opinion for eight long years of undeviated practice".

The unstamped press of the early eighteen-thirties, and the *Guardian* in particular, were the school in which the Chartist schoolmaster taught. Under O'Brien, the *Guardian* advanced beyond the workers' approach in Peterloo days, when their main fire was directed at the boroughmongers and unjust taxes. The old evils came to be seen not as causes but rather as symptoms of an unjust society in which the working man was simultaneously robbed of the right to vote and of the products of his labour. The paper also challenged the "science" of middle-class Political Economy, which, in words used by the unstamped *Man*, "sought to prove that a starving man is and ought to be the most contented being in existence".

There had been papers before the *Guardian* as well loved and as influential in stirring and spreading the spirit of revolt, but none, before or since, played so politically central and creative a part. More than any other mental force of its time, it hammered out of the diverse trends of Owenism and the Co-operative movement, trade union organisation, and the whole rich inheritance received from the American, French and Irish revolutions via Cobbett and Paine, a distinctive self-consciousness for the new class. A legend already in its own day, its fame and memory inspired the later struggles: the Chartist Oastler wrote after its demise that O'Brien should "put the soul of the *Poor Man's Guardian* into the *Northern Star*", chief organ of the Chartist movement. In the *Guardian's* correspondence columns, the loyalty that it captured among workers, the feeling that it communicated to them of their stature as society's present *producers* and future *masters*, is reflected in hundreds of letters. In its last number but one, a member of the National Union, Thomas Goldspink, wrote to express his "gratitude to you as a political and moral preceptor, from which I have derived much of the information I possess." He added that he felt sure the paper would be resorted to in after times as a useful corrective of the histories that would be written by hireling scribes. The author of the first history of the newspaper press, James Grant, recalled that one of the parties connected with the paper told him in exulting tones in 1833: "O Sir, the Guardian is rapidly tearing society up by the roots."*

In his own paper, *Bronterre's National Reformer*, O'Brien developed his views that only "through the conquest of political power will the working class create a society in which each man, while being guaranteed the product of his labour, would be prevented from appropriating the labour of others. The working class must destroy the power of the middle class." Francis Place blamed Bronterre O'Brien more than any other politician for the spread in the late thirties of "mischievous doctrines concerning property".

In the *Guardian* the teaching that wealth was created by labour, but through the oligarchic political system continually stolen from its creators, stimulated some of the liveliest of the letters to the editor. A contribution from "One of the Oppressed" (April 14, 1832) told the readers that the *remote* cause of their poverty was their "not having seats, *personally*, in that which ought to be your house", while the immediate cause was the "exorbitant rents, tithes, interest on money, profits on labour and profits on trade" imposed on them by "the landstealers, merchants, manufacturers and tradesmen, in that house from which you are excluded".

The history of mankind, O'Brien wrote in the following year,

"shows that from the beginning of the world, the rich of all countries have been in a permanent state of conspiracy to keep down the poor of all countries, and for this plain reason—because the poverty of the poor man is essential to the riches of the rich man. No matter by what means they may disguise their operations, the rich are everlastingly plundering, debasing and brutalising the poor. All the crimes and superstitions of human nature have their origin in this cannibal warfare of riches against poverty. The desire of one man to live on the fruits of another's labour is the original sin of the world."

And again in the same journal in October, 1834:

"All oppressed of every kind should look with distrust upon the measures

* *The Newspaper Press: its origins, progress and present position*, 3 vols., 1871–2.

of change which originate with their oppressors, and if the work of reform is to be done well for them, they must do it themselves."

Such knowledge was hard to win, and amid the Reform Bill period of excitement and popular hopes followed by disillusion, numerous and varied were the offered solutions and bitter the dissensions around them. In O'Brien's columns one may follow a remarkable progression from the common Radical programme of "Extirpation of the Fiend Aristocracy"—first aim in the programme of the National Union published in the *Guardian* on March 3, 1831—to the firm belief in manhood suffrage as a route to control of the state by working men, and the relief of their hunger and distress by this means, at which the grandsons of the stalwarts of the London Corresponding Society had now arrived.

The paper published a dozen editorials denouncing the Reform Bill. Its letter columns, however, sometimes reflected the view that something might be won from the Bill. A letter from William Carpenter, a former *Trades Newspaper* editor, argued that the lower class of labourers did not yet possess the power to obtain their just claims; the Bill admitted the theoretical necessity of reform, and this lower class ought in justice to themselves and to "society at large" to "abstain from everything that would produce a rupture that could only terminate in evil, and loss to all". The letter concluded: "The Bill conceded, *to some extent*, the right of representation on the basis of *population*; and this concession once made, in however trifling a degree, *must* be carried onward to its full extent."

This theme of salvation through middle-class allies had a very short run with the London working men of the early eighteen-thirties, though it was to revive strongly later. We may take a look here at one of the liveliest of the penny weeklies, the *Working Man's Friend and Political Magazine*, started by James Watson, another former shopman of Carlile, in December 1832 amid the furious fray over the Bill and its consequences.

"The whole thing [the paper declared] is from beginning to end humbuggery of the worst description. . . . One thing self-evident is that there is not the slightest pretence to make even an attempt at relieving the suffering millions from any part of their burdens. . . . We are then right glad to perceive that the National Union of the Working Classes think with us and have felt themselves compelled to call upon the 'people' in all parts of the country to prepare themselves for a National Convention" (April 27, 1833).

The journal started on December 22, 1832, and had run its brief course by the following August. Its eight quarto pages for a penny, illustrated with woodcut portraits of Radical personalities, publicised the movement for repeal of the Act of Union and a half page of its first issue was devoted to a meeting of the National Repeal Union.

Watson's journal tackled the press freedom question vigorously. Denouncing a prosecution launched against the *Guardian*, he pointed out that the Whigs, who had been such clamorous advocates for a free press, "have since their accession to power proved themselves to be its most malignant opponents. . . . To us, the Whigs are not objects merely of cordial execration, we pity the idiots, they dream that by attempting to prolong the existence of a stamped, shackled Press, they will be able to realise their dream. It is but a dream. Were they awake, they would see that during the last two years, victim after victim has been consigned to prison for publishing and vending unstamped Political Papers; and that in spite of the persecution, the 'objectionable' publications are more deeply rooted in public patronage than ever" (December 29, 1832).

Its January 26 number carried an account of a special meeting called by the National Union on the tyrannical conduct of the Whig government towards Hetherington, who had just been jailed for twelve months. The Rev. Dr. Wade was in the chair. He urged the meeting to "agitate, unceasingly agitate, the question of the repeal of the taxes upon knowledge" and said that if the working classes did this they would eventually get their rights. And he emphasised that the *Poor Man's Guardian*, the *Working Man's Friend*, and the stamped *True Sun* were not in competition and the National Union supported all of them. A speaker proposed a motion condemning the Whigs and declaring that there must be a "free trade in knowledge in order that honest men might enlighten their fellow-countrymen". (This was a shrewd dig at the Whigs and the Political Economy school, which pressed tirelessly for free trade and the ending of all state restrictions on commercial enterprise but rigorously excluded newspapers from this principle.)

A seconding speaker gave his opinion that the whole people had become "slaves to the progeny of William the Conqueror" and would remain in that degraded condition unless they rose and emancipated themselves. He went on:

"When he saw wealth and profligacy rolling in chariots and industry bare-
foot and begging in the streets what could he think of the sufferings of the
people and the inhumanity of their oppressors? . . . If they had the Press
free and unshackled, would those evils, he would ask, and thousands more
by which they were afflicted, have existed (Cries of No!) Without an
effort, different from any which had yet been made, they would never
release the Press from its trammels."

Rarely can the idea that press liberties and a better livelihood go
hand in hand have been more forcefully put. The speaker then condemned the attempts being made by military despotism to suppress
liberty in Ireland, and resolutions were carried supporting Hetherington's fight—"he exposed the fallacy and humbuggery of the Reform
Bill—he dared to show the causes which immersed the working
classes in misery and wretchedness"—calling for the repeal of the Act
of Union, and ending, to cap what must have been a memorable
evening, with "three cheers for Mr. Hetherington, three cheers for
Daniel O'Connell and the Irish Volunteers, and three cheers for the
Heroes of the Three Days of July in Paris!"

From his inevitable imprisonment Watson wrote a piece in the
February 23 issue under the heading "A VOICE FROM THE BASTILLE". He
declared that "he is happy that he is a single man and so can aid those
admirable men, both dead and living, who by their pens or their
tongues have aided the great cause of human liberty and universal
happiness". On March 2 he reported that he was preparing and
gathering new materials for renewed agitation. "I shall come forth
from my prison-house with increased knowledge, and a more deadly
hatred to the public robbers who despoil and misgovern my country.
The accursed Stamp Laws must be entirely abolished. We will yield
to no half-measures, we will have the press free and unshackled from
all fiscal extortions; or we will never cease to war with its injustice."

How closely this paper was knit with the trade union activities
appears in this passage from a report in the same number of a local
meeting of the National Union:

"On Tuesday evening the usual weekly meeting was held in the Chapel,
Chapel Court, High Street, Borough. Previous to the chair being taken,
Mr Turner a Victim of the Stamp Acts, entertained the audience by singing,
in good style, from the Gallery a Patriotic Hymn. The splendid banners of
several of the Borough, Walworth and Camberwell classes were hung round

the Chapel, and gave the meeting an appearance of the gathering of the Sons of Freedom."

A month later the journal carried a petition from its imprisoned publisher. He pointed out that as a general bookseller he had been selling no fewer than twenty penny periodicals including the *Penny Magazine* and other journals under the patronage of ministers. Magistrates had admitted that all equally violated the Act and this showed that "it is the opinions advocated in the *Poor Man's Guardian* that the Commissioners of Stamp and the Government are anxious to suppress".

The letters in Watson's paper reflect some of the ceaseless polemics among the London working men in the bitter aftermath of the Reform Bill. One signed COUNCILLOR protested that Carlile, editor of the *Gauntlet*, had deigned to inform him finally, after what was apparently a long correspondence, that he had lit his fire with a letter that COUNCILLOR had written to him, in reply to an attack in the *Gauntlet* on political unions. The letter criticised Carlile's "one-eyed vision". It told the crusty old Cyclops that it might suit him to reduce all unions to "tippling clubs"—because they met in public houses—but he had to do better than this if he were "to convince us (the Unionists) that several links are stronger than a chain and that we are idle drunkards instead of ardent searchers after knowledge, zealously determined to obtain and defend our rights as Englishmen and fellow-citizens".

Combative to the last, and linking as always the great events of the day with the press freedom fight, the paper's last issue but one announced: "The Friends of Freedom will meet at White Conduit Tea Gardens on Monday, July 29th, at two o'clock to celebrate the Third Anniversary of the glorious resistance of the unwashed Artizans of Paris against Kingly Domination and Ministerial misrule on the 28th, 29th and 30th July 1830; also to celebrate the triumphant acquittal of the intended victim of Whig tyranny GEORGE FURSEY" (a Stamp Act victim).

The last issue thanked the readers and advised trade unionists among them to have "a friendly communication with all the villages round their respective neighbourhoods". Watson thanked the Whigs for their persecution, which had contributed to "that mental emancipation of which I am an humble and sincere advocate" and concluded: "I have a line of duty marked out, and whilst I have health, strength, and any means at my disposal, I will continue to work for the benefit of *my order*."

In tune with the change in the content of the workers' papers, and their breakaway from middle-class Radicalism, their traditional internationalism took on a new colour. The initial enthusiasm for the French Revolution of 1830 was tempered later as the workers understood that it had brought to power men of the same kind as their own enemies at home. The *Guardian* (November 21, 1835) said that Louis Philippe was "but an instrument in the hands of the moneyed classes, whose system he must carry out or else abdicate his throne. Louis Philippe is the plunderers' king. He is the king of the pot-bellied bourgeoisie."

This straight class feeling stayed uppermost in working people's minds for most of the thirties and forties, as did recognition of the government and all state power as an instrument of the ruling class. Labour movement historians G. D. H. Cole and Raymond Postgate have estimated* that in these years "the opposition between the middle class (the word capitalist was rarely used) and the working class was more universally taken to be the key to current history than it has ever been before or since". The extraordinarily rapid formation just over a year after the Reform Bill of the Grand National Consolidated Trades Union, with possibly as many as half a million members, was the widest of all the reactions to that grand disappointment. Many workers took new hope from Robert Owen's prophecies that the Grand National could remove their burdens by taking over industry and running it co-operatively. The *Pioneer*, the paper of the Builders' Union founded in 1832, became the organ of the Grand National. A ferocious onslaught by the employers, including the presentation of "the document" requiring workers to abjure trade unionism, quickly knocked such visionary hopes on the head. Owen quarrelled both with James Morrison, editor of the *Pioneer*, and lecturer J. E. Smith who edited Owen's journal *The Crisis*;† he cut the first journal off from all connection with the Grand National and closed down the second. The two editors had been urging reform of the Grand National to make it an effective strike weapon, but Owen would have none of this.

On the other flank, the *Pioneer* in particular came under fire from the *Poor Man's Guardian* for seeing the exploitation of the workers as a

* *The Common People, 1746–1946*, p. 261.

† This 4-page large quarto weekly sub-titled "The Change from Error and Misery to Truth and Happiness" and published from the same office as the *Pioneer* was started on April 14, 1832. Its price was 1*d.* and later 1½*d.*

distinct sphere unconnected with the political struggle for manhood
suffrage. For nearly six months, O'Brien's leading articles crossed
swords with the builders' journal and tried to harness the Grand
National to the campaign for the vote. The dispute did not stop the
Guardian from carrying advertisements for the Grand National, reporting the rapid formation of new trade unions then occurring, and
raising money for their activities. But the long shadow of later differences between the "politicians" and the trade union wing of the movement can be seen already falling on the columns recording these
controversies.

Frequently the *Guardian* warned its trade unionist readers of the
danger of refusing to work for the vote. If they were not represented
in Parliament, it argued, trade unions could be wiped out by the
masters whenever Parliament chose. However, it was in advance even
of many Socialist journals of later date, including the *Commonweal*
and *Justice*, in its close and detailed following of trade union activities.
(Nine of its thirteen editorials between November 1833 and February
1834 were devoted to trade union subjects.)

The basic escapism of Robert Owen's teaching—its refusal to recognise any irreconcilable conflict between masters and men and rejection
of "politics"—delayed the formation of a labour political movement.
The *Crisis* went through the final peak moments of the Reform Bill
crisis without referring to it. The *Pioneer*, in the bitter Derby turn-out
of the winter of 1834-5 proposed that the strikers should be settled to
work as Co-operative producers, and the Grand National had to take
this barren scheme over. And the same paper, commenting on the
February 1834 Convention of the Grand National, consoled itself for
the Reform Bill disappointment with the following reflection: "There
are two parliaments at present sitting, and we have no hesitation in
stating that the Trades Parliament is by far the most important. It is
more national than the other . . . and the constitution is much larger.
The Union is composed of nearly a million members and Universal
Suffrage prevails among them."

The delusions of grandeur here expressed rapidly faded, together
with the Grand National itself, in the merciless class struggles of the
middle and late thirties to which the Reform Bill crisis formed a
prelude.

The first engagement in these struggles, before they mounted into the upheaval in support of the People's Charter, was fought over the press. Over 700 people had suffered imprisonment and other penalties in the unstamped newspapers cause before its victorious conclusion. The unstamped were counted in hundreds, and in addition to the seventy or so overtly political papers, that is, those campaigning for parliamentary reform, there was a host of other publications: anti-clerical papers like the *Slap at the Church* and the *Christian Corrector*, trade union and Co-operative journals, humorous papers such as *Dibdin's Penny Trumpet*, and crime sheets like the *Newgate Calendar*. The great majority of the unstamped, however, spoke for some organised body of opinion and struggle, and within about five years they had worn down authority by the collective weight of their mutiny.

While many of them tried to maintain that they were not news-papers because they contained no *news*, there was one publisher at least who tried to prove on the contrary that his product could not be a newspaper because it contained no *paper*. Henry Berthold published his *Political Handkerchief* on calico. The September 5, 1831, number told readers: "Your wives and daughters may become moving monu-ments of political knowledge. One shall be dressed in a description of kingcraft, another in a description of priestcraft, a third in a description of lordcraft, or general aristocracy. . . . The nakedness of mankind shall be covered both as to body and mind." And he added a promise that if the ink washed out he would buy back handkerchiefs and reprint them. Another journal, produced by two vendors, bore the title *Political Touchwood* because it was printed on thin plywood.

The Battle of the Unstamped opened with the launching, eight weeks before Hetherington's celebrated journal, of William Carpenter's *Political Letters*. Carpenter claimed that the letters, which took the form of addresses to the Duke of Wellington and other reactionary notabilities, were not a newspaper within the meaning of the Act. The Stamp Office won a case against him and he was fined £120 and sent to prison. Many editors before him had tried this and similar ploys to circumvent the law. Hetherington deigned no such subterfuge. His press launching opened with a fanfare:

"No more evasion: we will not trespass, but deny the authority of our 'lords' to enclose the common against us; we will demand our right, nor treat but with contempt the despotic 'law' which would deprive us of it."

George Jacob Holyoake, a leader of the sustained lobbying against the taxes on knowledge that was to go on until the repeal of their last remnant in 1869, declared in his memoirs published in 1870 that "the unstamped *Poor Man's Guardian* was the first messenger of popular and political intelligence which reached the working classes".

Three convictions were soon obtained against Hetherington and he was twice imprisoned for six months. William Lovett recalled later that the names of Hetherington, Watson and Cleave "were in the mouths of every news vendor and mechanic in the three kingdoms, Hetherington's name being always mentioned first . . . This was not a profitable business. He had to leave his shop disguised, and return to it disguised—sometimes as a Quaker, a waggoner, or a costermonger. After one of the flights he went to see his dying mother, when a Bow Street runner seized him as he was knocking at the door. To distribute his paper, dummy parcels were sent off by persons instructed to make all resistance they could to constables who seized them, and in the meantime real parcels were sent by another road."

Many of the men and women who were jailed came from far and wide in answer to advertisements in the paper for volunteers ready to face imprisonment. One called for: "some hundreds of Poor Men out of employ who have nothing to risk, some of those unfortunate wretches to whom Distress has made a Prison a desirable Home. . . . A subscription is opened to the relief, support and reward of all such persons as may become Victims of the Whig Tyranny." Lovett said that this fund was "kept up by small weekly subscriptions during the many years the contest lasted, and contributed in no small degree to the success of that contest".

The police gave a sovereign for every vendor convicted. "Many persons were also induced, by the offer of places in the police, to volunteer the sale of these publications, so as to be the better able to . . . betray the poor fellows who were endeavouring to earn their bread by selling them." Lovett quoted newspaper reports that an employee of the Stamp Office called Thomas Coley "admitted that he had been the means of convicting *seventy persons* for selling unstamped publications; and that he had received *a pound for each* at the Stamp Office". Hetherington himself, Lovett wrote, "was hunted from place to place by the police like a wild beast, and was obliged to have resource to all kinds of manœuvres in order to see or correspond with his family".

Another vivid picture from the life of a working-class Radical editor on the run is Lovett's recollection of the sailor turned book-seller and publisher, John Cleave:

"He was indefatigable in going about in all directions advocating the cause of an unshackled Press and in promoting the sale of the unstamped. Owing to our Victim Fund meeting at his coffee house and the victims coming there to be paid (many of them poor, ragged and dirty) the best portion of his customers were led to desert him; and few were the Radicals who sought to supply their place. John Cleave (though, like most of us, not without his faults) was also warm-hearted and benevolent; and that without much means at his disposal. I have known him, and his kind-hearted wife, to pre-serve from perishing many of the poor starving boys that were often to be found about the pens of Smithfield; by taking them into his kitchen when cold, hungry, and filthy; by feeding and cleansing them; while he has gone round among his friends to beg some old clothes to cover them, taken care of them, till he had finally got them berths at sea. And these poor boys he has generously fed or otherwise provided for them the means of earning their living."*

Among the many unemployed workers who served as Hethering-ton's vendors was at least one veteran of earlier persecutions—Joseph Swann—who had served four and a half years' imprisonment in Chester Castle. Here are the final words he spoke at his trial:

DEFENDANT (*asked why he sold the Unstamped*): . . . I have been out of employment for some time, neither can I obtain work; my family are all starving. . . . And for another reason, the weightiest of all, I sell them for the good of my countrymen; to let them see how they are misrepresented in Parliament. . . .

BENCH: Hold your tongue a moment.

DEFENDANT: I shall not! for I wish every man to read these publications.

BENCH: You are very insolent, therefore you are committed to three months' imprisonment . . . to hard labour.

DEFENDANT: I've nothing to thank you for; and whenever I come out I'll hawk them again. And, mind you, the first that I hawk shall be to your house.

The courage and ingenuity of the sellers baffled the authorities. Seizures of the unstamped papers in 1835 amounted to no more than

---

* How like a scene from *Oliver Twist*! More to the point perhaps, it was from such real-life episodes, exhibiting "freeborn Englishmen" in all their characterful-ness, amid the bottomless squalor and degradation of Victorian London, that Dickens drew inspiration.

a week's sale of their circulation for the year. The Treasury prosecutions proved no more able than the sedition cases of the twenties to silence the democratic press. About the mid-thirties the stamped newspapers themselves began to press for a reduction in the stamp duty, because they feared the vaulting sales of their contraband rivals. Some efforts, though abortive, made in 1835 to bring out *daily* unstamped papers appear further to have sharpened the anxieties of the daily newspaper proprietors. This change of front was also connected with an increase in the size and competitiveness as newspapers of the unstamped papers. In 1833, a wholesale stationer, Charles Penney, started his *People's Police Gazette* in broadsheet, the same size as *The Times*. Filled with police news and court reports, it achieved a circulation of 20,000 in a few months. Following suit, the unstamped publishers produced broadsheets of their own—including Hetherington's *Twopenny Dispatch* and Cleave's *Police Gazette* which was selling 40,000 by 1836, according to Francis Place. Broadsheet journals quickly replaced the unstamped quartos and were sold not on the streets like the penny papers but in shops, newsagents, barbers and beershops. When the government called in blacksmiths to smash Hetherington's presses in August 1833—Cleave's were also seized—they were quickly replaced by public subscription.

The government started to seize the unstamped broadsheets in the streets, its agents dogging the printers' boys on their rounds to the bookshops, and chasing and stopping suspicious cabs. In the battle of wits between the press and its suppressors, the Radical papers were sometimes smuggled over the rooftops, disguised as parcels, hidden beneath baskets of old clothes or apples, or concealed in hatboxes. Cleave at one time despatched the *Police Gazette* in coffins provided by a sympathetic undertaker—the ruse was discovered only when neighbours observing a delivery of coffins and suspecting an unreported epidemic called in the parish authorities.

By the beginning of 1836 the Hetherington and Cleave broadsheets were each selling more in one day than *The Times* did all week and the *Morning Chronicle* all month. The circulation of the leading six unstamped journals was said to total some 200,000 and one of them, the *Weekly Herald*, said (July 3, 1836) that a stamped newspaper was regarded as a curiosity in Bath, Birmingham, Manchester, Liverpool, Newcastle, Hull and Portsmouth.

The Stamp Office's campaign had earlier been blunted by a court

decision in favour of the *Poor Man's Guardian* in June 1834, declaring
that it was not a newspaper. The paper emitted a shout of joy:

TRIUMPH OF THE PRESS!—HURRAH! THE GUARDIAN A LEGAL PUBLICATION.
"Well, men of England, at last we have had a real triumph. After all the
badgerings of the last three years—after all the fines and incarcerations—
after all the spying and blood-money, *The Poor Man's Guardian* was pronounced, on Tuesday by the Court of Exchequer (and by a *Special* Jury too)
to be a perfectly legal publication. . . . "

It crowed over the Whig hirelings who used to "split the ears of the
groundlings about the 'palladium of our liberties', telling us 'a free
press was like the air we breathe; if we have it not we die'—all these
impostors were humbled in the dust by Tuesday's verdict." It went on
in this vein of rejoicing, telling the men of England that "at last we
have a free People's Press" and wishing it could shake hands with all of
them after their long and anxious labours to establish it.

The paper also showed its determination to build on a victory which
it knew to be partial one.

"The verdict . . . establishes that the poor may henceforward have unstamped
politics, though not unstamped *news*, as well as the rich. You may have
cheap pamphlets, but not cheap newspapers. This is a point gained at any
rate. It is victory No. 1. With God's blessing you will shortly have victory
No. 2. By bearding the 'law' we have established the legality of cheap
political pamphlets. By the same process we shall, with God's blessing and
people's support, compel the rogues to give you cheap political newspapers."

In July 1835, the paper reported that the Whig Chancellor of the
Exchequer, Spring Rice, might consider changes in his next Budget.
It was the old Westminster wirepuller Francis Place, knowing his
Whigs, who saw the need for a public campaign if this half-promise
was to mean anything. Through his contacts with the London working
men he initiated petitioning to Parliament in which over 130,000
people signed demands for changes. The Chancellor decided to devote
part of his Budget surplus to reducing the newspaper duties—despite
a demand by *The Times* that not the pestiferous news-sheets but
health-giving *soap* should be relieved of taxation. In the 1836 Budget,
the stamp duty on newspapers was cut from 4*d*. to 1*d*. and the other
duties were similarly reduced.

Two years earlier, the Lord Chancellor, Lord Brougham, had argued for full repeal. He said then that it was no longer a question of whether the workers should read or not, of whether they should be politicians and take part in the discussion of their own interests. This had been decided long ago. "The only question to answer . . . is how they shall read in the best manner; how they shall be instructed politically and have political habits formed the most safe for the constitution of the country." Spring Rice told the MPs, in an unintended tribute to the organised character of the Unstamped struggles, that "subscriptions had been entered into, and the fines which were imposed had been paid by the contributions of the people; so that it was, in fact, a system which enlisted the sympathies of mankind against the law, and it behoved every good subject to endeavour to put an end to it".

The middle-class Radical C. D. Collet, whose *History of the Taxes on Knowledge* remains the best account of the marathon lobbying for the final repeal of these taxes, recalled in this work that the newspaper stamp duty frustrated "those public-minded men who were anxious to educate the people and permit them to educate themselves". They saw the stamp duty as an obstacle. "A penny paper could not pay for a fourpenny stamp. The field of instruction was therefore left open only to those who were poor enough to have little to lose by breaking the law."*

We may turn to a reader of the *Poor Man's Guardian* called John Dimmock, writing a letter published in the paper's last issue on the day after Christmas 1835, for a closer-in view of the devotion that the paper commanded:

"Sir—I am, with many more of my friends and brother-Radicals, sorry to hear that the *Poor Man's Guardian* is to be continued no longer . . . it has been my leading star, and I have no doubt of hundreds more like me . . . I hope and trust that when the name and fame of such men as the bloodstained hero of Waterloo shall be sunk in oblivion, or only thought of with contempt, the name of the Editor of the *Poor Man's Guardian* will be celebrated with songs of joy. That you may meet with success in your next undertaking, is the sincere wish of a working man."

* Collet catalogued all the "intricate absurdities" of the legislation and noted that the Stamp Office had and used powers to exempt papers that the government considered "not to come under the true intent and purpose of the Act". The Act, Collet also noted sardonically, did not apply to monthly periodicals, and this "left gentlemen pamphleteers at liberty to free their souls, though not to reach the masses of the people".

In the same issue the publisher of this paper that called itself "the parent of all the penny sheets" recorded that he had started out five years earlier with the deliberate intention that "the people's right to a free press should no longer remain a dead letter" and "resolved to exercise it in defence of our common interests, and for the purpose of obtaining our political enfranchisement".

The paper's sale had by then dwindled to about 3,000, partly because of a certain retreat from "politics" in the years of the workers' disillusion with political Radicalism and attachment to the Owenite mirage, and partly because of the new competition from unstamped broadsheets. Financially, a sale of 3,000 was only just above Hetherington's break-even point. His costs have been estimated★ at about £14 for 10,000 copies (paper £8, printing and composing £4 10s., ink, placards, hire of type £1 10s.). If he sold 1,000 copies over the counter and 9,000 at the usual rate of 13 for 8d. to the vendors, he would make a profit of £24. Wages were a small item, two of his editors, Lorymer and Mayhew, never receiving any, and O'Brien being paid only irregularly.

Hetherington had printed the paper at first on two Stanhope iron presses at his establishment and later at outside printing shops. In mid-1834 he acquired a Napier double-cylinder machine capable of printing broadsheet size at the rate of 2,500 sides an hour. On this press he brought out his *Twopenny Despatch*, with which the *Poor Man's Guardian* was amalgamated, and seemed set fair for success in his business. It was believed that he could have been a rich man had he spent more time on his publishing and less on the political affairs of the London working men which were his main interest. He rejected offers of all the official printing business he could handle, made on condition that he gave up his unstamped activities. According to Bronterre O'Brien, writing in 1836, he owned £5,000 worth of stock and a press worth £1,500 and had an income of £1,500 a year. Yet when he died in 1849 he was almost a pauper.

When the battle shifted in the mid-thirties from the field dominated by the quarto news-pamphlet to the broadsheet newspaper field, the "destructive" press, as the Tory papers called the little law-breakers, faced conditions in which they could not long survive. The mid-thirties brought the steepest jump in production costs since the

★ Patricia Hollis, *Poor Man's Guardian* fascimile edition, Merlin Press—Introduction.

D

beginning of newspapers, marked the point at which substantial sums began to be needed to launch and sustain new journals, and sounded the knell of the small paper produced almost solo by a newspaper writer in the Cobbett and Wooler tradition. A competitively newsy journal required both investment and organisation on a far wider scale, which has increased continuously from that day to this. The Napier press installed by Hetherington cost 350 guineas—against £30 for the Stanhope press. Sales of the unstamped rose sharply at moments of excitement or crisis—like the *Republican*'s 15,000 after Carlile's arrest, the *Guardian*'s 16,000 in the May days of 1832, or the boosted sale of most unstamped papers after the arrest of an editor—and fell off when the emotion had passed. Radical publishers well knew by the mid-thirties that news and "all human life" are what sells papers. Hetherington accepted the challenge gaily. His penny *Destructive* announcing in June 1833 the plans for its broadsheet successor, the *Twopenny Dispatch*, said that it would be "a repository of all the gems and treasures, and fun and frolic", and "news and occurrences" of the week. "It shall abound in Police Intelligence, in Murders, Rapes, Suicides, Burnings, Maimings, Theatricals, Races, Pugilism and all manner of 'accidents by flood and field'. In short it will be stuffed with every sort of devilment that will make it sell. . . . Our object is not to make money, but to beat the Government."

Scandal and politics, in varying proportion, had sold newspapers ever since the early eighteenth century. Now the journal relying principally on political comment and the commitment of its readers was beginning to feel the draught.

The 1836 reduction of the stamp duty reduced the yawning price gap between unstamped and stamped journals. And it was this which, together with the penny sheets' prohibited politics, had made them commercially viable and even lucrative. The change brought the working-class Radical publishers face to face with a wide new field of competition.

The technical developments coincided, too, with the advance into political life of middle-class reformers who were now getting their second breath after the big struggle of 1830–2 and pushing causes in opposition both to the reigning aristocracy on their right and the workers' movements on their left. Increasingly, the press landscape showed the fractures in Radicalism, though the divisions did not run on too straight lines. So long as the "Fiend Aristocracy" kept its grip on the tops of both the parliamentary parties, working-class and middle-class parliamentary Radicals continued to have causes in common: demands for a wider franchise and for repeal of the Corn Laws, for example. The victors of 1832, however, quickly developed a strong press devoted to spreading the ideas of Political Economy and combating Owenite Socialism. Its leading organ, the Whig *Morning Chronicle*, set out to show in the winter of 1833–4 that reduced corn import duties would mean cheaper bread, cause production and trade to pick up, and so relieve the workers' distress. It strengthened this appeal with "Letters on the Corn Laws and the Rights of the Working Classes" which it carried as inserts. Directing its appeal to the widening audience for reform politics among the manufacturing and professional middle sections, the *Morning Chronicle* gave *The Times* a close run in the mid-thirties: its average circulation for the first half of 1835 rose to 5,490, against 7,353 for *The Times*. "The Thunderer" had been steady for the oligarchy, apart from an outburst of indignation about Peterloo, during the twenties. But it felt the turn of the tide in 1830 and supported the Reform Bill, sometimes in strong language. In doing so, its editor Thomas Barnes, a former Radical, spoke for the growing numbers from the middle-class who flocked into the reform fold as it became respectable and as the anti-Jacobin mania subsided. In the new manufacturing areas several established journals, such as the *Manchester Guardian*, the *Leeds Mercury*, and the *Nottingham Review*, caught the same message in the wind.

Alongside the Great Unstamped many legal Radical publications were successfully launched in the early thirties. They included the *Morning Advertiser* and from 1833 an evening sheet, the *True Sun*. Greater than these in circulation was the *Weekly Despatch*, in which sensationalist accounts of the wicked doings of court and nobility and wealthy ran side by side with attacks on the post-1832 government. By 1836 it had risen in six years to a circulation of 30,000, selling at $8\frac{1}{2}d$. Selling for 6d. after the stamp duty came down to a penny, it went on to reach 66,000 in 1842, giving it a readership many times that figure through the thousands of copies that went into public houses.*

By the late thirties every effort to curb the rebel press had failed:

* R. K. Webb, *The British Working Class Reader, 1798–1848*, quotes a contemporary calculation that the London papers were each read by an average of thirty people, and the provincial papers by anything from eight to thirty.

trials for sedition and blasphemy, the taxes on knowledge, and all the
ceaseless preaching, for almost a century of the divine rights of the
propertied classes. Up to the Reform Bill this had been mainly Tory
work. Afterwards a more middle-class approach to the problem, under
Whig auspices, got under way. Efforts to inform the labouring poor on
their duties, which first tried to keep them in ignorance and then, after
this attempt had failed, to ensure their "useful instruction", were
pursued relentlessly: it was the resistance to this oppression that gave
the "Knowledge is Power" watchword its enormous force for the
working population.

After the Reform Bill, two departments for informing, or misin-
forming, the poor were at work. They corresponded roughly to the
two ruling groups in Parliament. From the Tory side, organisations
like the Religious Tract Society, founded in 1799 to combat the flood
of treasonous and infidel reading, worked to deny all knowledge to
the people. For their failure a very large part of the credit must go to
the press indomitables. The historian of the Religious Tract Society
in a prize essay written in 1850 cited figures to show how much greater
was the circulation of the unstamped press than that of the entire
religious output. The "corrupting" press, he wrote, found its way in
very large proportion to the homes and haunts of the poor, while the
pious pamphlets and periodicals reached mainly professing middle-
class Christians. The religious tract with its "inflexible style of phraseology, together with the uniform mode of thought" spoke in such a
way as to "bar its access to any mind unfamiliar with the dialect of the
sanctuary", according to a work entitled *The Working Classes of
Great Britain* published in 1850. The pious press had as little success in
competing with the avalanche of popular almanacs (stamped and unstamped) which found an eager market for their mixture of folk
wisdom and superstition and were sold in yearly hundreds of
thousands.

It was after the more lordly and bishoply ways of treating the multitude as incapable of reason had visibly failed that the approach that was
to become the more common one in the Victorian era became predominant. But Tory and Whiggish ways of checking the workers'
social and political pretensions went on in harness side by side for most
of the century. They caught the audience in a kind of pincer—
resembling the recurring alliance of Toryism and right-wing Labour
in later days—to undermine the workers' self-confidence as a class. On

the Whig side, Charles Knight of the Society for the Diffusion of Useful Knowledge, wrote in the *London Magazine* of April 1828 that working people having been taught to read and consequently to think had loosed a new power in society and this "could not be stopped although it might be given direction". (A labourer correspondent in Poplar wrote in the *Guardian* (April 14, 1832) that the aim of Knight's tracts was to "prop up the present cannibal order of things" by reconciling the poor to their poverty.) Knight opposed the "impolitic" stamp law on the ground that it "lets loose upon us a great many of the evils that some persons dread from the licentiousness of the press, without any of the advantages of the cheaper, and therefore more extended, diffusion of political knowledge". James Mill wrote to Lord Brougham on September 3, 1832, to deprecate "the illicit cheap publications in which the doctrines of the right of the labouring people, who say they are the only producers, are very generally preached. The alarming nature of this evil you will understand when I inform you that these publications are superseding the Sunday newspapers, and every other channel through which the people might get better information. . . . I am sure it is not good policy to give the power of teaching the people exclusively to persons violating the law, and of such desperate circumstances and character that neither the legal nor the moral sanction has sufficient hold upon them. The only effectual remedy is to remove the tax which gives them this deplorable power."

One of the reasons for the failure of the Mechanics' Institutes founded in considerable numbers in the twenties was the many struggles that broke out between the middle-class improvers and workers interested mainly in political and social matters. Sometimes, too, the Institutes came under fire from diehard Tories. A Yorkshire clergyman denouncing one of Brougham's schemes said that for every one genius whose advance would be facilitated, ninety-nine lesser men would develop "discontent, insubordination, pride, and probably a disbelief in revelation", in exchange for "the tranquillity which a happy ignorance of Political Economy and party politics was accustomed to procure them."

When the London Mechanics Institution was founded in 1825, the Tory *St. James Chronicle* said that "a scheme more adapted for the destruction of this empire could not have been invented by the author of evil himself". Many on the Tory side regarded the mere existence of the Institutions as subversive, and rival bodies were often set up with

Church backing. The fare provided in the Institutions, a smattering of "scientific" instruction, and some general knowledge of a safe and edifying character, appears today insipid to the last degree: the fact that it caused such apprehension shows how enormous were the obstacles to popular education. Small wonder that many workers decided that they would get no worthwhile education except what they provided themselves. A correspondent in the *Poor Man's Guardian* (December 19, 1835) declared: "Many of us are already saturated with as much of what is called science as we can carry." And a few years later Cleave's *Penny Gazette* (March 19, 1842) spoke of the working man's "utter and just repugnance to institutions supported in great measure by patronage and conducted by patronage". If further proof were needed of the conspiracy of the rich patrons of all trends to bar politics, it is the refusal of the Institutions to admit newspapers of any kind: in Manchester they were not admitted until 1840, sixteen years after the Institution's foundation, and in Newcastle not until 1847, twenty-three years after the foundation.

When the Useful Knowledge society ended a debt-ridden existence in 1846, its *Penny Magazine*—which altogether avoided political discussion—had fallen from a peak 200,000 claimed by Knight to about 40,000. A report on the Mechanics Institutions by the society in 1841 admitted, somewhat late in the day, that political matters could no longer be kept from the working classes. What the workers meant by politics was crisply explained by an Owenite Socialist, William Pare, attacking the *Library of Useful Knowledge*, at two meetings of the Birmingham Political Union in 1832. Opposing the society's ban on politics he explained that he was not talking about partisan discussion of current issues, but the "great principles of the social connection, which intimately concern the working classes". From the other side spoke someone on whom the society's teachings had apparently worked better: Mr. Albert Fry replied to Pare that "the Insect Creation (published by the society) alone was full of the deepest interest, and gave a high, refined and softened tone to the mind; while the study of politics had the effect of hardening the heart. The political student seemed to be always in armour."

An interesting letter to a friend survives from Alexander and John Bethune, two poor Scots labourers turned authors who planned in 1837 to give a series of political lectures. The friend had advised them not to be "too red-hot in your political speculations". The brothers replied that religion and education did not move the working men, "but only speak to them of politics, and their excited countenances and kindling eyes testify in a moment how deeply they are interested. . . . In these days, no man can be considered a patriot or a friend of the poor who is not also a politician." The writers yielded to advice and the work they produced was a failure.

O'Brien wrote in the penny *Destructive* (June 7, 1834):

> "Some simpletons talk of knowledge as rendering the working classes more obedient, more dutiful. . . . But such knowledge is trash; the only knowledge which is of any service to the working people is that which makes them more dissatisfied and makes them worse slaves. This is the knowledge we shall give them."

He told his *Guardian* readers that without knowledge there could be no union, without union no strength and without strength no radical reform—"would that the oppressed knew this as well as the oppressors!"

The Bethunes' letter was written in a year of bitter struggle. A strike by the Glasgow cotton spinners was smashed when their entire strike committee was arrested and five men were transported for alleged violence against blacklegs. It was written, too, in the year before the Charter was launched and the poor became politicians in their millions. To this main sequel of the Reform Bill deception, and the part played in the Chartist movement by a press that for democratic ardour and class militancy is still beyond compare, our narrative now turns.

6

This Mighty Auxiliary

All eyes are on, all hopes are in the press;
Let that be free—and who can doubt success? . . .

The genius of the press shall yet prevail
And conquer where the boldest armies fail;
For despots, though united, feel distress
And tremble when the thunder of the press
Rolls through their kingdoms in the civil storm
Proclaiming justice, freedom and reform.

From "The Freedom of the Press"—verses by EBENEZER ELLIOT
in the Northern Star, July 4, 1846

WITH CHARTISM the Radical programme that had aimed for
some sixty years to turn Britain into a democracy joined up with the
big battalions of the labouring population, and the frontal conflict
which the rulers had tried for so long to avoid at last took place. The
challenge failed; and many of the examples set by the Chartists—their
class approach to politics, their rough but basic grasp of the meaning of
state power, their democratic spirit and profound internationalism—
were half-buried in the middle-class triumph that succeeded their
defeat. Of the partly lost heritage, the significance of the great press
of Chartism remains probably the least understood and appreciated
by today's labour, trade union and progressive movement.

Its hundreds of products, ranging for two decades from stamped
broadsheets to monthly magazines and from unstamped penny papers
of the old kind to printed bills for public posting, enjoyed an immense
circulation and influence, particularly in the movement's earlier years.
The publishers and editors of this press—Feargus O'Connor, Bronterre
O'Brien, George Julian Harney, Henry Vincent and dozens more—
were also the movement's charismatic leaders and orators, frequently
known to the people far and wide by their first names.

Their papers reflected the seething, incurable disunity in Chartism's top counsels, and yet all in all formed a single campaigning press for the manhood suffrage cause which united all the Chartists, and served as their principal means of debate, education and organisation.

As Hetherington and O'Brien fought their round for press freedom in the Unstamped battle, blows fell thick and fast from the masters of the post-1832 parliament. Less than two years after the Reform Bill victory, the Tolpuddle Martyrs were rushed off to Botany Bay, convicted on trumped-up charges of illegal oath-taking. By this action the Whig government of Lord Melbourne hoped to defeat what the *Poor Man's Guardian* called "the spirit of combination [that] has grown up among the working classes, of which there has been no example in former times". Months later, the Grand National Consolidated Trades Union—peak achievement of nearly a decade of strikes, organising of trade unions, and growing solidarity among them—fell to pieces. The same year brought the Poor Law Amendment Act, which abolished outdoor relief and replaced it with the workhouse system: it was aimed against the independent or semi-independent modes of life to which hundreds of thousands of poor folk were clinging rather than be pitched into the factories. O'Brien called it the "Poor Man's Destruction Bill".

A year later, there began a trade slump that was to last for nearly seven years. In a great strike in 1837, one of the strongest of the new crop of trade unions, the Potters Union, was defeated and crushed. The government began in the same year to apply the new law to the north of England amid riots, street battles and demolitions of workhouses (which became known as the "Poor Law Bastilles") by angry crowds of near-starving people. It was as the champion of the poor against this threat that the *Northern Star*, which was to be the most influential voice of the democratic movement for the next fifteen years, began life in Leeds on November 18, 1837, and early in the following year was publishing instructions on the formation of local committees of resistance in townships, villages and hamlets to the activities of the Poor Law commissioners.

The revolt merged rapidly with an upsurge in the demands of the London working men and Birmingham Radicals for a real reform of Parliament. Especially after the arrests of the Glasgow spinners, no trace of belief remained among the working population in the Parliament dominated by those whom Lovett called "the hypocritical, conniving and liberty undermining Whigs". A pamphlet to which the *Northern Star* and other working-class Radical weeklies gave great prominence in this year was a devastating exposure of the regime entitled *The Rotten House of Commons*. It was published by the London Working Men's Association, shortly after this body had been established as a kind of select club of the more active working-class politicians in the capital. Most of them had been associated both with the Grand National Consolidated Trades Union and with the struggles for a free press. Within a year, about 150 similar clubs had been established all over the country devoted to winning political power through a democratic reform of Parliament.

On February 28, 1837, a meeting called by the London Association at the Crown and Anchor Tavern in the Strand endorsed with 3,000 immediate signatures a six-point petition calling for universal manhood suffrage, annual parliaments, vote by secret ballot, payment of MPs, abolition of property qualifications for MPs, and equal electoral districts. Bronterre O'Brien claimed in an article written for the *London Mercury* that the principles he had fought for "almost alone for six years" obtained universal support at this historic occasion, which he contrasted with previous gatherings where "discrepancy, division and irresolution were our predominant characteristics".

The parent association of the London Working Men's Association was the Society for the Promoting of a Cheap and Honest Press. This had been formed in the previous year—just before the stamp duty was cut to 1*d.*—to pay the fines of Hetherington and Cleave. Article 3 of its declaration of aims pledged that every possible means would be devised "to remove those cruel laws that prevent the free circulation of thought through the medium of a *cheap and honest press*". The bid for power thus sprang directly out of the struggle for a free press and the crusade for political knowledge of the Great Unstamped; and if the working people of the capital, despite wide social and economic disparities and diverse ways of thinking, were now uniting behind a single demand, this was due before all else to the work of the working-class Radical news-pamphleteers and editors since the mid-twenties.

By May of the following year, the six-point petition had become a parliamentary Bill drawn up in due form. This was appropriately given its first public presentation at a Glasgow meeting on May 21, attended both by leaders of the embattled Spinners Union and delegates from the London trades. At this meeting, in the strife centre of the day, a National Petition on similar lines which had been drawn up by the revived Birmingham Political Union was also presented and enthusiastically acclaimed. Meetings of 80,000 in Newcastle, 100,000 at Bradford, 200,000 at Birmingham and 250,000 on Kersal Moor near Manchester, endorsed the six points, which became known as the People's Charter. In the winter, preparations went on for a national convention from which to launch the programme in force. By the following spring, the *Northern Star*, as the principal organ of this vast movement of working people's militancy and grass-roots democracy, had rapidly quadrupled its sales to reach a weekly total, enormous for the day, of 48,000.

The paper played a main part in this first gathering of forces. The speeches of its owner, "Lion of the North" Feargus O'Connor, at the country-wide mass meetings—Francis Place called him "the constant, travelling dominant leader of the movement"—inspired hundreds of thousands to action and confidence. His paper served as the official organ of Chartism, though it was never so designated. It paid the penny stamp, and cost $4\frac{1}{2}d.$, but from its first issue it denounced the "little red spot in the corner of your newspaper—the Whig *beauty* spot, your *plague* spot". Chartists everywhere learnt through its pages of their brothers' activities elsewhere in Britain and received full news and comment on the main events of the day. The paper was the chief vehicle, through its hundreds of reports of meetings large and small, its letters, and all the magnetic oratory that it printed in close-set column after column, for the heady belief in imminent victory for the Charter that seized multitudes of working people in 1839–40 and again to a lesser degree in 1846–8.

Alongside the *Northern Star* appeared a wide array of journals which either declared support for the six points or were begun expressly to promote them, though none of them ever rivalled the circulation or influence of O'Connor's journal. All the diverse and swiftly changing trends of Chartism were reflected in these papers, their controversies and bitter quarrels, and their rise and fall was often rapid.

Where did they spring from, the hosts that sustained a challenge to middle-class domination during a twenty-year age and confronted it head-on in three main crises? One of the forces in the Chartist alliance, the least important and the first to fade out, was that led by the Birmingham middle-class Radicals who had made the running in the united democratic effort of 1830 to 1832. Another, which exercised at first the strongest formative influence in the field of ideas, followed the London working-class politicians led by Lovett and Hetherington, with a tradition of support from the skilled trades going back half a century. Associated with it were some often remarkable leaders from the artisan class in the older towns and from among the operatives and trade unionists in the new manufacturing centres. The third, immense, contingent was formed by the hundreds of thousands of handloom weavers and domestic out-workers who were fighting a desperate rearguard action against the advance of factory production, almost untouched by trade union organisation, and seeing their one hope in the Charter. Their main centre was the north, and the *Northern Star* was very particularly their spokesman. The fourth stream was composed of the mass of the workers in factory production and of miners (ever to the fore in schemes for insurrection). The factory operatives and skilled workers as a whole stayed loyal to the dream of the Charter, but their unions, serving principally the élite of the skilled men, tended in good trade times to keep aloof; and the divided and inconsistent attitudes of many of the Chartist leaders towards the trade unions helped from their side to prevent the movement from ever knitting with trade unionism except on a local and sporadic scale.

Torn between these forces at the same time as it represented them all, Chartism never became a real party or produced any agreed social theory or programme outside the six points. Better than any other journal, the *Northern Star* mirrored both the basic success and the basic failure. It provided a common roof for all the revolts, old and new: the central cause of parliamentary reform, the republican, anti-clerical ideas of Paine, an angry nostalgia for Cobbett's old England,★ and the ideas of early Socialism. What it never did was to achieve a Chartist unity of programme or tactics.

★ Some leaders of the agitation against the new Poor Law had Tory backgrounds like Cobbett. Alongside the Tory-Radical estate manager Richard Oastler, big spell-binders at the immense demonstrations against the law were John Fielden the Radical millowner of Todmorden, and the "non-political" expelled Methodist minister James Rayner Stephens. In the Lovett group in mid-1838 there was much resentment over O'Connor's insistence that Oastler and Stephens be brought into the campaign for the Charter. Opposition to any alliance with the middle-class had been loudly voiced in the National Union of the Working Classes and the *Poor Man's Guardian* in the early thirties.

Labour movement historian R. H. Tawney has written of Chartism: "It was, as Marx pointed out, the entry in politics, not merely of a new party, but of a new class. The English counterpart of the continental revolutions of 1848, it was at once the last movement which drew its conception and phraseology from the inexhaustible armoury of the French Revolution, and the first political attack upon the social order which emerged from the growth of capitalist industry. The declaration that 'all men are born equally free and have certain natural and inalienable rights' marched hand in hand with the doctrine that 'labour is the source of all wealth'. . . . Behind it lay two generations of social misery and thirty years of economic discussion which had percolated into the mind of the working classes partly through popular papers, such as *The Poor Man's Guardian* and the *Co-operative Magazine*, partly through the teachings of the early English socialists, Thompson, Hodgskin, Gray, and above all, Robert Owen. The essence of Chartism was in fact, an attempt to make possible a social revolution by the overthrow of the political oligarchy".*

Round One in the attempt to overthrow the oligarchy began when the first Chartist Convention met in London in February 1839. After presenting a petition to Parliament signed by 1,250,000 people, the Convention moved on May 7 to Birmingham, in an increasingly tense situation as the government mustered troops and armed volunteers. Its move to the old citadel of parliamentary reform was accompanied by almost continuous mass meetings in the city's Bull Ring, and it was there on July 4 that the government struck its first heavy blow, when it dispersed the crowds with great violence, employing a force of sixty police brought from London. In September, after some hesitant moves to call a general strike and after a wave of arrests had begun which was to put some 500 Chartists behind bars, the Convention dissolved itself.

That a great willingness existed among the workers to link their strikes to Chartism is certain. In July, Lovett's paper *The Charter* carried a letter addressed to the secretary of the convention saying that nearly all the colliers in the north were determined "not to commence work again until they have gained their rights". It went on:

"We have done all in our power to try to get them to wait for the commands of the Convention. The answer is, that they have waited long enough for

* *Life and Struggles of William Lovett*, Introduction, p. x.

aught they have to expect from their tyrants. . . . There are more than 25,000 pitmen alone on strike, besides the town trades, who are in expectation of your orders daily. It is earnestly requested that the time of the strike be not delayed, but that it be put into force by Monday next, or the consequences for this district will be dreadful to contemplate; and if the Convention wish to retain the confidence of the people, here, they must speedily act. . . . "

The hope that the Charter stirred in trade unionists is also attested by a letter from the West London Boot and Shoemakers Charter Association to the Trades of London published in the same journal in the following April. It said that most of them had hitherto been content to defend their trade union but they had recently perceived that "even the very *existence of our unions* is dependent on the mere caprice or despotic will of an *irresponsible government*, which at any moment has the power to enact the most grievous laws for our annihilation". The unjust system had been permitted for so long "simply, fellow workmen, because the *working classes conceived they had nothing to do with politics*. . . . A political movement is now making throughout the length and breadth of the land to give the working men an equality of political rights, a right in making the laws they are compelled to obey. We would therefore call on you earnestly to join, as we have done, in this struggle for freedom, to form as we have formed, a Chartists Association in connection with your own trade. . . . "

No systematic plan of action, now or later, ever reached the organised workers from Chartism. After the 1839 Convention had faded out, Radicalism found itself back at a familiar old crossroads. Always it had harboured within it an alternative policy, which almost all the Chartist leaders were ready with greater or less eagerness to consider, and which their speeches and papers kept always in view. This was the idea of insurrection as a right—"peaceably if we can, forcibly if we must" as O'Brien defined the dilemma. The conception had been present in every movement for reform since the London Corresponding Society, not least in the alliance of the middle- and working-class that forced the Reform Bill through. It could boast most respectable antecedents. As we have seen, it connected with the English Revolution against the monarchy in the sixteenth century, and beyond that, in popular legend and belief, to Magna Carta itself. It had been appealed to by those Englishmen who supported the American Revolution, including a Whig minority in the British House of

Commons. And it had received an enormous impetus, via Tom Paine, from the French Revolution. Even Cobbett subscribed to the necessity and justice of insurrection if tyranny made it inevitable, and some of the middle-class Chartists brandished the insurrection threat more fervidly than any other leaders. The *Northern Star* (January 6, 1838) quoted Stephens as saying at a meeting at Ashton-under-Lyne:

> "If the people who produce all wealth could not be allowed according to God's word, to have the kindly fruits of the earth which they had, in obedience to God's word, raised by the sweat of their brow, then war to the knife with their enemies, who were the enemies of God. If the musket and the pistol, the sword and the pike were of no avail, let the woman take the scissors, the child the pin or needles. If all failed, then the firebrand—aye, the firebrand—the firebrand I repeat. The palace shall be in flames."

This was the inflammatory extreme. But there was a sense in which the so-called "physical force" party within Chartism expressed no more than the conventional attitude on the inalienable rights of Englishmen. It let the enemy know the immense potential strength of the labouring population. And it was strongly influenced by memories of the effect which the Whigs had produced by brandishing the revolution threat in 1832: physical force was an inherited *stance* of Chartism rather than an ideology or programme. The April 9 resolution of the convention, "that the right of the people of this country to possess arms is established by the highest legal authority beyond all doubt" (*The Charter*, April 14), expressed a belief regarded by most Chartists as commonplace truth.

After the convention's September fiasco, the insurrectionary idea and temper came uppermost as it had done earlier after the big repressions. Schemes for an uprising were afoot in Bradford, South Wales, and Birmingham, and government spies as in the Luddite and Cato Street days were fomenting and betraying them. On November 3 came the abortive Newport rising led by John Frost in which 14 Chartists were killed and 50 wounded.

The story of the condemnation of Frost, Zephania Williams and William Jones, their transportation, and the two million signatures demanding their return collected by May 1841, need not be retold here. One incident is worth recalling, however, for the light it throws on the status of the Chartist press as a means both of organisation and information. The celebrated wood-engraver, poet and Chartist

W. J. Linton* describing in later years how the news came to Watson's bookselling shop in the City Road that the death sentence on the Newport men was really to be carried out, and how then, in the little sitting-room behind the shop, "we copied out a petition for reprieve, to which, the subscriptions received in not many hours became so numerous that the Government was feign to send the announcement of a stay in the death sentence to Hetherington's more prominent place of business in the Strand, to be there exhibited to allay popular excitement".

One aim of the march on Newport had been to free from Monmouth jail the talented orator Henry Vincent, known to some as "the young Demosthenes", a print worker who had shot to the front among the East End London Radicals and later won great popularity with the colliers and ironworkers of Monmouthshire. His *Western Vindicator*, published unstamped at $1\frac{1}{2}d$. in Bath, had been launched a few months before his arrest in May and continued to appear during the Frost trial, carrying appeals, like all the Chartist papers, for the Defence Fund established for the Newport men. In the *Northern Star* of December 7, O'Connor gave a promise to Chartists everywhere that he would save Frost's life and contributed a week's profit from his paper to the fund. *The Charter* reported (February 3, 1840) that 30,171 signatures to the petition to save Frost had been obtained in Birmingham in six days and 13,166 in Merthyr.

In Round One a great Convention directly representing the vastest popular gatherings ever seen in Britain sat, split into factions, and abdicated because it could not decide how to proceed further. Some abortive attempts at rebellion took place, and most of the leading personalities of the movement went to prison. Many Chartist publications ceased, including the *Operative*, and the *Southern Star* edited by O'Brien, the Manchester *Champion*, founded by Cobbett's two sons, the *London Despatch*, and the *Northern Liberator*,† organ of the Newcastle Chartists which was published, like the *Northern Star*, in Leeds.

The next throw had a more marked working-class character: on

* Joined the Hetherington–Watson circle in about 1836 and three years later started a short-lived periodical, *The National*, in which extracts from political and philosophical work were republished for working men. Worked as an artist for *The Illustrated News* from its launching in 1842.

† Holyoake said that this journal, under the editorship of the Irish Chartist Thomas Ainge Devyr, was "the most readable of all the insurgent newspapers of that period".

one flank, the middle-class Political Union allies fell away, and on the other Lovett and many of his sympathisers among the better-off artisans withdrew from the main movement to devote themselves largely to educational activities. In the summer of 1840, Round Two was inaugurated with the foundation of the National Charter Association, an attempt to organise Chartism on national party lines, with hundreds of branches and members paying a penny a week subscription. A second petition for the six points, more strongly worded than the first and advancing the factory workers' grievances together with the manhood suffrage case, was presented to Parliament in May 1842, to be rejected by 287 to 49 votes.

Once again the movement was halted before the stonewall at Westminster with no plan prepared for further action. At this point, at the peak of the long slump, with over a million unemployed and the masters cutting wages all over the country, many areas were engulfed in strikes on a scale without precedent. Meeting after meeting in the mining and iron-working areas of Staffordshire and Warwickshire and later in Lancashire and Yorkshire, Scotland and Wales, passed resolutions demanding that all labour cease until the People's Charter became the law of the land. The National Charter Association, however, failed to link up in any organised way with the strike movement. Meeting in Manchester in August 12, 1842, to unveil a monument to Orator Hunt on the anniversary of Peterloo, the delegates of the association found themselves in the midst of a Lancashire strike-and-riot maelstrom for which they were quite unprepared.

They issued a splendid manifesto. It declared:

"Englishmen, the blood of your brothers reddens the streets of Preston and Blackburn and the murderers thirst for more. Be firm, be courageous, be men! . . . Our machinery is all arranged, and your cause will in three days be impelled onward by all the intellect we can summon to its aid."

But little or nothing had been arranged. The *Northern Star* carried an attack by O'Connor on the strike itself, which he said the millowners had deliberately provoked. The battle went on through August and September, but politically leaderless and amid growing Chartist quarrels. Over 1,500 arrests were made in the wave of repression, aimed at subduing both Chartism and the strikes, that followed.

Three things happened in four years of decline of the movement after 1842. An attempt by middle-class Radicals to capture Chartism through the Complete Suffrage Union formed by a Quaker Radical, Joseph Sturge, late in 1841—its planks were the repeal of the Corn Laws and an *extension* of the suffrage—drew off a few leading Chartists but failed with the majority of the movement's followers. Roughly at the same time, the long trade depression came to an end and some improvement in wages and conditions took place, leading many workers and the skilled trades in particular to turn their main attention to strengthening trade union defences. And in these years, too, government-subsidised emigration and a boom in mining and railways construction absorbed numbers of the unskilled jobless whose sufferings had given the "Hungry Forties" their name. The third change was the deep involvement of O'Connor and his journal, in the middle forties, in a scheme for solving the miseries of the uprooted and defenceless poor by setting them up as agricultural smallholders. The object, as the *Northern Star* defined it, was "to demonstrate to the working classes of the kingdom, firstly the value of the land as a means of making them independent of the grinding capitalist; and, secondly to show them the necessity of securing the speedy enactment of the People's Charter".

The scheme, with which the *Star* came to be largely taken up, gave a new twist to the old idea that working people, and people without work, could escape from the grip of the system by a kind of internal emigration into a small peasant life on the land; the hope that it inspired was that it would spare them both the inhuman hours of labour and no less inhuman long spells of worklessness in the new factories and towns—now becoming the lot, no longer of a minority of the urban workers, but of their great and growing majority. The scheme had a wide popular appeal; but it sapped the strength of the Chartist movement by diverting its quest for political power and sharpening the dissensions among the leaders.

When Round Three began with preparations in 1847 to present a third national petition to Parliament, none of the old weaknesses at the top had been cured and the movement's organisation—with the effectiveness of its press in particular much diminished—proved unequal to carrying through its last overt bid for power supported by the working population in force. Moreover, when the famous mass assembly took place on London's Kennington Common on April 10, 1848, with the intention of marching to Westminster to present the petition, Chartism faced an enemy incomparably better prepared and led than

before. One of the mainsprings of Chartism's third wave was the
Europe-wide revolutions in all the leading Continental nations and
many smaller ones in 1848. The old magic from Paris still worked
strongly. But the government and its press had also learnt their lesson;
when demonstrations of unemployed in London and Glasgow led to
prolonged rioting, the government seized its chance to present the
Chartists as rioters and associates of foreign revolutionaries. Panic was
worked up on a scale unknown since Peterloo, with the particularly
important aid of a middle-class press that had, for reasons we shall see,
greatly strengthened its circulation and influence. In addition, against
what The Times called the "armed poverty" of Chartism, the authorities were able to range the armed middle classes. It was not the
frightened squirelings of the Manchester Yeomanry that the Duke of
Wellington put in the field, but 150,000 armed special constables who
together with troops barred the way into London to the vast and
peaceable assembly on Kennington Common.

The calling-off of the march, the subsequent charges that many of
the nearly two million signatures to the petition had been forged, and
the victory at once claimed over a "threat of revolution", were to be
long celebrated by the victors and used as showpiece evidence in a
sustained and largely successful attempt to minimise the significance of
Chartism and bury its memory.

However, today's labour and progressive movement will find even
more riches in the legacy of post-1848 Chartism—diminished in scale
though it was—than in that of the earlier years. Certainly this is true
of the later Chartist press, which has closer affinities, in the ideas and
hopes that it communicated, with modern Socialism than with the
Radicalism that had reached its most advanced point with Bronterre
O'Brien. But April 10 on Kennington Common did mark the movement's last open confrontation with government. After that dismal
day, the scene was to change; the press scene almost beyond recognition.

Before examining this transformation, and the better to see its significance, we shall take a look at the Chartist papers at their peak of
circulation, influence and optimism, their means of survival, and some
of their leading editors in action. They formed a single national press
to a degree not achieved by the earlier Radical journals, with the six
points to unite them. It was a weekly press that lived by a different
law from that of the daily newspapers, with their small circulations

and dependence for survival partly on government bribes and partly on advertisement revenue. Publishers and editors who almost to a man had come up through the school of the unstamped papers knew how vital to their purposes, which commanded neither of these sources of support, were large circulations. The first number of O'Brien's *Southern Star*, an ambitious 16-page double-quarto newspaper selling at sixpence, said that "to speak the plainnest language we can, the fate of the *Southern Star* will altogether depend on its circulation during the first month". This was about 2,000 and apparently did not rise in later weeks.

Similar appeals were made by *The Charter*, started in January 1839 by a committee of management drawn from the London trades, which carried the words ESTABLISHED BY THE WORKING CLASSES below its title-piece. In one of its most eloquent pleas for help, it gave a still good definition of labour's need to possess and control its own press.

"Whenever the newspaper press is employed to separate the interests of society as a whole, and to secure for one class immunities and enjoyment not equally distributed amongst all, it then becomes an instrument of surpassing evil, disorganizing the community, and creating and calling into active operation all those maleficent influences which have in bygone times involved states and empires in intestine wars and ultimate ruin . . . every class, save the *labouring class*, has its representative in the newspaper press. . . . Why are the working classes alone destitute of this mighty auxiliary?"

This cry from the heart went on:

"The newspaper press, daily and weekly, is the property of capitalists who have embarked on the enterprise upon purely commercial principles, and with the purpose of making it contributory to their own personal and pecuniary interests. It is the course that is *profitable*, therefore, and not the course that is *just* that necessarily secures their preference. . . . It has many a time happened, therefore, that when the working population stood most in need of an organ of communication, a shield of defence, or a weapon of attack, the one upon which their reliance was placed has wholly failed them; and in the day of their utmost extremity has been handed over to their antagonists."

Even when this did not happen, *The Charter* said, the question must obviously be asked

"why so large and really powerful a section of society, as that constituted by the labouring classes, should consent to remain in a position which compels them to receive as a favour what they might secure as a right? Why should they not—like the other and more favoured classes in society—have their own Press, instead of being reduced to a passive and humiliating reliance on the Press of those who can have but little sympathy with their wants and wishes."*

Passion like this for press freedom and great expectations about what it could achieve formed one of the strongest cements of the movement. The papers exchanged their news and views and wished each other well on a great scale. O'Brien's *Star* reprinted many articles from its namesake in the north. It carried columns of reports on O'Brien's own trial at Newcastle on a sedition charge and the brother papers retold the story. His triumphant acquittal, after he had conducted his own defence with Irish wit and eloquence and democratic fervour, was described at length in a despatch that he wrote retailing "the glorious victory" to "the Radical Reformers of Brighton and the Isle of Wight", datelined Newcastle, March 3, 1840. One issue of *The Charter*, which was a rather larger stamped weekly than the *Southern Star*, selling at sixpence, carried fourteen reports under its "Chartist Movements" heading. They covered meetings from Dumbarton and Halifax in the northern storm centres to Rottingdean and Chelsea—where "a meeting of the industrious classes . . . was held in the Swan Tavern for the purpose of carrying out the Charter. The meeting was crowded to suffocation." The same issue relayed news from Vincent's *Western Vindicator* and from the *Sheffield Iris*.

From the north, O'Connor's *Star*, announcing the rules of the National Charter Association on August 1, 1840, designated as advocates of the Charter "especially the *Northern Star*, *Scottish Patriot*, *Northern Liberator*, *True Scotsman*, and the following cheap and talented periodicals, viz.: *The Penny Northern Star*, *Western Patriot*, *Trumpet of*

---

* The idea of reliance on employers' newspapers appears, however, to be blessed with eternal life. When the *Daily Worker* was suppressed in January 1941, Fleet Street came in force to a *Worker* press conference with pen poised to write patriotic reports justifying Home Secretary Herbert Morrison's action. Phyllis Davies—the patriot from the *Daily Mail*—which had earlier won notoriety for its friendly attitude both to Hitler and to homegrown fascists—delivered an impassioned declaration that, since the workers' point of view must be covered by the press, "the *Daily Mail* will see, as it has always done, that it is put". More recent examples of this greatest of all impertinences of lordly newspapers would be too many to list.

Wales, Advocate and *Merthyr Free News, Chartist Circular*, Hethering-ton's *Odd Fellow* and Cleave's *Gazette*, and they would further recom-mend the Executive Council, as a speedily as possible, to divide the country into Districts, engage Missionaries, and bring out the Press, to the utmost extent, in the cause of the people". This piece was head-lined: "Some means to the achievement of the great end."

If the Chartist papers were many, their casualty rate was high. The more successful and long-lived usually owed their good fortune to an outstanding national or local personality who set his imprint on the paper, in the old tradition of Radical journalism. Journals conducted under corporate ownership or control did less well. *The Charter*, run for fourteen months by the better-off London skilled men whom O'Connor later called "the pompous trades and proud mechanics who are now willing forgers of their own betters" (*Northern Star*, November 1, 1845), provides a classical example of their troubles. A sad farewell editorial article on March 15, 1840, said that *The Charter's* circulation of 6,000 copies should have yielded a profit of £20 a week according to the committee's best calculations. But the "liberal character" of the £30 a week paid by William Carpenter for literary contributions not always of a corresponding quality had turned the expected profit into a loss of £40 a week. Then there had been "a continued series of accidents, by the machine breaking, and the consequent loss of sub-scribers from inability to supply them."

The newspaper blamed even more strongly its own "proud mechan-ics", the compositors, who by their "constant practice of striking, and refusing to proceed with the composition of the paper, when a sum of only three or four shillings a man has been due to them, had caused delays". Especially to blame were the "established" men getting 36s. a week who "did no work till the middle or latter end of the week", and then demanded and received a full week's wages. Addi-tional hands had to be taken on, "entailing the loss of the early edition and continued decrease of the circulation".

The committee said that it fully admitted the right of men to the wages of their labour, and expressed its anxiety to satisfy every just claim on the paper, but felt that the men had by their conduct "disen-titled themselves to any sympathy or consideration, having occasioned the loss of hundreds of pounds to the paper; besides, in a great measure, contributing to its failure".

An address "to the operatives of the United Kingdom" said that the committee had maintained its post without flinching but the difficulties had been too great. It concluded—raising a problem that was to remain with labour journalism for a long time—"that the attempt to establish a newspaper by the co-operation of a numerous body of the working classes, and conducted under the supervision of a committee, should have failed as a commercial proposition, is no more than those experienced in newspaper proprietorship anticipated from the first".

For the superior vigour and longevity of the *Northern Star* there were many reasons, including the fact that the majority of its readers lived in the strife-torn centres of the new industrialism. Its position as undisputed head of the rebel press fraternity, its accessibility to most of the views in the movement, and its effective editorship were other causes of the great lead that it had over the other Chartist papers. This was a real newspaper, with a width and scale of news coverage greater than that of any earlier Radical journal.

The Manchester publisher, Abel Heywood, praising the paper at a rally to welcome released Chartists (*Northern Star*, August 22, 1840), said that the whole people owed a debt to the men of Lancashire and Yorkshire who helped to establish the *Star*.

"Would to God they had a *Northern Star* in every town throughout the kingdom! Would to God that every town could write upon the pillars of their churches, A *Northern Star* to be obtained here. The very existence of such papers would be a guarantee that the Charter would be obtained."

The paper was said to spend more on its reporting coverage from all over the country than any newspaper except *The Times*. Numerous worker correspondents wrote in its columns, contributing news of the movement in places large and small. It was selling 10,000 copies a week within four months of its foundation and established itself as an institution at all meetings of workers, at the great open-air gatherings, at readings in public houses and meetings of the trades whose struggles it reported widely, and in humble cottages.

For the *Northern Star* the trade unions, which O'Connor inadequately understood, figured as an ally to be won for alliance to win the Charter rather than a movement with its own special needs and limitations. However, O'Connor could not but see the unions' growing strength. Especially in 1844 and 1845, when trade union activities were on the upswing, he took notice of it. In pursuit of trade union support he changed the paper's name in November 1844 to *The Northern Star and National Trades Union Journal* and moved its head-quarters to Great Windham Street in London.

> "I invite you [he wrote] to keep your eye steadily fixed upon the great Trades' Movement now manifesting itself throughout the country, and I will implore you to act by all other trades as you have acted by the Colliers. Attend their meetings, swell their numbers, and give them your sympathy; but upon no account interpose the Charter as an obstacle to their pro-ceedings. All labour and labourers must unite; and they will speedily dis-cover that the Charter is the only standard upon which they can successfully rally. . . . I assert without fear of contradiction that a combination of the Trades of England . . . would be the greatest move ever witnessed within the last century. It would be practical Chartism."

As a running record of the movement's growth and clashing ideas the *Northern Star* has no rival. It opened its columns wide to all the debates. George Julian Harney who edited the paper for the major part of its career, was in the thick of the Chartist battle of ideas from the movement's earliest days. His career best reflects the progress within Chartism from the classic democratic spirit of Radicalism to democratic Socialism.

The son of a Deptford sailor, Harney was born in the year of Peterloo. He entered political life, after a spell as a cabin boy, along the well-trodden path through Hetherington's publishing concern. As a shopboy in the Unstamped struggle he imbibed devotion to a free press in his working teens, became Bronterre's devoted disciple in about 1832, and for hawking the illegal papers had served two prison sentences by 1836, the year before the launching of the Charter, when he was still only nineteen. Following the still strong Painite fashion, he took Marat, leader of the extreme left *sans-culotte* wing of the old French Jacobins, as his model. In 1837 he formed with the Spencean cobbler Allen Davenport and the republican Charles Neesom the East London Democratic Association. This lined him up with the poverty-stricken host formed by the Spitalfields silk weavers and the workers living in Clerkenwell, Tower Hamlets and other areas of constant bitter distress, and set him in opposition to the Lovett-Hetherington circle, who never accepted that this ragged army*

* A constable reported to the Home Office that he knew an East End Chartist procession to be unarmed because "their clothing was so thin that had they had any dangerous weapons upon them, I must have observed them".

belonged to those whom Lovett called "the *intelligent* and *influential* portion of the working classes in town and country". Only after protracted public recriminations—harbingers of later more serious splits— were the Jacobin-style rebels, who had reformed in May 1838 as the London Democratic Association, finally admitted with reluctance and misgivings to the London Working Men's Association. The disputes were partly over the new Poor Law—which Lovett opposed lukewarmly at the best—partly over the trade unions, and partly over the narrow interpretation that the skilled élite were placing on the "Knowledge is Power" idea. "Depend upon it, Fellow Democrats", George Julian wrote in the *Northern Star* (March 24, 1838), "that which our enemies will not yield to justice, they will never yield to *moral persuasion*." The ruling class, he said, would never grant to the workers "the kind of education by which they will learn their political rights".

This was the stage at which one of the basic alliances of Chartism was struck, when Harney and the LDA joined hands with the Northern Chartism of O'Connor, which had sprung from the struggle against the new Poor Law as the London artisans' movement had sprung from the struggles of the unstamped papers and the early trade union movement. Another alliance, of great import in the long term, was sealed at the same time. Harney became a member of the Polish Democratic Society*—he was apparently its only English member—and entered on a long association with Continental revolutionaries who already saw Chartism as the precursor of a new democratic upheaval in Europe.

Harney led the extremist wing of the 1839 Convention in London, and his *London Democrat* (April 20, 1839) carried his famous appeal: "ARM! ARM! ARM! . . . Let the one universal rallying cry, from the Firth of Forth to the Land's End be Equality or Death." However, he himself played little part in the clandestine plotting after the convention, partly because he had come under suspicion of being one of the Home Office spies with which the movement was riddled. On a speaking tour in Scotland in 1840 he appears to have been influenced by the characteristic Scottish emphasis on the need for organisation and education and told a Glasgow audience that he was much wiser in the

---

* Some Poles in this organisation took part in Chartist activities. When consequently they were struck off the relief fund for exiles administered by the Treasury Harney vigorously denounced this persecution in Bronterre's *Operative* (December 9, 1838).

year 1840 than he had been at the commencement of 1839. His inflammatory appeals gave place to a growing emphasis on the prime need for organisation and on the class character of the struggle.

In an address to the Democrats of Great Britain published in the *Scottish Patriot* his contribution to the inquest on the failure of the convention was to declare that the "vile shopocracy" was the main enemy of the Chartists in the "war of class against class" and chiefly to blame for the "continuing cannibal state of affairs". After his return from Scotland, he became Chartist organiser for the West Riding, and correspondent for the *Northern Star* from Sheffield. Two years later he joined the paper as assistant editor at the age of twenty-six and became editor in 1845. He was by then nationally known as a stalwart for the "class against class" approach, combating both the Complete Suffrage Union and the bid to siphon off Chartist energies into agitation for the repeal of the Corn Laws. The paper's circulation, which had fallen to about 10,000 with the easing of the trade slump in 1844, picked up under the editorship of Harney, who quickly established himself as the liveliest journalistic talent since Cobbett. He was a master of the racy phrase and the old Radical mockery of the upper orders. As Queen Victoria's children appeared at regular intervals, for example, he usually signalled the event appropriately for her poverty-stricken subjects. Once he suggested that instead of reciting prayers of thanksgiving, church congregations should sing "hymns of despair for their misfortune in being saddled with another addition to the brood of Royal Cormorants".* During the depression of 1846-7 the paper compared the rich diet of the royal hounds with the workers' meagre fare, and later in the *Democratic Review of British Politics, History and Literature*† Harney greeted the newly-born Prince Arthur as "a royal

---

* *The Times* printed the news (August 6, 1844) under the headline "The ACCOUCHEMENT OF HER MAJESTY" and said it was "indebted to the extraordinary power of the Electro-Magnetic Telegraph for the rapid communication of this important announcement". Apparently overcome by awe, the paper printed in its second edition a further despatch from Windsor, under the same headline, alongside the first report and adding nothing except that "Her Majesty and Infant are perfectly well". How the editor of the *Northern Star* might have appreciated the *Morning Star*'s headline on a royal wedding nearly 150 years later—amid gloom conditions and attacks on the workers—IT'S MORE LIKE A BLOODY FUNERAL !

† A threepenny 40-page monthly magazine which ran for sixteen months, from June 1849.

burden, from whom the greatest and most potent monarch in the world has condescendingly allowed herself, in her magnanimous deference to natural law, to be relieved".

The most important innovation under his editorship, however, was the paper's coverage of events abroad, with the intention, as he wrote in 1844, of making the English Democrats "aware of the part that was being played by their brethren on the different stages of the political world". The paper, Harney's biographer has written, has "a unique claim to having been the first mass-circulation organ of international socialist movements in England".*

Reports from his pen on international events took on a new tone and authority, stemming from his friendships with Polish, German, French and other exiled Continental democrats living in England. In 1843 he had met Frederick Engels and the warm friendship that grew up between them fed this new involvement richly. Engels began writing for the *Northern Star* early in 1844, and the paper published in June his celebrated account of the Silesian weavers' strike. He told his English readers that capitalist development in Germany was "bringing the same oppression and toil for the many and riches for the few" as in Britain.

The continuous profound hold that sympathy with revolution abroad exerted on British working-class opinion after France's 1789 —reviving at every new upheaval in Europe—has already emerged in this record. Engels, whose *Condition of the Working Class in England* exposing the human ruin wreaked by capitalism belongs in spirit half to English Chartism and half to the clearer later vision of Marxism, paid tribute to this internationalism of the British workers. In a dedication in English "to the Working Class of Great Britain" accompanying the celebrated work's first edition in German he declared: "With the greatest of pleasure I observe you to be free from that blasting curse, national prejudice and national pride, which after all means nothing but *wholesale selfishness*. . . . I found you to be more than mere *Englishmen*, members of a single, isolated nation. I found you to be MEN, members of the great and universal family of Mankind, who know their interest and that of all the human race to be the same."

This was the spirit which Harney expressed when he faced the Whig Foreign Secretary Lord Palmerston on the hustings at Tiverton in Devon in the general election of 1847. He exposed Palmerston's

* Dr. R. Schoyen, *The Chartist Challenge*, p. 127.

support for reaction in Europe in a two-hour speech, to which the haughty lord had perforce to reply in a five-column statement in *The Times*. "A blow struck at liberty on the Tagus," Harney said in one of his most resounding phrases, "is an injury to the friends of freedom on the Thames."

Two years earlier, freedom's friends on the Thames had united forces, on September 22, 1845, in the Society of Fraternal Democrats, bringing together revolutionary democrats and Socialists in a group that remained in being until 1852 and prepared the way for the First International. The Fraternal Democrats were in session when the news of Louis Philippe's abdication in Paris, which triggered the 1848 revolutionary wave in Europe, was brought into the hall. Frost re-called later in his *Forty Years Recollections*:

"The effect was electrical. Frenchmen, Germans, Poles, Magyars, sprang to their feet, embraced, shouted and gesticulated in the wildest enthusiasm. . . . Then the doors were opened and the whole assemblage . . . with linked arms and colours flying, marched to the meeting place of the Westminster Char-tists in Dean Street, Soho. There another enthusiastic fraternisation took place and great was the clinking of glasses that night in and around Soho and Leicester Square."

It was the Chartism of the Fraternal Democrats, led by men whom O'Connor contemptuously called "Socialists first and Chartists second", that gained the upper hand in the movement after the Kennington Common collapse. This part of the story is linked above all with the names of Harney and of Ernest Jones. A recruit to Chartism from an upper-class background (his father was equerry to the Duke of Cumberland), Ernest Jones entered the movement in 1846 and was arrested in the post-1848 repression. As speaker, organiser and editor he was the most significant figure in later Chartism and his career formed a bridge between Chartism and the modern labour and Socialist movement, notably in the field of the press. When Jones was released from prison in 1850, Harney caught in an editorial in his *Friend of the People* the essence of the transition for which Jones more than anyone else stood. After deriding middle-class claims that Char-tism was dead, Harney went on:

"In 1848, ERNEST JONES was sent to prison for having spoken figuratively and with a poet's licence, of the coming day when the green flag of Chartism should fly over Downing Street. In 1850 the released patriot was received by thousands of Yorkshiremen under waving folds of the red banner. The change in the popular symbol was vastly significant. In 1848 a Chartist Convention was content to ask for the Charter, and nothing but the Charter, leaving the social question to the chances of the future. In 1851 the delegates of the people (at the Manchester convention) lift up their voices for THE CHARTER AND SOMETHING MORE. . . . Propositions which the mind of every thinking man can compass, have been enunciated by the Executive, adopted by the Convention and will speedily evoke the action of the people. Behold, ye victors of the 'Tenth of April'—behold the fruits of your victory."

For a while Harney and Jones led the "red flag" side jointly, in opposition to O'Connor. Harney continued, however, as editor of the now failing *Northern Star* and maintained its coverage of European events, with contributions from Engels, Mazzini, Louis Blanc and other Continental democrats. In June 1850 Harney started his *Red Republican*, the title itself constituting a challenge to the O'Connorites. Its aim, he said, would be to "popularise the principles of Red Republicanism, to unfurl a banner, announce a faith, and clear the way for those more powerful who will follow". The paper was an unstamped penny quarto and carried little news because of the stamp legislation. In June 1950 it published the first English translation of the *Communist Manifesto*, with an editorial comment that it was the most revolutionary document ever published.

The paper printed many strike reports, and made a serious effort to win the trades to the side of Chartism in its new, Socialist phase. It emphasised, however, that "trades organisations may mitigate but they cannot uproot existing evils. For the working classes there is but one way of righting their wrongs, that of obtaining mastery of the State". It declared:

"It is not any amelioration of the condition of the most miserable that will satisfy us: it is justice to all we demand. It is not the mere improvement of the social life of our class that we seek: but the abolition of classes and the destruction of those wicked distinctions which have divided the human race into the princes and paupers, landlords and labourers, masters and slaves. It is not any patching and cobbling of the present system we aspire to accomplish, but the annihilation of that system, and the substitution instead of an order of things in which all shall labour and all enjoy, and the happiness of each guarantee the welfare of the entire community" (October 12, 1850).

Later the paper under its new name *The Friend of the People* (adopted partly in consequence of refusals by newsagents to accept the "Red"

label amid the reaction that followed the collapse of the European
revolutions) wrote that trades combinations "retarded the ascendancy
of all-devouring capital", although the workmen were always van-
quished in any great struggle. "Trades Unions may continue to
afford some degree of protection in any ordinary contest between
labourers and capitalists, but from their very nature they must be
impotent to effect any general social change from the advantage of
the wealth producers." In an England on the brink of an unprecedented capitalist expansion, which had overcome the frontal attack
of Chartism, this declaration made small impression on organised
workers now concentrating their energies on fighting for the best
bargain they could obtain within the triumphant system.

The readership for Chartist publications was shrinking fast. A
quarrel between Harney and Jones which began late in 1851 was
partly connected with this decline. When Harney acquired the
Northern Star on April 1, 1852, when its sale was down to 1,200 copies,
with the intention of merging it with the *Friend of the People* as the
Star of Freedom, Jones accused him bitterly of trying to undermine his
own projected *People's Paper*. There was not room for two weekly
papers in the movement and the success of one would be at the expense of the other, Jones said. The incident shows how matters had
altered since the days when people used to assemble at the stage-coach
stops to collect copies of the *Northern Star* and O'Connor gave his
general blessing to all the Chartist papers in the peak year of 1839.

How different, too, from the tone of the early years is that of the
July 6 number of the *Red Republican* as it denounced the press ("a few,
a *very* few journals excepted") as "the worst of all the enemies arrayed
against the political and social claims of the masses . . . this most influential institution is the most gigantic evil of this age." The cry, in
sharp contrast to the joy that followed the victory of the Unstamped
in 1836, is one of despair. Harney harked back to the period of the
"youth of the press" when it had been "the great instrument of progression" laying bare "the atrocities of aristocratical usurpation", and
unmasking "the frauds of sacerdotal craft". Looking back with nostalgia to the times of Paine, Cobbett and Carlile, Harney exclaimed
colourfully that in those days

> "a new and terrible power carried dismay into the recesses of royal cabinets,
> and caused fear and quaking in the breasts of the mighty of the earth. . . .
> As long as the Press was under the ban of tyrants it flourished in spite of

Illustrations

i. The "Freed Press Terror", as seen by an early Radical cartoonist (with acknowledgments to the James Klugmann Collection).

ii. *Pig's Meat*, frontispiece to the collected edition, and the first issue.

iii. France's July 14, the event that provided British Radicals with an almost inexhaustible inspiration and was widely celebrated for over half a century after 1789, as in this front page of C. J. Linton's Chartist magazine, *The National*, in 1839.

iv. One of the most audacious pages in Radical journalism—the *Republican* letter to the Prince Regent on September 3, 1819, blasting his support for the Peterloo yeomanry and magistrates.
Below: No. 20 of T. J. Wooler's *Black Dwarf* leading with one of the accounts that the editor wrote from prison about his trial.

v. The *Poor Man's Guardian* of July 5, 1834, celebrating Henry Hetherington's court victory for cheap political pamphlets.
Below: First issues of Watson's *Working Man's Friend* (1832) and of Robert Owen's *The Crisis* hailing the imminence of "some great change in the condition of man".

vi. Title-pieces of four Chartist weekly journals and of Potter's *Beehive*.

vii. The November 9, 1850, issue of Harney's *Red Republican* containing the first English publication of the *Communist Manifesto* of 1848.
Below: a cartoon on the back page of the same paper's November 2 number. It presents in the form of the royal arms the Queen, bishops, lawyers and British soldiery in Ireland. The verse caption reads in part: "For England's lions—donkeys, sanguine, on a field of gold/For Ireland's harp—a peasant strung upon a gallows old."

viii. Front page of the SDF journal *Justice*, March 14, 1896. The Latin motto reads: "Let justice be done though the heavens fall." The leading article, headed "Pity the Poor Landlords", criticises the tax reliefs worth £3 million which had just been given to them. It also attacks grants given to the landlords to improve their property, commenting:
"This is grand. Any similar proposal for the purpose of organising the labour of the unemployed on the land or feeding starving children would be met by howls of protest and appeals against pauperising the people and sapping their independence. There is no fear of pauperising the landlords!"

ix. A late *Commonweal*, still with William Morris's famous foliated title-piece, and leading with a cartoon on the press.

x. The November 15, 1888, issue of the *Labour Elector*. A *Clarion* front of April 8, 1893. The drawing in column 1 satirises working men paid to march in an Ulster Loyalist demonstration against Home Rule for Ireland. An accompanying comment says that these "disloyal Loyalists" openly avow their intention of resisting the Home Rule Bill even after it has become the law of England.

Sylvia Pankhurst's *Workers' Dreadnought* celebrating the Hungarian workers' rising of 1919, with artist's illustration of the progress of Socialism among the women of eastern Europe.

xi. Two historic "firsts":
No. 1 of the *Daily Herald*, brought out by the London compositors in their 1911 strike, and invoking in its first sentence the Communist William Morris, "that noble old English Master Printer . . . who treated his men as men", after citing his "What is this—the sound and rumour?" verses presaging the approach of the Socialist revolution.
No. 1, nineteen years later, of the Communist *Daily Worker*.

xii. Front page of the British Socialist Party's weekly *The Call* (December 18, 1919) produced amid the labour movement's campaign to prevent Churchill going to war against Soviet Russia. "The Junkers" in the headline are not the Prussians but "Churchill, Lloyd George and Co.—the British section of the Junker International". It reports that "every trade union deputation that meets the Prime Minister comes away from the Presence with a sickening sensation of having been tricked" and warns that Churchill "is determined to carry fire and sword into Soviet Russia on the first available opportunity".

Below: the *Daily Herald* of February 28, 1921, with its exposure of the part played by Scotland Yard's secret printing press in producing bogus *Pravdas* for use in support of counter-revolution in Russia.

xiii. The *Workers' Weekly* issue for Armistice Day, 1924, in a Britain careering towards the 1926 general strike, marked the event with a splash celebrating the successes of the Socialist Revolution and a dramatic, biting cartoon ("The Hypocrites") on the ceremony at the Cenotaph in London's Whitehall.

xiv. The imposing front of *Lansbury's Labour Weekly*, the journal launched by the former *Herald* editor after his disillusionment with this paper as the Labour Party and the TUC conducted it after 1923.

Below: No. 2 of the *Sunday Worker*, illustrating this paper's attempt to compete on general news terms with the mass-circulation capitalist Sundays and draw Socialist conclusions at the same time.

xv. The re-designed *Reynolds News* of 1936, at the start of its attempt as the organ of the Co-operative movement to build an anti-fascist popular front.
The first issue of the *Daily Worker* after the labour and trade union movement's hard-won victory against its suppression.
The same paper's April 14, 1954, issue, first of four award-winning issues in the 'fifties and 'sixties (in the Newspaper Design Award) with which chief sub-editor Allen Hutt established the technical pre-eminence of Britain's first working-class daily newspaper owned by it readers.

xvi. Three "fronts" of the labour movement papers that campaigned in the 'seventies for legislative changes to help the labour movement press and win a democratic new deal ending the monopolist stranglehold.

Photographs by E. Greenwood

THE MAN WOTS GOT THE WHIP HAND OF 'EM ALL

RADICAL CARTOON OF THE POWER OF THE FREE PRESS.

This is that matchless Pigs meat
So famous far and near.

Oppressors hearts it fills with Dread,
But poor Mens hearts does cheer.

ONE PENNYWORTH

OF

PIG's MEAT;

OR,

LESSONS

FOR THE

SWINISH MULTITUDE.

COLLECTED BY THE POOR MAN'S ADVOCATE, IN
THE COURSE OF HIS READING FOR MORE THAN
TWENTY YEARS.

INTENDED

To promote among the Labouring Part of Mankind proper Ideas of their Situation, of their Importance, and of
their Rights.

AND TO CONVINCE THEM

That their forlorn Condition has not been entirely over-
looked and forgotten, nor their just Cause unpleaded, neither by their Maker nor by the best and most enlightened
of Men in all Ages.

STORMING OF THE BASTILLE,
July 14, 1789.

The Republican.

No. 2. Vol. I.]   LONDON, FRIDAY, SEPT. 3, 1819.   [PRICE 2D.

A LETTER TO HIS ROYAL HIGHNESS THE PRINCE REGENT,

On his thanking the Magisterial and Yeomanry Assassins of Manchester for MURDERS COMMITTED *by them on the 16th of August last.*

London, August 30, 1819.

SIR,

THE general indignation and disgust excited in the public mind, in consequence of the *atrocious Murders* committed by the Yeomanry Cavalry, at the instigation of the Magistrates of Manchester, on the bodies of the inhabitants of that town, assembled in a legal and peaceable meeting, for the purpose of discussing the best means to obtain a redress of their grievances, and a radical reform of the representative system, could have been exceeded by nothing but the Chief Magistrate of the Country sanctioning, and actually returning thanks to the *murderers!!!*—This, Sir, it appears you have done, through the medium of your Secretary of State for the Home Department, the ever-memorable SIDMOUTH ; and as the document cannot be too generally read, or too much known, I shall here insert it, and make such observations upon it, as to me seem necessary.

THE BLACK DWARF.

A London Weekly Publication.

EDITED, PRINTED, AND PUBLISHED, BY T. J. WOOLER, GATEWAY, 81, BISHOPSGATE WITHOUT; AND ELLENBOROUGH COLLEGE, SURREY.

No. 20.   WEDNESDAY, JUNE 11, 1817.   PRICE 4d.

Satire's my weapon; but I'm too discreet, | I only wear it in a land of Hectors,
To run a-muck, and tilt at all I meet ; | Thieves, Supercargoes, Sharpers, and Directors. Pope.

TRIAL OF THE EDITOR.

" Whosoever thou art, that lovest Liberty ;—desirest to be happy without Riches ;—powerful without subjects ;—a subject without a master ;—dare to court my death. Kings then will tremble before thee, whilst thou alone wilt fear no one."

OMAR.

This important case, as it regards the grand question of the liberty, or the slavery of the British Press, came on, as expected, on Thursday morning last before Mr. Justice Abbott, and a special Jury. The Editor received notice of most polished habits —of the most candid demeanor. He expected to find in him indeed, a decided, a powerful, but an open, an honest foe. He was prepared to meet argument and eloquence.—He expected brilliance of wit, and extraordinary powers of self-possession—with a full knowledge of all the political circumstances under which he had arrayed himself as the opponent of the liberty of the Press. In all this, he was most severely disappointed. Instead of the polished manners, and easy elegance of the gentleman, he met with the overbearing insolence of a man who had not found time to adjust the weight and emoluments of his office to his shoulders :—instead of the candid opposition of one anxious for the preservation of good order, and opposing pernicious principles from a strong sense of their mischievous

THE
POOR MAN'S GUARDIAN,
A WEEKLY PAPER FOR THE PEOPLE.

This Paper (after sustaining a Government persecution of three years and a half duration, in which upwards of 500 persons were unjustly imprisoned, and cruelly treated for vending it) was, on the Trial of an Ex-Officio Information filed by

HIS MAJESTY'S ATTORNEY-GENERAL against HENRY HETHERINGTON,

IN THE COURT OF EXCHEQUER,

Before LORD LYNDHURST and a Special Jury,

DECLARED TO BE

A STRICTLY LEGAL PUBLICATION.

Printed and Published by H. Hetherington, 126, Strand.

No. 161.]	Saturday, *July 5*, 1831.	[Price 1*d*.

PROGRESS OF DESPOTISM IN AMERICA. THE MIDDLE CLASSES SHOWN TO BE THE REAL AUTHORS OF SLAVERY IN ALL NATIONS. READ AND LEARN, &c.

Friends, Brethren, and Fellow-Countrymen,

In these dreadful times when liberty is, as it were, hunted out of the world, when the best part of man-

oppression engender that almost despair which animates unarmed citizens to rush on bayonets. It is said the people of France are turbulent, seditious, and uneasy. So are the people of Ireland, and so are those of every other country where there is the spirit of men abiding, and abuses of authority to call it into action. The end of all government is the happiness of mankind, so far as that depends on those enjoyments which are equally essential to all, namely, the ordinary necessaries of food, lodging, and clothing. Whenever the ordinances and institutions

---

THE
WORKING MAN'S FRIEND;
AND
POLITICAL MAGAZINE.

Train up thy children, England,
In the ways of righteousness—and feed them
With the bread of wholesome doctrine.
Where hast thou thy mines—but in their industry?
Thy bulwarks where—but in their breasts? Thy might—
But in their arms?
Must not their numbers, therefore, be thy Wealth,
Thy Strength, thy Power, thy Safety, and thy Pride?
Oh! grief them grief and shame,
If in this flourishing land there should be dwellings,
Where the new-born babe doth bring unto its parent's soul
No joy! where squalid Poverty receives it at the birth,
And on her withered knees
Gives it the scanty bread of discontent.

SOUTHEY.

" Liberty with danger is to be preferred to slavery with security."—SALLUST.

No. 1.]	LONDON, DECEMBER 22, 1832.	[PRICE ONE PENNY.

THE  CRISIS,

[Institution of the Industrious Classes, Gray's-Inn Road.]

OR THE CHANGE FROM
ERROR AND MISERY, TO TRUTH AND HAPPINESS.

"IF WE CANNOT YET RECONCILE ALL OPINIONS, LET US NOW ENDEAVOUR TO UNITE ALL HEARTS."

VOL. I.—No. 1.]	EDITED BY ROBERT OWEN.—SATURDAY, APRIL 14, 1832.	[ONE PENNY.

PROSPECTUS.

IT is now evident to every one who observes passing events, and who reflects upon the new public opinion which is arising throughout the various Nations of the World, that some great Change in the condition of man, either for good or for evil, is about to take place—in fact, that a *momentous* CRISIS is at hand. Be it our task

"THE CRISIS" will therefore be no party paper: it will be occupied in developing, in plain simple language, the great principles of human nature, and the means of applying them, with equal simplicity, in practice, to all the affairs of domestic life, and to society in all its ramifications.

"THE CRISIS" will upon all occasions *discourage religious ani-*

THE CHARTER.

ESTABLISHED BY THE WORKING CLASSES.

No. 10.   SUNDAY, MARCH 31, 1839.   PRICE 6D.

The Northern Star,
AND LEEDS GENERAL ADVERTISER.

Vol. I. No. 8.   SATURDAY, JANUARY 6, 1838.   PRICE FOURPENCE HALFPENNY, OR FIVE SHILLINGS PER QUARTER.

THE
SOUTHERN STAR,
AND LONDON AND BRIGHTON PATRIOT.

No. 1.]   THE SOUTHERN STAR, SUNDAY, JANUARY 19, 1840.   [PRICE 6D.

THE PEOPLE'S PAPER
THE CHAMPION OF
Political Justice & Universal Right.

No. 1.]   SATURDAY, MAY 8, 1852.   [PRICE THREEPENCE.

The Bee-Hive
THE PEOPLE'S PAPER,
ORGAN OF TRADES, FRIENDLY, CO-OPERATIVE SOCIETIES, WORKING MEN'S CLUBS, AND OTHER ASSOCIATIONS OF THE INDUSTRIAL CLASSES.

REGISTERED FOR   ESTABLISHED 1861.   TRANSMISSION ABROAD.

No. 501.   SATURDAY, MAY 20, 1871.   PRICE ONE PENNY.

THE RED REPUBLICAN.

EQUALITY, LIBERTY, FRATERNITY.

EDITED BY G. JULIAN HARNEY.

No. 21.—Vol. I.]   SATURDAY, NOVEMBER 9, 1850.   [PRICE ONE PENNY.

German Communism.

MANIFESTO OF THE GERMAN COMMUNIST PARTY.

(Published in February 1848.)

Two things appear on considering these facts. I. The ruling Powers of Europe acknowledge Communism to be also a Power. II. It is time for the Communists to lay before the world an account of their aims and tendencies, and to oppose these silly fables about the bugbear of Communism, by a manifesto of the Communist Party.

ments of the modern Bourgeoisie. The discover of the New World, the circumnavigation of Afric gave the Middleclass—then coming into being-new fields of action. The colonization of America the opening up of the East Indian and Chines Markets, the Colonial Trade, the increase of com modities generally and of the means of exchange

TO MR. G. JULIAN HARNEY.

MY DEAR SIR,—The enclosed rhymed letter came to me by post, undated, with a simple request that I would forward it to you. I do not like to vouch for its genuineness. It may be, or it may not. My own opinion is, to speak truth, against it; but, then there is the internal evidence, which, however, does not go for much. Lord Brougham has tried his hand at so many things. Nevertheless, it does not follow that all which is put forth as his should be written by him. Sir James Graham's famous pamphlet was, I know, written by somebody else. This letter can, however, hardly be the work of a mere secretary. Such as it is, I send it to you. Your readers can form their own opinion on the matter.

October 27th (22nd Sunday after Advent), 1850   Your constant admirer, M.P.

GOD AND MY RIGHT

JUSTICE

THE ORGAN OF THE SOCIAL DEMOCRACY.

No. 635, Vol. XIII.]   LONDON, SATURDAY, MAR. 14, 1896.   [Price One Penny.

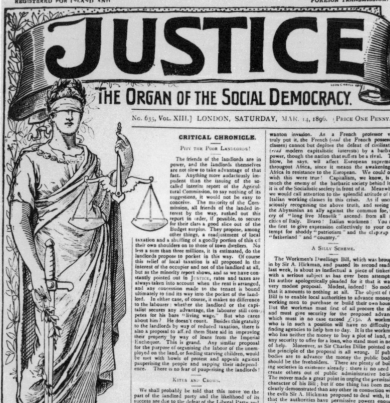

FIAT JUSTITIA RUAT CŒLUM.

CRITICAL CHRONICLE.

PITY THE POOR LANDLORDS!

The friends of the landlords are in power, and the landlords themselves are not slow to take advantage of that fact. Anything more audaciously impudent than the issuing of the so-called interim report of the Agricultural Commission, to say nothing of its suggestions, it would not be easy to conceive. The majority of the Commission, all friends of the landed interest by the way, rushed out this report in order, if possible, to secure for their class a good slice out of the Budget surplus. They propose, among other things, a readjustment of local taxation and a shifting of a goodly portion of this on their own shoulders on to those of town dwellers. No less a sum than three millions, it is estimated, do the landlords propose to pocket in this way. Of course this *relief* of local taxation is all proposed in the interest of the occupier and not of the landlord at all, but as the minority report shows, and as we have constantly pointed out in JUSTICE, rates and taxes are always taken into account when the rent is arranged, and any concession made to the tenant is bound ultimately to find its way into the pocket of the landlord. In either case, of course, it makes no difference to the labourer : whether the landlord or the capitalist secures any advantage, the labourer still competes for his bare "living wage." But who cares about him ? He doesn't count. Besides this gratuity to the landlords by way of reduced taxation, there is also a proposal to afford them State aid in improving their property by way of loans from the Imperial Exchequer. This is grand. Any similar proposal for the purpose of organising the labour of the unemployed on the land, or feeding starving children, would be met with howls of protest and appeals against pauperising the people and sapping their independence. There is no fear of pauperising the landlords !

KITES AND CROWS.

We shall probably be told that this move on the part of the landlord party and the likelihood of its success are due to the defeat of the Liberal Party and once more the cry will be raised "See what you have done ; you have put the landlords into power, and now they are using that power for their own class interests." Precisely ; and the only alternative was to put the capitalists once more in power in order that they might use it for *their* class interests. While the workers are the victims of the kites and crows, it is a matter of little importance to them whether kites or crows are in the ascendancy. In either case their bones will be picked pretty clean. If this dodge of the landlord party to help themselves out of the national till should have the effect of impressing upon the workers a sense of the readiness with which the propertied plunderers will use for their own ends the political power which they are constantly warning the workers against using at all, it will do some little good. Whether the landlord gets State aid to augment his rent, or the capitalist screws it to enhance his profits, whether local taxation is reduced in the rural districts for the sake of the landlord or increased in the interest of the capitalist makes no difference to the worker. He has to bear it in any case, and it is about time he learned how little he is affected by the battles of the kites and crows.

HOW THE HARPIES HANG TOGETHER.

The Italian defeat has more morals than one. It is instructive to notice how all the representatives of capitalistic civilisation, however much at loggerheads they may be otherwise, "stand in" and hug each other, in face of the common barbaric enemy just as they do in face of the common Socialistic enemy. Queen Victoria and the Austrian Emperor send condolences to Umberto on the failure of his marauding expedition against a power with which they have at peace, and a potentate with whom they have no ground of quarrel. Even the French bourgeoise press, bitterly incensed against the Italians as it professes itself on other occasions, is by no means elated over the success of Menelik in repelling their

wanton invasion. As a French professor very truly put it, the French (read the French possessing classes) cannot but deplore the defeat of civilisation (read modern capitalistic interests) by a barbaric power, though the nation that suffers be a rival. The blow, he says, will affect European supremacy throughout Africa, since it means the awakening of Africa in resistance to the European. We could only wish this were true ! Capitalism, we know, is as much the enemy of the barbaric society behind it as it is of the Socialistic society in front of it. Meanwhile we would call attention to the splendid attitude of the Italian working classes in this crisis. As if unconsciously recognising the above truth, and seeing in the Abyssinian an ally against the common foe, the cry of "long live Menelik" ascends from all the cities of Italy. Bravo ! Italian workmen ! You are the first to give expression collectively to your contempt for shoddy "patriotism" and the clap-trap of "fatherland " and "country."

A SILLY SCHEME.

The Workmen's Dwellings Bill, which was brought in by Sir A. Hickman, and passed its second reading last week, is about as ineffectual a piece of tinkering with a serious subject as has ever been attempted. Its author apologetically pleaded for it that it was a very modest proposal. Modest, indeed ! So modest that it amounts to nothing at all. The object of the Bill is to enable local authorities to advance money to working men to purchase or build their own houses. But the workman must first of all procure the site, and must give security for the proposed advance, which must in no case exceed £150. A workman who is in such a position will have no difficulty in finding agencies to help him to buy. It is the workman who has neither the money to buy a plot of land, nor any security to offer for a loan, who stand most in need of help. Moreover, as Sir Charles Dilke pointed out, the principle of the proposal is all wrong. If public bodies are to advance the money the public bodies should be the freeholders. There are plenty of building societies in existence already ; there is no need to create others out of public administrative bodies. The mover made a great point in urging the permissive character of his Bill ; but if one thing has been more clearly demonstrated than any other in connection with the evils Sir A. Hickman proposed to deal with, it is that the authorities have permissive powers enough and to spare, but that the evils will never be effectually dealt with until these powers are made compulsory.

THE RADICAL ROUT.

The fatuous folly which lent the support of the bulk of the Liberal Opposition to this silly scheme is only another evidence of the utter break up and rout of the Radical Party. That party seems to become more completely demoralised every day. There is talk of disruption and disintegration on every hand, and lately we hear a good deal of the Radical revolt. But the poor Rads seem too abject and spiritless to revolt or do anything but bemoan their sad fate and weep for the leader who is lost to them. They are certainly doing all in their power to demonstrate the utter worthlessness and incapacity of their party, and it is to be hoped that working men followers of that organised hypocrisy will have sense enough to profit by the lesson which is so steadily being drummed into them, and will cease any longer to be humbugged by the pretensions of Liberalism. If working men Radicals will put their class first, as do the Tory landlords and the Liberal capitalists, and, as these do, "stand by their order," we shall soon have all our enemies in one camp, and all our friends by our side.

There was a crowd of City and West-end mobsmen and women to greet Dr. Jameson and his fellow accused at Bow Street Police-court again on Tuesday. These people seem to make themselves quite at home in a police court. They evidently know where they ought to be. But they had the decency to behave with a little more propriety on this than on a previous occasion. There was very little interest manifested, and already the popularity of the raiders seems to be on the wane. There was an addition of two to the number of prisoners on Tuesday, but what most people are eagerly awaiting is the appearance of Cecil Rhodes—for, after all, it is he and the Chartered Company who are really on their trial.

THE COMMONWEAL

Have you not heard how it has gone with many a Cause before now : First, few men heed it ; Next, most men contemn it ; Lastly, all men ACCEPT IT—and the Cause is Won.

Vol. 7.—No. 322.   SATURDAY, JULY 16, 1892.   Weekly : One Penny.

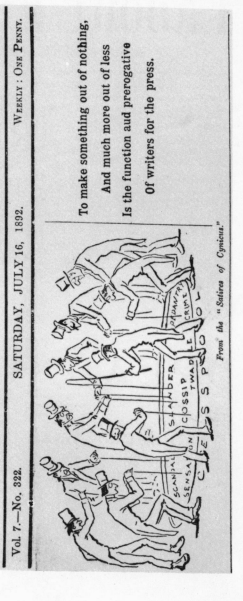

To make something out of nothing,

And much more out of less

Is the function aud prerogative

Of writers for the press.

From the "Satires of Cynicus."

THE
Labour Elector
THE ORGAN OF PRACTICAL SOCIALISM.

Vol. I.—No. 7.]   LONDON, 15th NOVEMBER, 1888.   [Price One Penny.

The CLARION
EDITED BY NUNQUAM.

No. 70.   SATURDAY, APRIL 8, 1893.   PRICE ONE PENNY.

MILD AND BITTER.

[MAY-DAY NUMBER.

"THE TIGER'S" REVENGE.

THE WORKERS'
DREADNOUGHT
For International Socialism.

Vol. VI.—No. 6   SATURDAY, MAY 3rd, 1919   Price Twopence.

THE HUNGARIAN REVOLUTION.

THE FIRST FIVE DAYS OF THE HUNGARIAN REVOLUTION.

Extract from the account of an eye-witness, Henry Charles Schmitt.

[The events here described are the events of the first revolution which created a Hungarian Republic with a National Assembly as instrument of government, and which has since been succeeded by a second Revolution based on the Soviets. The events of the first Hungarian Revolution are, however, very closely interwoven with those of the second. The pamphlet from which these extracts are taken will shortly be published by the Workers' Socialist Federation.]

....And so I come to the actual picture-gallery of the revolutionary events.

The Daily Herald.

No. 1.   LONDON, WEDNESDAY, JANUARY 25, 1911.   PRICE ONE HALFPENNY.

To "ONE AND ALL."

What is this—the sound and rumour ?
What is this that all men hear,
Like the wind in hollow valleys
When the storm is drawing near;
Like the rolling on of ocean
In the eventide of fear ?—
'Tis the People marching on.

* * * *

Men of the L.S.C.

What nobler inspirer for the hour and the object—your modest, legitimate demand for a shorter working day—than the author of the above, that noble Old English Master Printer, William Morris, who treated his men as men, "fellow craftsmen," in that famous Kelmscott Press, down Hammersmith way ?

Yes, after many years of that tranquility which leads to sleep but not to death, "the sound and rumour" is of war !—war not of the workers' seeking, unless the worker is *ever* to receive no improvement in his everlasting drudgery.

is a Labour Party in the House, and it holds supreme power.

On we march, then—we, the workers,
And the rumour that ye hear
Is the blended soul of battle
And deliverance drawing near,
For the hope of every creature
In the banner that we bear:

> 50—48.

Yours, fellow workers, in the hope that conquers.   W. F. REAN.

STRIKING PARAGRAPHS.

WE have arrived. At last we have a daily paper of our own. If we differ at all from the orthodox daily press, it will be in the fact that we shall give the *correct* position of affairs day by day.

— :o: —

We ask our readers to be kind, and excuse our imperfections. We have met the usual difficulties that always attend the production of a first number. Still, we have arrived.

— :o: —

The necessity for our existence was brought

We are surprised to see, in one of the letters issued by the Master Printers' Association, that employers who concede the men's terms may be made to suffer for their temerity. Is this a threat ?

— :o: —

One of the most conspicuous features of the dispute has been the loyalty of the L.S.C. members. The notices have been tendered almost without exception. In only one instance has it come to our knowledge that certain members of the chapel failed to respond to the call. The proprietors of that establishment have decided that they will convert the establishment into an "open house." Here let it be known, once and for all, that the question of the "open house" will be fought as strenuously as the hours question itself. Members who have tendered notices will not withdraw them if any non-union man is retained in the department. Chapel Officers should make a note of this and act accordingly.

— :o: —

Our members must be prepared for certain methods of deception that are being practised. To one office, at least, a bogus telegram was sent to the Father of the Chapel ordering him to cancel notices—a trick of a most discredit-

---

DAILY WORKER

Workers of the World Unite !

No. 1   WEDNESDAY, JANUARY 1, 1930   One Penny

WOOLLEN WORKERS TAKE THE FIELD

REVOLUTION IN INDIA GROWS

Congress Chiefs Feel Mass Pressure

The All-India National Congress, which opened at Lahore yesterday, adopted by 942 votes, against 79, the resolution moved by Gandhi; deploring the throwing of a bomb at the Viceroy and congratulating him on his escape. The minority, waving Red Flags, raised angry protests. Gandhi's second motion is to deal with the new manoeuvre of withdrawal of "Dominion status" in favour of independence.

The reports of meetings of the Congress Committee in Session since Christmas Day, shows that the enormous rising tide of the Indian masses, led by the heroic Indian proletariat whose determined fight, marked by mass political strikes, is the enormous motive force which has compelled the leaders of the Indian bourgeoisie, who have in the past two years gone over to the side of British Imperialism, to make a desperate attempt to retain their hold on the masses by a show of opposition.

The resolution of the bourgeois nationalist leaders in favour of independence and boycott of legislature significantly leaves the campaign for civil disobedience and non-payment of taxes to the discretion of the Congress Committee, "as and when necessary."

At the Sikh Conference meeting yesterday, also in Lahore, Kharak Singh, the president, stated that out of thirty-one recent death sentences on revolutionary Indian nationalists, twenty-seven were Sikhs.

When Sir Frederick Sykes, Governor of Bengal, visited Ahmedabad two days ago he was met by a demonstration outside the station waving flags and with shouts of "Frederick Sykes, go back."

PRINCE'S JAUNT

To Travel Into Impenetrable Jungle—By Train

WITH HIS VALET !

On Friday the Prince of Wales will again start a jaunt that will cost thousands of pounds of the money the workers have earned for him.

He is going to Capetown, and from there will journey into the jungle—by train !

There he will display his intrepidity against the wild beasts of Africa. His valet is to accompany him, probable to hold the rifle.

An official of the "Kenilworth Castle," on which he is to travel, states that he is expected to play a prominent part in the "strenuous" deck games which are to be played on board.

"Otherwise, he will use an ordinary first-class cabin with the usual dressing-room."

SHOOTING THE UNEMPLOYED

Social Democrat Police Chief Orders Massacre in Cologne

BERLIN, Tuesday.—Yesterday evening 10,000 unemployed workers demonstrated in front of the Cologne Town Hall in order to support the proposal of the Communist faction for winter assistance for the unemployed.

The Social Democratic Police President was in charge of large forces of police, who tried to prevent the demonstrators from reaching the Town Hall. At first the police used their batons, but when their efforts proved ineffective the Social Democrat gave the order to fire.

Many workers were wounded by the

MASS STRIKES AGAINST WAGE REDUCTIONS

Police Attack Pickets

ALL WORKERS SOLID AND DETERMINED TO WIN FIGHT

OVER two thousand woollen textile workers are on strike. The attempt to cut wages is meeting with real mass resistance The workers are in a militant mood and maintain the utmost solidarity against employers, Labour Government, trade union bureaucrats and police

The young workers are especially active and are giving increasing support to the Communist Party Campaign for rank and file Committees of Action

BONDFIELD, SCAB;

Labour Prepares to Smash Wool Strike

(From Our Own Correspondent.)

BRADFORD.—The council of the wool textile employers has not yet commented on the letter of the Minister of Labour proposing to set up a court of enquiry into the situation in the woollen industry under Part 2 of the Industrial Courts Act, 1919

Before availing themselves of the offer to impose the wage reduction by means of arbitration the woollen bosses are anxiously watching the strikes which are repeatedly breaking out and being carried on with remarkable determination. I understand that Margaret Bondfield is going ahead with the setting up of the Court and that the constitution and terms of reference will be announced shortly.

DEFIANT SPIRIT

Determined to Resist Lower Wages

(From Our Own Correspondent.)

SADDLEWORTH.—The attempt of the Saddleworth millowners to break the strike in nine mills against a wage cut of two shillings in the pound has completely failed. Although the mills were opened on Monday morning not one of the thirteen hundred strikers, mostly women and girls, returned.

The police have repeatedly attacked the pickets and mass arrests have been made The defiant attitude of Lily Hutton, a young woman worker, when "on trial" for assaulting a burly police inspector, typifies the spirit of the workers.

A long period of short time and low wages has made them determined to resist to the utmost.

DYE WORKERS STRIKE

---

xi

Published by The Executive Committee of the British Socialist Party.

The Call

AN ORGAN of INTERNATIONAL SOCIALISM

No. 193 THURSDAY, DECEMBER 18th, 1919 TWOPENCE

"THEY WILL CHEAT YOU YET—THOSE JUNKERS"

By FRED WILLIS

The Junkers in this particular case being Winston Churchill, Lloyd George and Co.— the British section of the Junker International.

Has one single statement of theirs, on Russia, been consistent with their actions? Or vice-versa? Is there one sane man or woman in these islands who believes a word they say on any subject whatever? Every trade union deputation that meets the Prime Minister comes away from the Presence with a sickening sensation of having been tricked. And everyone knows that Churchill, despite his statements to the contrary, is determined to carry fire and sword into Soviet Russia on the first available opportunity. His aristocratic soul is finely contemptuous of the great demonstrations of popular feeling that are sweeping the country against intervention or interference of any sort. He is well aware that there is even a growing trend of opinion among the workers towards downright pro-Bolshevism. Ward's reception at the Trade Union Conference must have convinced both him and Ward of the affectionate regard which the ordinary, unsentimental trade unionists entertain towards himself, his policy, and his camp followers. The light has spread; the truth prevails. The campaign of calumny has all but spent its ... there. Similarly, the French "Populaire" publishes the names of French units which are under orders for the great adventure. Unless the workers of this country, and of France, act, and act decisively, they will find themselves committed to a Spring campaign in Russia for the express purpose of crushing Revolution abroad as a preliminary to stifling unrest at home. Surely we owe a duty in this matter to our own men who are being sent unwillingly across the seas on an errand they dislike, at the behest of masters for whom, in their heart of hearts, they feel nothing but contempt. Clemenceau's visit is regarded in some quarters as a sign that our own governing class has decided to do

THIS WEEK'S FEATURES

under present circumstances, self-supporting. The waste and corruption of the war period has to be made up; the inevitable dislocation of the time of revolution to be repaired, and this means that machinery and implements of all kinds must be imported in exchange for her own native products. The blockade is intended to prevent Socialist reconstruction. The subsidising, open or secret, of the counter-revolution is maintained for the same sinister purpose. The Baltic States are deliberately bullied into continuing a state of war against the Soviet Republic. All this, and much more that history will have to record, for the sake of beating the Russian workers in their heroic fight against the old Tsardom and the New Capitalism.

Let us not only cry Peace, but force Peace upon our unwilling masters. Let our special Trade Union Conferences be gatherings to initiate action, and not to conduct pretty debates.

For it is not only the Russians they are trying to beat; it is we who are being cheated. They cheat us—these tricky politicians—of all we fought for through forty years of Socialist propaganda. They filch our dreams from us; they rob us of the dawn. And they will cheat us still, and our children's children, unless the organised workers of this country realise that the cause

---

DAILY HERALD

No. 1,598 (No. 595—New Series) ♦ LONDON, MONDAY, FEBRUARY 28, 1921. TWOPENCE

Dyspepsia

THE SCOTLAND YARD PRINTING PRESS

How the Special Branch Assists Russian Reactionaries

PAPER'S GUILLOTINED IMPRINT

This is another show up of the Special Branch of Scotland Yard, and another exposure of imitation "documents."

Last autumn our Government was threatening to break off the Russian Trade negotiation because of alleged Bolshevik propaganda.

At that very moment the Government's own Secret Service was collaborating with Russian émigrés in producing and sending abroad for propaganda purposes bogus copies of a Bolshevik official paper.

"PRAVDAS" PRINTED IN LONDON

Some little while ago these came into the DAILY HERALD office ...

10 EXECUTIONS TO-DAY?

Vindicating the "Law" in Ireland

PRISON SECRETS

From Our Own Correspondent

DUBLIN, Sunday.—It is reported here, but not confirmed, that four political prisoners under sentence of death will be executed to-morrow in Mountjoy Prison.

There are, in addition, six executions fixed for Cork Gaol for to-morrow.

Battle in a Bog

THE SECRET PRINTING OFFICE

LOCK-OUT OF MINERS

Announced for Next Month

LEADERS TO MEET

Delegate Conference to be Called

By a Special Correspondent

Class Conscious

Wigan Notices

THIS WEEK'S BY-ELECTIONS

GOOD PROSPECTS IN ALL DIVISIONS

EVERY HELPER NEEDED

WOMEN HELP KENNEDY

OUR BIRTHDAY

Have you yet sent for your Collecting Card for our Birthday Fund? Send to-day to 2 Gough-square, Fleet-street, E.C.4

---

xii

The Workers' Weekly, November 7, 1924

Workers of the World, Unite!

THE Workers' ⊕ Weekly

THE FORERUNNER OF THE WORKERS' DAILY.

OFFICIAL ORGAN OF THE COMMUNIST PARTY OF GREAT BRITAIN.

No. 92   FRIDAY, NOVEMBER 7, 1924   [Registered at the G.P.O. as a Newspaper]   One Penny

SEVEN YEARS' STABLE GOVERNMENT

The Hypocrites

SEVENTH ANNIVERSARY OF THE RUSSIAN REVOLUTION

HOW TO CELEBRATE

On November 7, the workers all over the world will be celebrating the seventh anniversary of the Russian Revolution. The last seven years have been years of profound instability in the world. Capitalist Governments have had their little hour and ceased to be. Labour and Social-Democratic parties have had their brief glimpses of power, either in coalition with their masters or by enjoying a shadowy independence and then have been forced to abandon office, without achieving any positive results for the working class.

Whilst all this uncertainty has been displaying itself in capitalist governments, the Soviet Power has gone on developing. Every year that has passed since 1921 has been a steady improvement in the workers' wages, increased production in industry, increasing mastery of the arts of politics and government. Whilst no results have been achieved anywhere by the application of the policy of the Social-Democrats, the results of the application of revolutionary Communist policy in Russia are inspiring. The workers who have followed the Social-Democratic leaders have lost almost everything; the workers who followed the Russian Communists have conquered one-sixth of the globe.

Every year since 1918 two events have been celebrated at the beginning of November—Armistice Day and the Anniversary of the Russian Revolution. The one commemorating the close of the murderous capitalist war, the other pointing the way out of capitalism and war. The workers should learn the lesson. We are living in a dangerous world. Imperialist rivalries are becoming more acute. Armaments are being piled up to an unheard of extent. The world is drifting to new slaughter. Only by treading the same path as the Russian workers, by setting up a workers' government based upon the organisations of the working class, by establishing a broad proletarian democracy for the workers and an iron dictatorship against the capitalists, can we achieve real freedom.

From November 7 to 14, our party will be celebrating the "Ten Days that Shook the World," not merely by demonstrations but by increasing its influence amongst the working class, recruiting new members, founding factory groups.

Every member must exert the greatest possible energy in order that our numbers will increase and the party be transformed into a real Bolshevik Party, able by its influence in the British Labour Movement not only to defend Soviet Russia but to lead the struggle for power in Britain itself.

The week following November 7 must be a week of energetic activity —and results.

THE "RED LETTER"

What is the Left Wing Doing?

The "Zinoviev letter" mystery is still unsolved.

The capitalist press is doing its best to confuse the issue still more. Every capitalist newspaper is busily turning the attention of its readers to the question of how the "document" got into the hands of the *Daily Mail*, by what channels it "came to England," and so on.

But the real mystery is not either of these. The document is a forgery, and those who forged it could just as easily as not pass on a copy to the *Daily Mail*. There is not even any mystery about MacDonald's part in the whole affair. He has confessed himself that he broke his word to Rakovsky, and had himself corrected a draft Note to the Soviet representative.

The mystery is not here. MacDonald was out to catch middle-class votes, even if it meant scrapping the chances of the Anglo-Soviet Treaty and of a Labour victory. That every intelligent worker sees.

The real mystery is—WHAT ARE THE LEFT WING DOING? Where is their loyalty to their class? Where are their oft-repeated

(Continued in next column)

(Continued from previous column) assurances of solidarity with Soviet Russia? Why have they not come out, as the Communist Party has done, demanding the withdrawal of the dirty forgery, an apology for Gregory's insolent Note, and the dismissal of the responsible officials? Why have they allowed MacDonald to get away with it?

We assert that, though this forgery was launched as an eleventh hour dodge, it is only the first move in a new attack on Soviet Russia. The minds of the workers are to be poisoned, as a preliminary to the open campaign. And we go further. We declare that it is common talk in the Tory clubs that the Tory Government's first act will be to demand that the Soviet Government take back its Note of breaking off relations.

The Tories are already preparing a big propaganda campaign, demanding that the Soviet Government should be made to accept new forgeries as genuine of the British Foreign Office acts its soul upon them. This is the secret of their ignoring Rakovsky's refutations.

Once again we ask. Where are the Left Wing? And we warn the workers—BE ON YOUR GUARD! PREPARE TO DEFEND SOVIET RUSSIA!

The Cabinet Committee

The Cabinet Committee investigating the Zinoviev letter has decided that "it is impossible on the evidence before them to come to a positive conclusion on the subject."

In other words Mr. MacDonald slabbed the Labour movement in the back by issuing to the world at once the election a note to Russia concerning a document whose authenticity the Government has been unable to prove.

True, the note was sent without Mr. MacDonald's consent, but he drafted the note, he it would to draft some condemning documents of probable authenticity and place them in the hands of the enemies of the working class to use against the Labour movement! Mr. MacDonald is either a knave or the most astounding bungler in the history of the Labour movement. In any case his place is at once at the helm of the Labour Party.

UNDER WHICH FLAG?

Armistice Day Reflections

On November 11 for two minutes there will be a "great silence" in memory of the "glorious dead." The traffic will be brought to a standstill in the streets, the busy factories will stop, and little knots of notables will place wreaths on the Cenotaph or the local war memorial.

Most of those who will take a prominent part in these Armistice Day ceremonies will be quite sincere in commemorating the memory of the dead, quite determined to ensure that never again shall the flower of the nation be sacrificed in war. Yet most of these who are moved by these nationalist sentiments will in their political capacity be supporting a policy which if allowed to develop must lead to fresh wars.

Most of those who are celebrating the Armistice have just voted on the winning side in an election in which the Union Jack, the flag of British Imperialism, has triumphed for a brief moment over the Red Flag, the standard of international working-class solidarity.

It may never occur to most of the participants in the Armistice celebrations that it is absurd to mow the dead old flag and deplore the loss of those who were sacrificed in the late war. It is precisely the waving of "good and evil" and the creation of a surrounding atmosphere of emotionalism which strains the outlook necessary for the preparation of new wars.

The Communist Party can pay tribute to the dead soldiers of the working class without inconsistency or hypocrisy, and will do so. It will wave no national flags. It will shed no ineffective tears. On Armistice Day we will not only mourn for those who have been sacrificed, but we will steel ourselves to carry on with renewed hope and energy the struggle against Imperialism which was the cause of their death.

Only those who are struggling against Imperialism with its scramble for trade and territory can really say that they have learned the lesson of the late war and are prepared to act upon it in their everyday life.

No one can logically mourn for the dead and uphold Empire, for the struggle for the maintenance and extension of Empire are the direct cause of the last war and is preparing the way for the next.

No one can logically mourn the dead and vote for capitalist armaments which menace the living.

In the factories and in the unemployed queues the workers must remember that while one section of the master class

(Continued at foot of next column)

preparing new wars, and are mocking the living and the dead.

The Communist Party can pay tribute to the dead soldiers of the working class without inconsistency or hypocrisy, and will do so. It will wave no national flags. It will shed no ineffective tears. On Armistice Day we will not only mourn for those who have been sacrificed, but we will steel ourselves to carry on with renewed hope and energy the struggle against Imperialism which was the cause of their death.

"The old flag" is the symbol of soulless predatory Imperialism. It has wasted over thousands of bloodstained battlefields on which workers have been sacrificed in order that their masters' lust for trade and territory might be satisfied. It now waves over slave-driven factories and sunless, fetid slums where the survivors of glorious wars and their dependants are condemned to vegetate in misery and degradation. The "old flag" of all capitalist countries are the symbols of war, slavery, and degradation, and those who wave them on Armistice Day are serving the cause of capitalist imperialism.

J. B. Campbell.

LANSBURY'S Labour Weekly

Vol. I.—No. 17.   SATURDAY, JUNE 20, 1925.   TWOPENCE

Registered at the G.P.O. as a Newspaper.

WITH THE RANK AND FILE

BY GEORGE LANSBURY

Sunday Worker, March 22

CAR-
TOONS
Pages
3, 5, 6

Sunday Worker

FINAL EDITION

MAGA-
ZINE
Pages
9, 10, 11

THE ONLY LABOUR SUNDAY NEWSPAPER

No. 2   SUNDAY, MARCH 22, 1925   Twopence

STENCH FROM LAW CASES GROWING THICKER

OUR FUTURE

No. 2 of the SUNDAY WORKER produced a volume of comment and criticism.

It could be divided into two equal portions. There were those who were disappointed with our size, and those who were more concerned with the fact that the first Sunday Labour newspaper in this country had appeared than with contrasting it, to its detriment, with the millionaire press.

One comrade went so far as to suggest that people thought they had been "taken in" when they saw the paper.

Another, when the paper was delivered, together with his capitalist paper, thought that the SUNDAY WORKER was no advertisement leaflet inserted by his newsagent.

Yet another suggested that it would serve money together and then started off with sixteen pages.

Let us face this position quite frankly. We are not able, neither will any other working class newspaper ever be able, to compete in size and volume of content with the millionaire-owned Sunday press.

If we had delayed making a start until the future of the paper was assured we should never have started.

We have staked our future on the goodwill and loyal support of the workers. We believe the workers will support a Sunday newspaper which gives the news from their angle and corrects the errors of the boss press.

Emboldened by our success last week, when we were able to get out 161,000 copies and received orders for 250,000, we have decided to increase the size of the paper to 12 pages.

ADULTERY AND LECHERY MULTIPLIED

Military Men, Titled Ladies, and Rich Idlers Mixed up in Trials that Smell to Heaven

Corruption, crookedness, multiple adultery, lechery, and trickery of the grossest description—these are the reigning elements of social life among the Upper Classes of the present day, if the testimony brought out in the courts during the past week is to be believed.

The state of Capitalist society in its greatest social centre—London—apparently matches anything that prevailed in Rome before its fall or in St. Petersburg before the Russian Workers rose and cleaned out the stables.

And it is this corrupt class which supplies the "brains" and the "guiding minds" which the working class are taught to look to for leadership in Politics, Industry, Diplomacy, Military Life, and Government!

MR. "A"
Robinson Appeal Dismissed

An echo of the Mr. "A" case was heard, at the Courts of Appeal, on Friday when judgment was given in the case of Robinson v. the Midland Bank (Limited). The appeal of Mr. Robinson was dismissed.

In giving judgment the Master of the Rolls said that the defence of the bank to Mr. Robinson's claim was that the money was the fruit of a wicked and shocking conspiracy to obtain money from Sir Hari Singh, that the money was paid into the bank for and on behalf of the conspirators, and that they had discharged themselves of all liability by paying out the money on the same authority and by the same machine as that on which they originally received it.

The jury found that there was a con-

GENERAL "X"
Money and Adultery in Dennistoun Case

Another long and exciting instalment of the "star" Society drama was shown at the Law Courts this week when the Dennistoun case was resumed.

Mrs. Dorothy Dennistoun, it will be remembered, is suing her ex-husband, Lt.-Col. Ian Dennistoun, late of the Grenadier Guards, for sums of money amounting to £1,305 which she says he owes her.

Mr. Justice McCardie intimated that he would put ten questions to the jury and remarked "There are far more and far graver questions in this case than many people here abhors thought."

Mr. Norman Birkett took over the task of addressing the jury on behalf of Col. Dennistoun.

THE NEXT
Waterhouse Case in Further Stage

Another Society case involving titled people came before the courts on Monday.

The judge had previously made efforts to get the case settled out of court and to prevent further revelations of the life led by "Society" coming before the public. He remarked that the public was "sick of this class of case."

In his opening statement Counsel said that this class of case was all too common lately, and added that if it represented in any way the normal state of English society, then he was tempted to think that with exposure after exposure a strengthening of the law was necessary.

The case was brought by Mrs. Muriel Waterhouse, of Hove, Brighton, to recover...

COOK'S BRAVE SPEECH

"The Workers are Starving"

RANK AND FILE MUST CONTROL

MacDonald's Moderation

Before a large and enthusiastic meeting in Tredegar, S. Wales, last night, A. J. Cook fiercely indicted Capitalism.

It has, he said, many powerful advocates, the Government, the Press, the Pulpit, and, alas, even in our own ranks, apologists for it are to be found.

Force is organised in every quarter for its protection.

It is not the method of capitalism to rely upon reason and truth. The forces of the Army, Navy, and Secret Service, have been, and will continue to be used without compunction.

The Workers will never forget Poterloo, Tonypandy, and the Railwaymen's, Dockers', and Miners' struggles.

WHAT IS THE NEW SUPPLEMENTARY RESERVE REQUIRED FOR?

The workers are starving, and suffering from unemployment, underemployment, and low wages. The Miners, Railwaymen, Shipbuilding workers, and Engineering workers, are all at grips with their masters. All the workers will be...

xiv

FIRE AND FRAUD See Page 9

REYNOLDS NEWS

GOVERNMENT OF THE PEOPLE, BY THE PEOPLE, FOR THE PEOPLE

RADIO—Page 29   LONDON SUNDAY MAY 3 1936   TODAY'S WEATHER: Fair, local frost at night.   PRICE 2d.

EMPEROR HAILE SELASSIE 'AN EXILE

Flight From Addis While Mob Shoot and Pillage

Cheerio, Kids!

EMPEROR Haile Selassie of Abyssinia is now an exile. With the Empress, the Crown Prince, and other members of the Royal Family he fled his capital, Addis Ababa early yesterday, for Djibouti, the French Somaliland port.

This sensational message was flashed to the British Foreign Office by Sir Sidney Barton, our Minister at Addis Ababa. Immediately it was received Mr. Anthony Eden, the Foreign Secretary, interrupted his week-end and returned to the Foreign Office to discuss the situation with his officials.

Although the Emperor was accompanied on his flight by his Foreign Minister, M. Herouy, and other officials of the Abyssinian Government, there is nothing to

£10 A WEEK MEN TO BE ON THE PANEL

New Plan Is Ready To Launch

HUNDREDS of thousands of people with incomes above £10 will benefit by a new scheme of medical service to be launched shortly.

Under a group system financed on a weekly contribution, have families with an income not exceeding £500 a year will be able to obtain general and even specialist advice from a doctor of their own choice.

The scheme, which was recently

MONDAY, SEPTEMBER 7, 1942

PASS THIS ON TO A FRIEND—

Daily Worker

No. 3431   MONDAY, SEPTEMBER 7, 1942

LATE EDITION

ONE PENNY

—TEN READERS FOR EVERY COPY!

STALINGRAD BEATS OFF ANOTHER MASS GERMAN ASSAULT

Von Bock's South-West Drive Fails

VON BOCK'S SECOND AND GREATEST MASS ONSLAUGHT AGAINST THE HEROIC CITY OF STALINGRAD HAS BEEN SMASHED AND THE RESISTANCE OF THE DEFENDERS IS STIFFENING, ACCORDING TO A DESPATCH FROM MOSCOW LATE LAST NIGHT.

Though the situation must remain grave while 50 German civilians with thousands of tanks and planes are ceaselessly battering at the gates of the city, the drive from the south-west has failed, cables Reuter's special sorress cnduct, that was confirmed by the Moscow communique yesterday.—

"All German attempts to break through to the city are meeting with staunch resistance from Soviet troops," it was reported. "During the past 24 hours the Germans have made four attempts to attack one fortified sector, all of which were unsuccessful.

From JOHN GIBBONS
Daily Worker Special Correspondent

MOSCOW, Sunday night.

THE great Stalingrad battle rages with undiminishing intensity. With first grey streaks of dawn German Junkers and Messerschmitts come over in their hundreds trying to bombing and machine-gunning to pulverise Soviet defences.

Soviet Tank Unit Struck At Full Speed

From HAROLD KING

Malta Gunners Greet Us

CABLE AND WIRELESS

Via Imperial

ELF. DAILY WORKER CAYTON STREET LONDON EC2

CONGRATULATIONS COMRADES ON SUCCESS GREETINGS
FROM MKERS OF MALTA BEST WISHES FOR FUTURE
STRUGGLE AGAINST FASCISM — ARUNDELL

Harry Pollitt's Appeal

I APPEAL on behalf of the Central Committee of the Communist Party to every member and Party sympathiser to use all the example in the way we all work for the success of the Daily Worker.

The Daily Worker is our fighting fund. We are all going to price an issue how to use it. How to apply it to every job on six on. It is a fund that every worker, skilled and unskilled, men or women, can afford.

It can be used to cramp our food, munitions, housing for the people's paper. Fighting for people's peace to people's victory and a people's peace.

How to Win the War

DAILY WORKER'S POLICY

The following declaration of the aims of the Daily Worker has been adopted by the Editorial Board

ON this historic day of republication the Daily Worker thanks all those of the Labour, trade union, co-operative and democratic movements whose magnificent support not only succeeded in removing the nineteen months' ban, but also very considerably strengthened the unity of the people.

£50,000

Drive Rommel Back From Our Minefields

THE CAIRO SEE-SAW see page two

Daily Worker

(PRINT)   M ★ ★ ★   WEDNESDAY APRIL 14 1954

THE ONLY DAILY PAPER OWNED BY ITS READERS

This is Gollan's line

From LEW GARDNER

EDEN AGREES TO 'A NEW KOREA'

Attlee says Yes, Bevan says No, to Indo-China action

Eden bows to Dulles

DULLES has achieved some success in dragging Britain toward participation in the dirty imperialist war in Indo-China. That is the meaning of Eden's statement in the Commons...

LABOUR M.P.s' shouts of "Another Korea" interrupted Mr. Anthony Eden, Foreign Secretary, in the Commons yesterday as he read a statement showing that he and Mr. Foster Dulles had agreed to joint action in Indo-China.

"There will be no national unity on this intervention," Mr. Ellis Smith (Lab, Stoke-on-Trent S.) called out, while another of his colleagues accused Mr. Eden of prejudicing the Geneva talks.

Top U.S. atomic scientist suspended

BECAUSE he opposed the development of the H-bomb in 1949 America's top atomic scientist, Dr. Robert Oppenheimer, has been suspended from all his official posts and is being subjected to a special investigation.

Best talks ever

MAN OF TODAY

XV

Morning Star

INCORPORATING THE DAILY WORKER

THURSDAY MAY 9 1974

FREEZE PRICES

AUEW assets handed back after anonymous offer

STRIKE TRIUMPHS – NIRC SOMERSAULTS

By MICK COSTELLO

TOTAL VICTORY was chalked up by the engineers yesterday in their battle with the National Industrial Relations Court, as a result of the massive response to their leaders' national strike instruction.

Even before the union's strike decision, back-door moves started to get the court off the hook and the manoeuvre eventually used to save the court's face was its grudging acceptance

of an anonymous donor's payment of the damages awarded against the engineers.

But no face was saved, as everyone is aware that it was the industrial action threat, and then the unprecedented strike in all industries, that forced through the solution.

Among the firms hit were Ford, Vauxhall, Chrysler, British Leyland, Massey-Ferguson, Rolls-Royce and GEC, as well as the newspaper industry, shipyards and power stations. As Britain ground to a halt, the court was powerless to do other than accept the anonymous £65,000.

In his court yesterday, Sir John Donaldson said: "An offer to pay the judgment debt of another is a novelty." He was worried that acceptance of the anonymous offer of £65,000 would "involve some surrender of the authority of the court."

But Mr. Peter Scott, who...

WE SAY
Damper on Donaldson

LABOUR'S INDEPENDENT WEEKLY

THE HYSTERIA OF WITCH-HUNT PAGE FOUR

Tribune

EIGHTPENCE   VOL 38 NO 5   FEBRUARY 1, 1974

The siren song of 'consensus'

Deflation? — nonsense

by **RICHARD CLEMENTS**

...state and much more besides.
Already some of these measures are in operation. Behind the smokescreen of the miners and oil prices and the so-called "explosion" of...

next year or so, if the "consensus" economists get their way, is a "stop" far more savage than we have ever seen before.

The special case of failure...

SIGNS OF THE UNCHANGING TIMES

 **Labour Weekly**

THE NEWSPAPER OF THE LABOUR PARTY   No. 121 March 22, 1974   5p

 TRIUMPH OR DISASTER?

How the 500 men of Meriden are fighting to keep their jobs — CENTRE PAGES

EXPRESSWAY TO DISASTER

THE PAPERS THAT DIED

Scottish Daily Express	Glasgow	1974	closure
Scottish Sunday Express	Glasgow	1974	closure
Evening Citizen	Glasgow	1974	merger
Guardian Journal	Nottingham	1973	closure
Daily Sketch	National	1971	merger
Evening Mail	Chatham	1969	closure
Scottish Daily Mail	Edinburgh	1968	closure
Sunday Citizen	National	1967	closure
Evening News	Carlisle	1967	merger
Evening News	Hereford	1966	merger
New Daily	National	1966	closure
Evening Dispatch	Edinburgh	1963	merger
Evening Dispatch	Birmingham	1963	closure
Evening Mail	Leicester	1963	merger
Evening Chronicle	Manchester	1963	closure
Yorks Evening News	Leeds	1963	

By MARTIN LINTON

THE IMMINENT CLOSURE of the *Scottish Daily Express* and the Glasgow *Evening Citizen* has put the thorny issue of Press monopoly into the lap of the new

Bread prices

them. As long, indeed, as the middle classes were under the heel of the 'superior orders' the Press remained faithful to its first mission:—the advocacy of Truth and Freedom. But new times arrived. The middle classes, aided by the Proletarians, conquered the power to share the supremacy of the State with those who were formerly their lords and masters. More crafty than the men of force, the men of fraud had recourse to corruption in lieu of persecution; and the Press, from being the pioneer of Progress and the champion of Right, became the lackey of oppression and the relentless enemy of Eternal Justice."

Such was the swansong of the Carlile tradition of worship for the press as a right whose mere exercise would by the "multiplication of mind" enable Reason to liberate mankind.

In support of the *Red Republican*'s change of name, G. J. Holyoake in an article on December 7, 1850, pleaded that the old name was "one which in this country would always keep those who bore it a small party and therefore it is good sense to change it". The new enemies of the Charter were "masters of profounder tactics than our old Tory opponents, and unless we grow, too, and learn to match them and check every new move, they will beat us".

Amid such expressions of woe, the naïve old hopes that "the genius of the press shall yet prevail and conquer where the boldest armies fail" were nearing their end. A new press era, with different ground rules, had begun, and it will be described in the next chapter.

But first we should take a brief look through the papers which served the working people for so long as their main source of news and encouragement to struggle. Their columns are filled with the flash and fire, the hope and song, the solidarity and spirit of defiance of the founding generation of today's labour and Socialist movement.

Verses published in the Chartist press were often intended not for private reading but for singing at the great public assemblies, in the branches of the National Charter Association, in public house meetings or in prison to pass around the message of revolt. Set to popular tunes like "Rule Britannia", "Auld Lang Syne", or "Ye Mariners of England", they covered a wide range of topics. One song, used in the campaign to bring home John Frost, said: "He lived for his country, for freedom he tried To raise up the wretched he wish'd" (*Northern Star*, May 2, 1840). Another song, by James Syme, satirised advice given to workers to sing at their toil and thereby make it almost a pastime. It ran

E

> Sing, brothers, sing I'd have
> But let your ditties be
> Such anthems as can only ring
> From spirits that are free
>
> Oppression's funeral dirge go sing,
> And peal the dying knell
> Of public plunder and each courtly thing
> Such songs would suit you well.
>
> (*Northern Star*, December 26, 1840)

Then there was a warning addressed, amid a wave of arrests, to "Ye white slaves of old England" against government spies:

> Be firm and unite, but be cautious in words,
> On your prudence depends the success of your cause.
>
> (*Northern Star*, November 5, 1842)

Other topical affairs dealt with ranged from the presentation of the National Petition in 1840 to the death of a little girl from starvation on a roadside near Llangefni ("Another soul hath winged its way / To God's bright seat on high. / Another heart is Mammon's prey, / And ye stand lamely by"), the deaths of the Chartists at Newport, and the European revolutions of 1848.

Many verses dealt with the middle-class myths about the benefits to be had from a repeal of the Corn Laws. One stanza in verses entitled "The Corn Laws and Emigration" ran:

> We might buy cheap, but landlords want great rents
> To spend on keeping grand establishments
> Their feasts, their fancies, jewels, balls and plays
> The poor man's nakedness and hunger pays.
>
> (*Northern Star*, January 1, 1842)

Verses written on March 30, 1841, apparently in celebration of a disastrous meeting held by the Anti-Corn Law League, ran in part:

> Who are that blustering, canting crew,
> Who keep the cheap loaf in our view
> And would from us more profits screw?
>   The League
>
> . . . .
>
> Who wish to gull the working man
> And burk the Charter, *if they can*

With their self-aggrandising plan?
The League

There are verses expressing horror of the new Moloch of factory industrialism, which "turns blood to gold":

> His bowels are of living fire
> And children are his food.

Two stanzas in this poem entitled "The Steam King", by Edward P. Meads, went:

> The sighs and groans of Labour's sons
> Are music in their ear,
> And the skeleton shades of lads and maids
> In the Steam King's hell appear.

> Those hells upon earth, since the Steam King's birth
> Have scattered around despair:
> For the human mind for heav'n designed,
> With the body, is murdered there.
>
> (*Northern Star*, February 11, 1843)

There are hymns to liberty, and sonnets to imprisoned Chartists, including several to O'Connor, whose words of greeting from his cell in York Castle to the "fustian jackets, blistered hands and unshorn shins", who were his "beloved friends" outside, have passed into the English language. In the earlier years, the strongest theme is perhaps that of the outraged rights of the freeborn Englishman and the denunciation of tyrants of every degree—kings, landlords, bishops, Whigs and European despots.

The Chartist papers were also the first firmly to stake a working-class claim to a companionship of purpose with the great creative spirits of art and literature, whose portraits were sometimes given as inserts with the *Northern Star* and other journals. Scotland's *Chartist Circular* acclaimed Shelley, over the publication of whose "blasphemous" works there was a long running fight between publishers and the law, as one who "believed that, sooner or later, a clash between the two classes was inevitable, and, without hesitation ranged himself on the people's side" (October 19, 1839). In a series in July of the following year on the "The Politics of Poets", it assailed "the gentlemen critics (who) complained that the union of poetry with politics is always hurtful to the politics and fatal to the poetry", and went on:

"But these great connoisseurs must be wrong if Homer, Dante, Shakespeare, Milton, Cowper and Burns were poets. Why should the sensitive bard take less interest than other men in those things which most nearly concern mankind? The contrary ought to be true, and is true. . . . All true and lasting poetry is rooted in the business of life. . . . It is not in vain that the great spirits of the world have raised their voices and cried 'Liberty!' . . . it is to take advantage of this great inherent power in our national poetry that we propose to bring before our readers the leading political principles developed in their writings."

Later pieces dealt with the work of Byron and Milton, Robert Burns, and Robert Tannahill, the muslin weaver and "sweet lyric songster" of Renfrewshire.

The *Chartist Circular* (February 20, 1841), writing on Burns, said: "Every Chartist mother should repeat his patriotic songs to her children, in the winter evenings, by the cottage hearth. His writing should be familiar to every young Chartist, and constitute part of his juvenile education." The *Northern Star* (August 24, 1844) said that Burns' "A man's a man for a' that" would always "electrify the sons of freedom wherever gathered", and in its December 21 issue it was hailing Charles Dickens, in a review of his *Christmas Carol*, as "the poet of the poor". Reporting the death of Wordsworth at his ripe and Tory old age of 80, Harney's *Democratic Review* (May 1850, p. 473) acknowledged that it did so with no very heavy sense of sorrow. Unlike Burns, Byron, and Shelley, "Wordsworth passes from amongst us unregretted by the great body of his countrymen, who have no tears for the salaried slave of Aristocracy and the pensioned parasite of Monarchy".

The *Labourer*, a monthly journal published by O'Connor in furtherance of his Land Scheme, ended one of its literary reviews with this homely advice:

"We say to the great minds of the day, come among the people, write for the people, and your flame will live for ever. The people's instinct will give life to your philosophy and the genius of the favoured few will hand down peace and plenty, knowledge and power as an heir-loom to posterity" (1847, p. 94).

In the *Northern Star* of September 19 we find a song—to the tune of "Auld Lang Syne"—written by John Arnott in honour of the Fraternal Democrats' celebration at London's White Conduit Tavern on April

21, 1846, of the anniversary of the French Republic. One stanza speaking of the cause of peace, goodwill and brotherhood, reads:

> To aid this cause we here behold
> British and French agree,
> Spaniard and German, Swiss and Pole
> With joy the day would see
> When mitres, thrones, misrule and wrong
> Will from this earth be hurled
> And peace, goodwill and brotherhood
> Extend throughout the world.

From their side, as we have seen, Continental revolutionaries of every brand followed the progress of Chartism with eager attention. The *Northern Star* (July 25, 1846) published a letter from the German Democratic Communists of Brussels congratulating O'Connor on his success in a Nottingham election.* Signed by Engels, Ph. Gigot, and Marx, the letter said that now that the Free Trade principles of the middle-class had triumphed (the Corn Laws had just been repealed) "the ground is now cleared by the retreat of the landed aristocracy from the contest; middle class and working class are the only classes betwixt whom there can be a possible struggle."

The letter went on:

"We hesitate not a moment in declaring that the *Star* is the only English newspaper . . . which is free from national and religious prejudice; which sympathises with the democrats and working men . . . all over the world; which in all these points speaks the mind of the English working class . . . We hereby declare that we shall do everything in our power to extend the circulation of the *Northern Star* on the continent, and to have extracts from it translated in as many continental papers as possible."

In the following year the *Northern Star* reported a speech made by Marx to the Fraternal Democrats while he was in London for the Second Congress of the Communist League, which commissioned him to write *The Communist Manifesto*. "Dr. Marx, the delegate from Brussels, then came forward, and was greeted with every demonstration of welcome, and delivered an energetic oration in the German language." In this he called on the Democrats of Britain to help to

---

* O'Connor was "elected" by acclamation by a Chartist throng at the hustings, but defeated at the subsequent poll. It was in the general election of the following year that he won the seat in the regular manner, to become Chartism's only MP.

establish "a congress of working men to establish liberty all over the world". He said that the Democrats of Belgium, whom he represented, felt that the Chartists of England were the real Democrats and that the moment they carried the six points of their Charter, the road to liberty would be opened to the whole world. "Effect this grand object, then, you working men of England and you will be hailed as the saviour of the whole human race", said the speaker (December 4, 1847).

Another aspect of Chartist internationalism was its close relations with the Irish national struggle. Writing in the *Operative* (November 4, 1838), Bronterre O'Brien implored the Chartists' Irish brethren to accept the hand of fellowship which, for the first time in the history of England, Scotland and Wales, was being offered them to recover their long-lost rights, by political bodies which "may be fairly said to represent nine-tenths of the British population".* He said that Ireland could not extricate itself from its state of oppression and bondage without the help of the British people and that "the converse of this proposition applies with almost equal force to the impoverished people of England and Scotland".

And in two sentences which still point to the heart of Britain's Irish problem and Ireland's British problem, he said:

"Well then, seeing that the productive classes of the two islands have the same wants and the same enemies; why should they not look forward to the same remedy, and make common cause against the common oppressor? How? . . . By a grand alliance between the oppressed or unrepresented classes of Ireland with the oppressed or unrepresented classes of Great Britain."

In Ireland's famine year, verses appeared in the *Northern Star* (April 25, 1846) entitled "Ireland in Chains", for singing to the tune of the *Marseillaise*. They began:

> Rise Britons rise with indignation.
> Hark! hark!! I hear the clanking chains
> That bind a generous nation,
> Where martial law and terror reign.

The Chartist missionary James Leach received a big welcome in Dublin in January 1848 and close ties with the republican Irish Con-

---

* The "hand of friendship" was the "Address by the Radical Reformers of England, Scotland and Wales", signed by 136 Chartist and workers' associations calling for Irish signatures to the first National Petition.

federates were formed. Chartist associations were established in many parts of Ireland and an Irish Democratic Confederation appeared among the Irish workers in England. The *United Irishman*, published by John Mitchel in Dublin, which carried weekly instructions on street fighting early in 1848, had a considerable sale in England. In the aftermath of the Kennington Common affair, Mitchel was arrested in May, after Habeas Corpus had been suspended, condemned to fourteen years' transportation and whisked away in a prison ship the same night with a haste even greater than had been taken earlier to remove from England the Tolpuddle Martyrs.

Ireland was not the only field in which liberation as both a patriotic and social aim won Chartist applause. In February, 1852, Gerald Massey wrote in the *Friend of the People* (February 7) of the poet-soldier of the Hungarian people's revolt against Austria, Franz Petofy, and promised to invite its readers at some time "to a Hungarian Banquet at which Petofy shall be Lord of the Feast". In the same paper W. J. Linton told with deep sympathy and remarkable penetration the story of the Tsar's bloody suppression of the Decembrist conspiracy of 1825, which he called "the baptism of the Russian revolutionary movement".

Such were some of the journals, and such in outline the vast movement of ideas of which they were the vehicle, in Chartism's great popular resistance movement to the onset of capitalist industrialism and its conquest of political power. They were years also in which the new power consolidated its grip, creating in Britain the economy that was to be the workshop of the world. In the 1848 clash the government took possession of London's electric telegraph office on the day before April 10. The Army, as Harney wrote years later, was "seated like a spider in the centre of its web, on the diverging lines of iron road". For our story these are symbols marking a turning point: the electric telegraph and the railways provided just two of the changed rules for press production already mentioned. These raised the power of the medium, extended its field, and faced the working-class and democratic papers with problems of a new kind amid transformed political and technical conditions.

7

A Tale of Three Papers

Welcome brutality—but Heaven preserve us from the "kind masters".
Brutal tyranny can enslave the body, but brutal kindness does worse, it
enslaves the mind. . . .

People's Paper, November 13, 1852

FOR HALF A CENTURY the papers at which we have looked
devoted themselves mainly to a people's struggle for political power
through manhood suffrage. With the eighteen-fifties the battle is lost
and the stage must be reset. Chartism, as an overt challenge and organised force, dwindles and dies within a decade. Its enormous gatherings
and militant papers live on in legend, providing a standard for later
achievement. A generation of almost uninterrupted economic expansion and amassment of wealth begins, in a Britain that will shortly
plant its flag, following a torrent of trade, over one-quarter of the
world. Free Trade, the gospel of this expansion, triumphs about 1860
as Chartism ends. In the twenty years or so after the mid-century the
trade union movement, in an advance where every inch is bitterly
contested, pieces itself together, with the Trades Union Congress
coming into being towards the end of this period.

Most of the working men's leaders, after the 1867 Reform Act has
widened the franchise, support the Liberal Party at elections and become that party's tail. But simultaneously Marx and Engels, as participants in Chartism and the movements that grew out of it, forge
weapons of liberation sharper than any known to working-class
Radicalism, and in the International Working Men's Association
(First International) founded in 1864 inaugurate the world movement
that today fights to end both national and social enslavement.

In these years the workers, whose stubborn daring broke the worst
fetters on the press, prove unable to found an independent newspaper
press on their victory. A flourishing, mainly Liberal, press of the
middle-class redefines press freedom itself to suit its outlook and in-

terests. The title itself of *democratic* press, which Radicals and Chartists used as a banner and their opponents often used as an epithet of abuse, acquires a different meaning, and from about the sixties the new masters and their newspapers feel that it is safe to appropriate the title to themselves.

The transformation is illustrated most clearly in the careers of three newspapers: the *People's Paper* of Ernest Jones; the *Beehive* newspaper, organ both of the trade union movement and of early Liberal-Labour politics; and *The Times* which announces the new press freedom doctrine.

Ernest Jones came out of Tothill Fields prison, Millbank, on July 9, 1850, after one of the cruellest imprisonments suffered by anyone in the Radical and Chartist struggles. He was put for nineteen months in a 13 ft. by 6 ft. solitary cell, where he was allowed neither pen, ink nor paper. Because he would never pick oakum he was repeatedly placed in a dark cell on a bread and water diet and during his second year was so broken in health that he was unable to stand upright. Earlier he had rejected offers of liberty on condition of abjuring his political life. When he came out, he joined forces with Harney's *Red Republican* group, and there was a project for them jointly to edit a new *Friend of the People*. Harney, who was keenly aware, as we have seen, that press power was slipping away from the movement, published in his paper (April 19, 1851) a prospectus for a "complete *news*paper" to contain, with news of Chartist organisation and progress, reports of parliamentary debates, public meetings and "Legal, Political, Mercantile and general intelligence".

The appeal was signed by 100 personalities from all over the country, but because of an estrangement between Jones and Harney the scheme was stillborn. On May 8, 1852, Jones launched his *People's Paper* in an effort to save the movement by giving it a firm organisation and developing the Socialist approach ("The Charter and Something More") which clearly marked the last important Chartist convention, in March 1851. Marx wrote many articles for the paper and shared the editorship with Jones for a few weeks in the summer of the following year.

Writing a little earlier in his magazine *Notes to the People* Jones had asked: "Why is a People's Paper Wanted?" His reply, in addition to giving the most forceful and eloquent statement of the case for an independent workers' paper yet heard, placed a new emphasis on the role of such a paper as organiser, agitator and teacher. He wrote:

"The very first, the most essential requisite of a movement is to have an organ to record its proceedings, to communicate through, with its several branches—to appeal through, to exhort through, to speak through, to defend through, and to teach through. It is the fundamental bond of union, the ensign of progress, and the means of organisation. It is that which gives party a local habitation and a name—it is that which enables it to hold up its head amid the whirl of parties, and to keep its various elements together. . . . A movement that has not the mighty organ of the press at its command is but half a movement—it is a disenfranchised cause, dependent on others, pensioned on others, pauper on others for the expression of its opinions."*

It was "utterly fatal to the cause" to leave Chartism without its newspaper, said Jones, making an appeal for £500 to launch "a *really* Chartist organ". His keen awareness of the struggle the paper faced emerged in a front-page article in the first issue, in which he asked the democratic movement to return to the democratic press some of the benefits that it had received from it.

"Let every reader remember the object for which this paper is started. Let him remember that it is established by public subscription of the sons of toil. Let him remember that we are precluded from the usual copiousness of advertisement and publicity. . . . Let him canvass among friends and acquaintances. Let him remember that this is indispensable, and to be of use must be immediate and then a surer success will attend this paper of the people than attends even the gold-supported papers of the wealthy classes."

The circulation probably never rose above 3,000, and Jones had to conduct a campaign for subscribers and a fighting fund—the need was a guaranteed £3 a week—to keep the journal going. Penny-a-week collections were organised in areas where Chartism was still strong and in some workshops. Activities of the branches of the movement were punctiliously reported. One of the supporters of the paper's fund, signing himself "A Working Man, Nottingham", wrote (July 30, 1853): "As a beginning I now send, and mean to send *sixpence* a week myself towards its support. In addition to this I am collecting in my shop and among all the readers of the paper in my locality that I know, their weekly PENNY."

* Vol. II, p. 753.

In 1854 Jones launched a £200 fund with the aim of increasing the paper's circulation by reducing the price. In May it was enlarged to 12 pages and had a pictorial supplement with engravings that included scenes from the Crimean War. It was at this point the largest working-class newspaper so far produced and a great journalistic and technical achievement. Readers responded well enough for the price to be reduced from 5d. to 3½d. in December, but the supplement had to be discontinued. The weekly loss continued, draining Jones's own pocket.

At the Chartist Convention in March 1858, Jones announced that he needed to raise £80 immediately, Within a fortnight £40 was contributed, but it was evidently not enough. In June the paper was taken over by J. Baxter Langley (of the Cobdenite *Morning Star*) with the proviso that Jones should have two columns for Chartist news. It struggled on under this arrangement until August when the paper carried a long letter saying that Langley had offered to let Jones have the paper back for £100, but Jones did not feel able to recommend to the localities that they should consider the offer. So on September 4, 1858, the *People's Paper* came to an end.

For six years it had almost alone tried to pull together a fragmented working-class movement and direct it towards the aim of political power. Before the end, Jones tried to join forces with middle-class Radicals to win a more limited parliamentary reform. And before the swelling tide of class collaboration overwhelmed him, as it did many other Chartists, he fought a tremendous battle, "keeping the old flag flying", as the Radical editor of the *Newcastle Weekly Chronicle*, W. E. Adams, recalled in his memoirs, "till he was almost starved into surrender". Chartism, which had emerged partly out of the struggle for a free press, made its last stand in Jones' magnificent newspaper. It maintained a Socialist and internationalist commentary on many of the big issues of the fifties: the great Preston weavers' strike of 1853, for which it also organised support; the demonstration of 200,000 people in Hyde Park which in 1855 killed a Bill to prohibit Sunday trading; the many solidarity meetings in support of Polish, Italian and other national and social liberation struggles abroad.

The paper also extended the old internationalism to the colonial sphere. Here is how it defended the people of India against frantic denunciations in the British press after the Indian rising of 1857:

"Was Poland right? Then so is Hindustan. Was Hungary justified? Then so is Hindustan. Was Italy deserving of support? Then so is Hindustan. For all that Poland, Hungary and Italy sought to gain, for that the Hindu strives. Nay! More. The Pole, the Hungarian, the Italian still own their soil. The Hindu does not. The former have rulers of their own, or kindred faith, above them. The Hindu has not. The former are still ruled by something like law, and by servants responsible to their masters. The Hindu is not. Naples and Florence, Lombardy and Poland, Hungary and Rome present no tyranny so hideous as that enacted by the miscreants of Leadenhall Street and Whitehall in Hindustan. . . . We bespeak the sympathy of the English people for their Hindu brethren. Their cause is yours—their success is, indirectly, yours as well. The fearful atrocities committed have nothing to do with the great cause at issue—that cause is just, it is holy, it is glorious" (September 5, 1857).

Commenting (February 17, 1855) on a London meeting of solidarity with European revolutionaries, Jones wrote:

"Is there a poor and oppressed man in England? Is there a robbed and ruined artisan in France? Well, then, they appertain to one race, one country, one creed, one past, one present, one future. The same with every nation, every colour, every section of the toiling world. Let them unite."

This rebel against the implacable "brutal kindness"—mixing concessions and forcible repression—that prevailed after the bourgeois victory of 1848–50 kept a flame alive. It spelt out the class character of Chartism, and its social implications. Here is how Ernest Jones put the matter in an open letter to Chartists after his release from prison (*Northern Star*, August 10, 1850):

"I believe that the less enlightened portions of the working classes feel little sympathy with political rights, unless they can be made to see the results in social benefits: I believe they do not yet fully understand the *connecting link between* POLITICAL POWER AND SOCIAL REFORM; I believe there is little use in holding before them the Cap of liberty, unless you hold THE BIG LOAF by the side of it."

It is true that Jones failed to understand how the trade unions fitted into this new requirement; like all the Chartist leaders he swung between denunciations of the narrow approach of trade unionists and their indifference to politics and attempts to win their support when hard times and strikes were setting their members in motion. Class hatred of the new rulers and sheer impatience for their overthrow led to Chartist impatience with the organised workers.

The *People's Paper* bitterly denounced all the newly fashionable talk about the "mutual confidence of employers and employed that certain portions of the working classes were indulging in amid the mass of factory tyranny which meets us on all sides" (November 13, 1852). Amid the defeat, every trend that saw a prospect of achieving social improvements without a head-on clash between masters and men revived strongly in many and varied forms, including the old hope for salvation through the Co-operative movement.

In combating this illusion, Marx worked closely with Ernest Jones in 1851 and 1852 on a series of articles in the *People's Paper*. In April 1856 he accepted an invitation to address an anniversary dinner of the *People's Paper*, attended by staff, compositors and a number of political refugees, at the Bell Hotel in the Strand. It was here that Marx paid his well-known tribute to the fighting generations of which the paper was the latest representative: "The English working men are the first-born sons of modern industry. . . . I know the heroic struggles the English working class has gone through since the middle of the last century; struggles not the less glorious because they are shrouded in obscurity by middle-class historians."*

"Organise! Organise! Organise!", Ernest Jones wrote in the *Northern Star* immediately after his release from prison. Working-class organisation took two main directions in the following quarter of a century. One was the First International. The other was the consolidation of the trade unions on the "New Model" lines pioneered by the engineers and other skilled workers. Neither development depended, to the extent that earlier movements had done, on a newspaper press. But the *Beehive* (1861–76) served the International for a period as its semi-official organ, as well as establishing itself as the most influential trade union journal of its day.

The paper began as a direct offspring of one of the most formative

---

* Marx broke with Jones in protest against his attempts before the last Chartist Convention to reach a compromise with middle-class Radicals on the suffrage question. Jones moved to Manchester in 1861 to become Lancashire's most influential leader in working-class and left Radical politics, and play an especially prominent part in rallying opinion behind the Northern States against the slave-holding South in the American Civil War. After his death in January 1869, Engels wrote to Marx that Jones's bourgeois phrases were "only hypocrisy after all and here in Manchester there is no-one who can take his place with the workers". Jones, he added, "was the only *educated* Englishman among the politicians who was, at bottom, entirely on our side".

of all the union disputes of the century. This was the long and bitter builders' strike and lockout in 1861 over the workers' demand for a reduction in hours, during which the employers again tried to force "the document" on the men, and solidarity action all over the country rose to its greatest height since the Preston strike of eight years earlier.

Started by George Potter "in the interest of the working classes" it appeared weekly until the end of 1876, when it was renamed the *Industrial Review*, to close down finally two years later. The *Beehive* was the organ of the London Trades Council (born from the builders' battle) until the autumn of 1865, and of the First International for most of that year. The paper served also as the voice of the Trades Union Congress (formed in 1868) in its campaign to defend trade union rights in 1871-5. And it was the organ, too, of the London Working Men's Association founded by Potter in 1866 to promote the parliamentary candidatures of working men with Liberal support.

During the builders' struggle, Potter, leader of a small carpenters' union and secretary of the Building Trade Conference, made a systematic attempt to obtain a fair hearing for the men's case in the principal London dailies and weeklies and was deeply impressed by his failure to do so. By July 1861 he had determined to launch a national trade union paper, controlled by working men. Some efforts to launch such a paper had been already made. The *Workingman*, a penny weekly begun in June 1861 by Joseph Collet, a political refugee from France had trade unionists on its committee of management; it tried to win acceptance as a general working-class organ, replacing its original sub-title of "Co-operative Newspaper" by that of "Political and Social Advocate of the Rights of Labour". But the *Workingman* lacked funds and a proposal to form a limited liability company to float it came to nothing. Other journals reflecting in various ways the same feeling that a hearing for the trade unions must be won through an independent press were the Manchester penny monthly *Weekly Wages* (August 1, 1861) started by a group of building workers, which also expired, with its third issue, for lack of finance, the *Flint Glass Makers' Magazine*, the *Bookbinders Trade Circular*, and the *Operative Bricklayers Trade Circular*. But none were newspapers and none could meet the demand for a national labour organ.

As a nationally known trade union militant, Potter was well placed to carry through the venture. He obtained some initial funds by subscription from some of the dozens of building trade societies, and a greater sum from an upholsterer of independent means, William Dell, who lent him £120 in September. A limited liability company was formed and Potter was made manager at a salary of 33s. a week—about the same money he would have earned if he had continued to work as a carpenter. No journalist himself, but aware of the importance of the new paper appearing as a professional product, Potter appointed as editor George Troup, who had edited papers in Scotland and after some twenty-five years' experience had the reputation of being a first-rate editor but a poor businessman. As assistant to Troup, ex-compositor Robert Hartwell who had been managing printer of the *Daily News* for fifteen years, joined the new paper. Hartwell had been publisher of the Lovett circle's short-lived *Charter* over twenty years earlier, had taken the chair at the Crown and Anchor meeting that launched the six points of the Charter, and was a General Council member of the International.

In its management and editorial methods, the Trades Newspaper Company, publisher of the *Beehive* picked up a tradition as old as John Gast and his Metropolitan Trades Committee, which had also set up a joint-stock company to run its *Trades Newspaper* in the mid-twenties and, like Potter, appointed a professional journalist as editor. The London Trades Council called for support for the *Beehive* in November, a month after it had been launched (reaching a circulation of 5,000), and for several years afterwards the council's minutes were often the printed reports cut from the *Beehive* and pasted into the minute book. The paper at this time combined "all the features of a popular weekly newspaper with the more specialised features of a trade union and working-class journal. In these issues of autumn 1862, sometimes as much as half the space was devoted to general news, particularly the more lurid details of police-court cases, rapes, murders, suicides, accidents and the like. The *Beehive* was in fact described in the subtitle which it carried at this time as 'A Weekly Newspaper of General Intelligence; and Trades, Friendly Society and Co-operative Journal ' ".† The directors listed in the 51st issue showed that many recruits from the trades had been added to the original board.

However, the paper ran early into money trouble because of the failure of union societies, and especially the richer ones, to take up

---

* Also Treasurer to the General Council of the International in 1865, and Joint Treasurer to the Reform League in 1866.

† Stephen Coltham, *Essays in Labour History*, pp. 194–5.

shares. The Amalgamated Society of Engineers, wealthiest of them all, took up no shares at all. Circulation had fallen to 2,700 within two years and by April 1862 debts of £827 had accumulated.

At this time the basic dispute in the trade union camp, that between Potter, supported by some of the more militant Northern unions, and the leaders of the large craft unions who became known as the Junta* was coming to a head over what the Junta saw as Potter's irresponsible support for all strikes under all circumstances. To offset his influence the craft union chieftains tried to use the *Workman's Advocate* (1865-7) which had begun in 1862 as the *British Miner* and was acquired by the Junta in September 1865.

Potter was in open breach with Applegarth in April 1864 when the leader of the Amalgamated Society worked for arbitration in a Birmingham builders strike and Potter in his journal opposed this course. A ding-dong row began in which Applegarth vowed to crush the *Beehive* and the *Beehive* (July 8, 1864), reminded the Junta leader that he was "the servant not the Master" of the Society and demanded to know who gave him authority to pay himself an extra 15s. a week.†

In the early part of 1864 a plan to turn the *Beehive* into the official journal of the International was wrecked by the rivalry between Potter and George Odger, the Radical politician, London Trades Council secretary and Junta leader, who wanted to use trade union organisation chiefly for parliamentary agitation. Between 1863 and 1869 the International, however, published its decisions and materials in the paper. The old internationalist tradition remained strong enough to make most of the trade union leaders anxious to appear at the head of the International as affiliated organisations. The Executive Council of the International had Applegarth, Odger, bricklayers' leader George Howell and W. R. Cremer, building worker, as members. The Junta members' other, more practical motive was to obtain the help of working-class bodies in other countries in keeping out foreign black-legs. Their enthusiasm waned after the Reform Act of 1867, which extended the franchise; they grew more and more involved in middle

---

* Leading members of the Junta (known at the time as "the Clique") included Robert Applegarth of the Amalgamated Society of Carpenters and Joiners, Edwin Coulson of the "London Order" of Bricklayers, William Allan of the Amalgamated Society of Engineers, and Daniel Guile of the Ironfounders.

† R. W. Postgate, *The Builders' History*, p. 286.

class Radical and later in official Liberal politics, with the aim of strengthening the position of the unions at law which came under fierce attack in the late sixties and early seventies. Two members of the General Council of the TUC (formed in 1868), Odger and Benjamin Lucraft, a former Chartist, resigned over the Paris Commune (1871), and trade union support for the International declined, partly in consequence of the almost universally hostile press barrage against the Commune, but probably to a greater degree for other reasons.*

Marx had already severed his connection with the *Beehive* when it was acquired in 1869 by the Liberal MP and hosiery millionaire Samuel Morley with support from his political friends. Engels wrote to Marx (July 30, 1869) that it was a disgrace that after nearly forty years of a political working-class movement in England "the only working-class paper which existed could be bought up by a bourgeois like S. Morley". In the reorganisation Potter lost his independence. The new owners installed over his head, as chief editor, the Unitarian Minister Henry Solly, founder of the Working Men's Club and Institute Union, and after 1869 the paper reflected the views of the Junta. Potter, too, eventually became submerged in Lib.-Lab. politics.

For some three years after the First International severed relations with the *Beehive*, unanimously and publicly, in May 1870, the General Council published its reports in the *Eastern Post*, a Radical weekly appearing in the East End of London. The journal became almost its official organ, though it maintained an "impartial" stance and also reported many of the disputes and controversies around the International in the early seventies.

Up to the takeover, the *Beehive* had done sterling service in many fields of working-class organisation. But neither it nor the Junta had come within a mile of the intention proclaimed by their predecessors in the Grand National Consolidated Trades Union of thirty years earlier to bring about "a DIFFERENT ORDER of things, in which the really useful and intelligent part of society only shall have the direction of its affairs".

It is worth looking a little more closely at the *Beehive* takeover in the light of twentieth-century labour press problems. On February 19, 1870, a notice appeared in the paper explaining the aims which it would serve. It carried an aura that was to become all too familiar in much later handovers of labour journals to capitalist management.

* See A. L. Morton, *Marxism Today*, March 1971.

The notice said that the paper, which cost twopence, would be terminated in its existing form and replaced by

"a PENNY BEEHIVE that shall combine, with new friends and resources, all its former supporters, and thus launch it afresh, with greatly increased strength, not only as the defender of Working Men's rights and interests, but also as a guide and stimulus to the performance of those public duties which their newly acquired political power [through the 1867 Reform Act] has imposed upon them."

The paper was to be improved in all its departments, the news would be "collected and condensed with care", some of the "ablest and best known friends of the Working men would write the leading articles", and the journal would be "in every sense of the word a first-class weekly newspaper, equal to any now published in general interest, and Superior to all in the attention it will give to questions in which the Working Classes of the country are Specially interested".

Aims were defined which included "relieving working men from the degradation and weakness of ignorance" and fair play for trade unions. The paper would, "when needed, defend them from the attacks of their enemies. But it will equally uphold the rights of non-Unionist workmen; and also of employers". Other points were the reporting of Co-operative proceedings, help for Friendly Societies, and the advocacy of "a judicious system of Emigration".

The notice concluded:

"It will be able to render essential service to Working-Men Candidates, and other Liberal Candidates for Parliament by articles in its columns and by fully reporting their speeches on working-class topics."

A pompous leader in the same issue spelt out its segregationist attitude to the workers as a "special interest" even more clearly:

"The industrial classes all over the country are alive to their needs, faults, and deficiencies, as they have never been before. If we can only serve *them* usefully we have no fear but that they will support *us* faithfully. If ever there was a faithful, generous nature, whatever their faults, it is the English workingman. To that we commit ourselves in unhesitating trust."

The article went on to give a pledge that it would "never be found promoting class animosities" and said that it would feel it had failed miserably if it did not assist in "reconciling Labour and Capital, in binding *all* classes together in bonds of brotherhood". It then promised to contend sternly "against the unrighteous spirit in which the more powerful class in the community is always tempted to push under the social and political claims of the people".

To this message the rest of the *Beehive*'s life was devoted. The police news, divorces, indecent assaults and other general news which it had carried were dropped as "unelevating" and their place taken by much dull sermonising. "Addresses, articles and lectures by the middle-class friends of the Junta, upon the present condition of the law, on foreign trade, on the proper policy of trade unions, and on all the points of the Liberal Party programme took the place of the old fighting editorials . . . public respectability was carried to the extreme. Employers were very rarely attacked but 'atrocities by trade unionists' were published and condemned."*

Its July 8, 1871, issue urged the government to take due note of "abominable outrages" in Sheffield—offences in that city which were widely quoted in the anti-union propaganda of the day. The paper, of the same size as one of today's tabloid papers, gave its readers 16 pages of this kind of instruction with their penny, largely lifted from other newspapers. It was somewhat reduced in size early in 1876 and often filled its front page with a handsome etching of a trade union leader or Liberal MP.

Before this sorry fate overtook it, the *Beehive* had provided the trade union movement to which its main service was done with a first-class, professionally edited and produced journal. In 1865–7 the paper was in the thick of the first major upsurge of working-class activity for political democracy since 1848, when it helped the National Reform League to force through the 1867 extension of the franchise. The two forces behind the *Beehive*—the International and the trade unions— were both deeply engaged in this battle, during which meetings and marches comparable in size and militancy with those of Chartist days took place. But after the victory the League faded away as its leaders placed themselves still more firmly in tow to the Liberal Party and devoted themselves to an effort to obtain more political weight for the "working-class interest" within the existing political structure.

About the same time as the middle-class gained this direct suzerainty over the principal working-class newspaper, it opened its counter-attack in the field of ideas, press and propaganda against Socialism. The Paris Commune of 1871 provided the occasion. By that event the

* Postgate, op. cit.

never entirely abandoned anti-Jacobin panic was transmuted without any break into anti-Communism. Its two threads were the sacred rights of property and depiction of internationalism as a conspiracy. Up to this time, both these conceptions had been firmly rejected by majority working-class opinion. "The longest-lived of the Chartist sentiments was their interest in foreign affairs. After they had despaired of success in England, they were still convinced that the revolution would shortly be victorious abroad."*

It is true that some workers were seduced into supporting Palmerston's war in the Crimea, which they supposed to be aimed at the ancient foe of all free men, the Tsarist autocracy. But the solid working-class support for the North in the American war showed the still stubborn fidelity to the democratic cause in the mid-sixties; workers widely identified aristocracy in its slave-owning shape in the American South with the still enormous oligarchic presence and power in the British Parliament.

After 1870 this old tradition came under mounting attack, starting with a pathological outburst against the Commune. In this, the press displayed for the first time in a massive way its ability to stage a total hate-chorus. Among all the press, only *Reynolds News* and the Radical *Examiner*, whose editor Fox-Bourne was in close touch with Marx at this time, backed the Commune. Writing in the *Beehive*, Professor E. S. Beesley denounced the "conspiracy of misrepresentation" in the press about the working men and women of Paris. Beesley, professor of history and political economy at University College, London, champion of the New Model trade union expansion, Positivist philosopher† and friend of Marx, contributed a series of articles to the paper brilliantly exposing the conspiracy. He knocked down in particular the atrocity stories in *The Times*, which maintained at first that the Commune was all got up by released jail-birds.

In a letter on June 12, 1871, Marx expressed admiration for one of the articles, and said that Beesley's continued co-operation with the *Beehive* was a "further sacrifice you are making to the good cause".

---

* G. D. H. Cole and Raymond Postgate, *The Common People, 1746–1946*, p. 387.

† Follower of the teachings of Auguste Comte who bitterly attacked the evils of the capitalist order but believed that an enlightened public opinion could "moralise" the capitalists and ensure that the new wealth was used in socially beneficial ways.

(The paper's main editorial line was as abusive of the Commune as the rest of the press and Beesley's articles were accompanied from the start by denunciatory letters in the correspondence columns.)

One of Beesley's articles contained this ringing statement of the position held by the International:

"The cause of labour is the same all the world over, and therefore the operations of a society like the International cannot fail to obtain an increasing support. Middle-class men may affect to denounce the solidarity of workmen as unpatriotic, but do they not themselves systematically treat workmen as an alien class? M. Jules Favre, for instance, is on quite confidential terms with the German authorities, and bombards Paris with an animosity and spite which they never showed; and our Press, which looked on coolly enough while he helped to conduct a mere national war, sides with him warmly in his attack upon the common enemy. Workmen would be foolish indeed if they did not knit close their bonds of union in the face of this concerted hostility."

As the French government forces stormed the outer defences of the world's first working-class government Beesley wrote that if there was one thing which respectable society desired more earnestly than a working-class defeat it was the dishonour of that class. "It desired that they should discredit themselves and their class before the world and be taught not only that they were slaves but that they deserved to be slaves—of which the labouring class of other countries might take note. This idiotic cackle has died away into blank and chapfallen dismay."*

Beesley told his readers that they were witnessing "the first act of the most momentous historical drama of modern times". He caused enormous wrath in those whom he called the friends of order and people in "shiny silk hats and delicately gloved hands" and barely managed to keep his university post. He also told the Junta leaders that they had brought down on themselves the anti-picketing Criminal Law Amendment Act—brought in by the Liberal government to balance concessions wrested from it in the Trade Union Act—by their indifference to the fate of working-class Paris.

After the collapse of the *People's Paper* and the eclipse of the *Beehive*, newspaper press power, so bitterly fought over ever since Cobbett's *Address to the Journeymen and Labourers*, passed at last to the middle-class, and its possession was not to be challenged for many years. By

* Royden Harrison, *Essays in Labour History*, p. 233.

1870 this press had grown mightily in circulation and influence, although its biggest expansion was still to come. The taxes on knowledge that remained after the 1836 cut in the stamp duty continued for long to keep daily newspapers expensive and their circulations low by modern standards. The initiative for the agitation for the total repeal of the taxes during the late forties and fifties came from the same London artisans' circle who had formed the Society for the Promoting of a Cheap and Honest Press of 1836; it was from the People's Charter Union of 1848 that the Association for the Repeal of the Taxes on Knowledge emerged three years later to lead the final efforts in this cause. The Union was formed mainly by London Chartist leaders who had kept clear of what Lovett called "the blundering demonstration" on Kennington Common. A meeting held hours after this affair set up the Union and elected a council. No fewer than eleven of its members, including Hetherington, Watson, Holyoake and Dobson Collet, the chronicler of this long fight's protracted final stages,* joined the repeal association.

The events of what Collet called this "entirely uphill fight" can be briefly told. Against the campaigners, although they had the support of Francis Place, of the Free Trade conquering hero Richard Cobden and of Charles Dickens, the odds proved heavy indeed. Publishers, newsagents and vendors fearing for their profit margins opposed repeal. However, it was the ingrained reluctance in ruling quarters to venture along a path that for so long had been considered perilous that repeatedly defeated the reformers.

In the Commons, when Radical backbenchers raised the matter, Liberals and Tories united against them. Disraeli thought that the tax was a necessary evil. It was Gladstone's opinion that it was not the stamp duty that made newspapers dear but the trade unionism of the printers which had raised their wages too high. The old governing class, Cobden said, always wanted to keep the tax "because they know that the stamp makes the daily Press the instrument and servant of the oligarchy."

During the Crimean War, however, so many unstamped jingo sheets of "war news" appeared that the law-abiding journals, as in 1835–6 themselves demanded repeal of the stamp laws. The stamp duty was abolished in 1855 and the tax on paper in 1861. The surety

* *History of the Taxes on Knowledge.*

for fines or libel was not removed until 1869, after a celebrated case in which Freethinker Charles Bradlaugh's *National Reformer* had run up penalties claimed by the Attorney General to total over £10 million. So ended one of the most stubbornly fought battles for democracy, with the jail sentences from the days of John Wilkes to those of Ernest Jones totalling many hundreds of years.

The repeal of the stamp duty brought an immediate increase in the competition offered to *The Times* and other established daily newspapers. The day before the repeal, the Tory *Daily Telegraph* was born, pronouncing in a leader that "the Press had shown itself to be the safeguard of the Throne, the improver of morality, and the guardian of the subject". It cost 2d.—half the usual price that had prevailed since 1836. Still with an apologetic gesture to the opinion that regarded all cheap newspapers with suspicion, the leader orated: "Let not, then, the new era of journalism which we this day inaugurate in the Metropolis of the world, be viewed in any other light than as an additional monitor of the people, and a loyal champion of the Sovereign and the Constitution."

When it became a penny newspaper on September 17, 1855, the *Telegraph* again pleaded, in a first-day editorial, that there was no reason "why a daily newspaper conducted with a high tone, should not be produced at a price which would place it within the means of every class of the community". The future stability of revered institutions, it said, must depend in future more on the enlightenment of the millions than on bayonets and legions. Within a few months, the paper had risen to a circulation of 27,000, about half that of *The Times*. Four years later is was claiming a sale larger than that of all the other daily newspapers combined. It reached 200,000 by the time of the Franco-Prussian war in 1870, and continued to say until 1896 that it had "the largest circulation in the world". That was the year in which Alfred Harmsworth's *Daily Mail* was born, to usher in the age of the newspaper barons and monster circulations.

Other newcomers after the 1855 repeal were the *Morning Star* and the *Evening Star* founded on March 17, 1856, to support the Radical politics of the Manchester school, opposed on numerous questions to the still deeply aristocratic politics of both the Tory and the Liberal top leaders. Richard Cobden and a number of friends put up part of the £80,000 required to start these papers, and Samuel Lucas, brother-in-law of John Bright, was appointed editor.

In the field of what can be called the commercial-Radical weekly newspapers—the only papers that most of the wage-earning population ever bought—the ending of the stamp duty led to reductions in price, a spate of new journals, and increases in circulation. *Reynolds Weekly Newspaper*, begun on May 5, 1850, cut its price from 2d. to 1d. a week before the paper duty was repealed in Gladstone's autumn budget of 1861. Its owner told readers in the first penny issue that he was "surrendering to the public all the immediate advantages that can possibly be derived from the abolition". (The abolition, incidentally further stacked the odds against the *Beehive*, which could not be produced for less than twopence. An editorial on November 1, 1862, named the "war of the weeklies" as one of the difficulties that kept down the circulation of Potter's weekly in its early years.)*

In the fifties, invention on the technical side brought cheap daily newspapers at last within reach. The type-revolving machines produced by Augustus Applegarth in Britain and the Hoe firm in America made possible newspaper runs at first of 8,000 to 10,000 copies an hour and then, later in the sixties, of 18,000 an hour. The development of stereotyping (casting of the surface to be printed as a curved plate to fit on the rotary printing machine) speeded the runs still further. By 1867 the *Daily Telegraph* was already casting up to ninety-six stereo plates a night to cope with the flood of editionised small advertisements. Reducing another limitation on size, the Fourdrinier papermaking machine, first erected in 1803, had gradually come into wide use. By the fifties British paper mills had over 400 of these machines in use, and they were followed in the seventies by machines to convert woodpulp into newsprint.

This was the material basis also for a great expansion of the Sunday newspapers. Their development as the stable working-class newspaper reading, which began early in the century, took off on a large scale in the middle of the Chartist years, and the Sunday papers mostly served the needs and tastes of an overwhelmingly Radical readership. Both the success, and the eventual failure of Chartism pointed them in the direction they took; the success showed the extent of the public demand for Radical politics; and the failure indicated to the more commercially-minded operators like G. W. M. Reynolds and Edward Lloyd that to maintain their circulations they would be well advised

---

* Coltham, op. cit., p. 183.

to stick more to the middle of the Radical road, avoid close political commitment, and exploit the lucrative pastures of police news, court cases, and the wicked lives of the wealthy.

Before Reynolds, Lloyd had launched his *Weekly News* (1842) and John Browne Bell his *News of the World* (1843) and quickly raised them to sales in the hundreds of thousands. The mere appearance of Sunday newspapers on this scale affronted the strong sabbatarian trend in the Victorian establishment, and as late as 1839 Sunday papers used to run a Saturday morning edition, "so labelled, on Friday nights, for pre-Sabbath sale to the unco guid".*

From about 1850 the reading field was further crowded by the many manuals and magazines published by John Cassell, including the *Workingman's Friend, Cassell's Popular Educator*, and *Cassell's Magazine*. These gained a steady and growing readership among the skilled workers who were the first to wrest some real improvement in wages and conditions of life from the mid-Victorian prosperity. Cassell induced many working men, whom he rewarded with small prizes, to contribute articles to his papers on subjects ranging from bee-keeping to poetry, from the virtues of temperance to the principles of Political Economy.

In the sixties and seventies, the material rewards for better qualifications increased—and the magazines which catered for workers bent on self-improvement thrived in consequence. The Christian Socialist and Temperance movements, which had been minority trends within Chartism, had prepared the way for this development, and a continuous impulse to the self-betterment approach arose as the gulf widened, between many of the skilled workers, with their relatively high wages and the profound poverty and squalor of the unorganised and irregularly employed.

So ended, captive to the middle class, one version of the "Knowledge is Power" liberation creed which had inspired the workers' first struggles as a class. The legal finis written to the taxes on knowledge proved the palest of answers to the real hopes of men who had always seen a free press and independent labour politics as two sides of a coin. Lovett and Hetherington, Harney, Jones and Potter had all regarded their journals as a form of representation, linked to the central aim of obtaining representation in Parliament. Labour's politics and labour's press fell together under middle-class management.

* Allen Hutt, *The Changing Newspaper*, p. 51.

The change was signalled by *The Times*, with a redefinition of freedom of the press that rapidly acquired classic status. It hauled down the "Birthright of a Briton" flag which had flown over so many audacious challenges since Wilkes, and replaced it with a banner proclaiming the press to be the "guardian of truth". What had been seen as an inalienable social *right*, sprung from the earliest democratic stirrings, was now decreed to be a sacred *institution*. What had been a voice out of the people, denouncing their wrongs and demanding justice in the knife-and-fork terms of Cobbett and the Chartists, was declared to be a voice almost from heaven.

It was two months before Ernest Jones started his *People's Paper* to give the workers a press that would not be "dependent on others, pensioned on others, pauper on others", that *The Times* delivered its pronouncement elevating the press out of the people's reach. The new doctrine was proclaimed in two articles written by Robert Lowe★ on the instructions of *Times* editor Thomas Delane. They were prompted by a dressing-down which Lord Derby had given to the paper after it had condemned both the *coup d'état* by Louis Napoleon in the previous December and the approval for the French usurper's action expressed by Lord Palmerston. The first article, on February 6, 1852, rejected ministerial demands that the press should "share the responsibilities of statesmen" and said:

"The responsibility we acknowledge . . . is estimated by a totally different standard of rectitude and duty. . . . The Press owes its first duty to the national interests which it represents, but nothing is indifferent to it which affects the cause of civilisation throughout the world. The Press of England, standing as it now does in the enjoyment of entire freedom, would grievously neglect its exalted privileges if it failed to recollect how much is due to the common interest of Europe."

The second article, on the following day, said that

"the ends which a really patriotic and enlightened journal should have in view are, we conceive, absolutely identical with the ends of an enlightened and patriotic Minister, but the means by which the journal and the Minister work out those ends, and the conditions under which they work are essentially and widely different. . . . The duty of the journalist is the same as that

---

★ Later Lord Sherbrooke, who distinguished himself even among the Whigs, during the agitation for the 1867 Reform Act, by the venom of his attack on the trade unions.

of the historian—to seek out truth above all things, and to present to his readers not such things as statecraft would wish them to know but the truth as near as he can attain it."

This founding document of the capitalist free press conception has two important aspects. On the one hand it broke with the oligarchy's idea of the newspaper press as a basically venal activity to be used at will by government or political faction; it declared the independence of newspapers from administrative control; it provided an ideology for the expansion of the press, under a multiplicity of ownerships and expressing all the many and diverse trends within the Liberal, Tory and non-Socialist Radical establishment, during the rest of the century: and it helped slowly to raise journalism from its menial Grub Street regions into a profession, with scope for higher standards of news reporting, exposition and comment. The hundreds of national and provincial weekly and daily newspapers presented a diversity, an apparently open door for news and views, which in the long Lib.-Lab. years caused the question of an independent working-class newspaper press—as distinct from small organs of opinion—to fade out of view.

On the other hand, *The Times* definition stated quite clearly that the ends of government were "absolutely identical" with those of the press—assuming that both were enlightened and patriotic. Of this question it made the press the arbiter.* It sowed the seeds of a free press conception that triumphed like Free Trade and at about the same time. In the same way as this main doctrine of Liberalism rested on the actual monopoly of world trade held by Britain in these years, the new teaching of *The Times* rested on the near-monopoly position that it held at this time in the press. By the early fifties, the paper had become a highly profitable enterprise based on sales of over 50,000 a day, compared with the tenth of that figure reached by its nearest Fleet Street rivals. Its commanding position rested on its pioneering work both in the gathering of news and in printing techniques; its status as "The Thunderer" stemmed from its occasional violent sallies on behalf of the new capitalist class against aristocratic privilege in the

---

* The august journal's belief in its own eternal mission in this field is exemplified amusingly in a brochure sent to advertisers in 1958. This declared that the "maintenance of the historic qualities of *The Times* is of first-class national interest. Britain cannot function without a strong, educated, efficient, informed, and morally healthy governing class. *The Times* was, is and will continue to be, the organ of that class. It will remain so even under a non-capitalist economy".

first half of the century.* It was consequently easy for Printing House Square to vaunt its "independence"—and good business, too, at a time when its competitors were still taking bribes (for instance the *Morning Post* and the *Morning Standard*, which received secret subsidies from Napoleon III's government in France). *The Times* itself, however, in the fifties and sixties, pursued under Delane—beneath the camouflage of what the paper's official *History* calls his passionate determination "to be independent of every influence except that of instructed public opinion"—a consistent line of appeasing Russian tsardom, a policy flatly opposed to the main attitude of British public opinion towards the gendarme of Europe. And Delane conducted this policy in close association with Baron Lionel, head of the Rothschild banking house, and a principal financier of the Tsar.

The papers that were independent in *The Times* institutional manner divorced themselves from overt political controls. They never did so, however, from the dependence on advertisers in which newspapers had always stood. Indeed, the very first elaborations of the new notion of freedom declared *dependence* on commercial advertisements to be a foundation of this freedom. Five years before Delane's Olympian manifesto, Walter Bagehot, founder of the *Economist* and re-moulder-in-chief of the theory of the constitution according to the new masters, wrote in his journal: "Whether a journal can be sold to its readers for one penny or sixpence with profit to its proprietors depends on the revenue it can obtain from advertising". This "sustains in wealth and independence that press which is the best guardian of public liberty", Bagehot added, and concluded that "either by the price of the newspaper or by the number of advertisements England must have a thoroughly independent press".

For half a century before this, democratic journals had paid a weekly forfeit for their opposition temerities—advertisers had simply placed their business elsewhere. What Bagehot and Delane did between them was to sanctify this built-in bias. The dependence on advertisers—in a period of many competing newspapers and a multiplicity of small and medium businesses—attached the press to the victors of 1848 as a class rather than to any one capitalist interest or state administration. It

---

* Hazlitt described the paper as "the mouthpiece, oracle and echo of the Stock Exchange" and added: "It takes up no falling cause; fights no uphill battle; advocates no great principle; holds out a helping hand to no oppressed or obscure individual."

permitted the emergence of "great editors" of the Delane breed and
of journalism as a respected and apparently free and self-sustaining
liberal profession following its own laws and devices. From this seed
of Free Trade, however, not noble champions but the dragon of
today's monopoly situation in the press eventually grew.

The free press which *The Times* proclaimed stifled the people's press
without whose defiance of the law and of the aristocratic party of
ignorance it could not have arisen. Once again the basic problem
which this survey has been following arises: freedom for whom?
These were years when, as a leading labour movement historian has
written, "Socialism and independent labour politics came to be regarded as exotic plants which could never flourish on British soil".*
In the press field, *The Times* view triumphed as part of this process.
After the *Beehive*, no journal appeared for a long time that either Jones
or Gast or Doherty would have accepted to be an independent working-class organ.

The climb out of this trough proved long and hard. It began about
the middle seventies, after the great depression of 1874 had knocked
the ground from under a trade union movement which had made
large, but precarious, advances in years when it could wrest economic
and legal concessions from an expanding economy. The story of the
trade unionist recovery, of the reappearance of a workers' political
movement aiming first at independent representation in Parliament
and going on to adopt Socialism as its aim, of the days when in Engels'
words "the grandsons of the Chartists again entered the line of battle",
forms the background for the next stage of the struggle, in which
workers' papers that were not "pauper on others" were once more to
appear.

* Max Beer, *History of British Socialism*, II, p. 196.

8

"The Cause" and its Press

Intelligence enough to conceive, courage enough to will, power enough to compel. If our ideas of a new Society are to be anything more than a dream, these three qualities must animate the due effective majority of the working people; and then, I say, the thing will be done.

WILLIAM MORRIS

THE FAMOUS PROPHECY by the Communist writer, artist and teacher points straight at the central problem, in his day and ours, of Britain's democratic and labour movement. We have seen the three qualities—knowledge, will and power—emerging as aims continually pursued with varying emphases by this movement and its papers. The genius of Morris fused into a single conception ideas which in various shapes had been expressed by leaders as diverse as Cobbett and Doherty, Paine and Lovett, Ernest Jones and Feargus O'Connor.

In the sixties and seventies of last century few people spoke about a labour movement in today's sense of a movement combining Socialist aims, independent trade unionism, and independent politics. The idea emerged only slowly, with many a setback. But it was present in what the Socialists from the eighties to World War I knew as "the Cause"; it was the impulse behind the long struggle for Labour representation in Parliament out of which the Labour Party arose; and it inspired many of the fighters for trade union rights. Each of these trends developed its distinctive organs of press and publicity, and they interacted strongly on each other. At the opening of this age no representative working-class newspaper of any kind existed; at the end, a movement gathering all the threads together possessed its first daily newspaper.

On January 7, 1865, the *Miner and Workman's Advocate* published an address of the National Council of Practical Miners saying:

> "We offer no antagonisms to capital. Capital and labour, are as far as interests are concerned, identical. Let the union of ALL be cemented, and a brighter day will dawn on the poor pitmen of this country."

The escape from this abyss of delusion took a long time and followed a complicated course; a new Socialist and labour press provided the principal means, the main forum, for a vast conflict of ideas, without which the recovery would not have been possible. The story interlocks with the decline of Britain's monopoly of world trade, and of the false image of "union of all" which was the basic success of the Victorian middle-class heyday and the source of its ugliness and hypocrisies. The image dissolved slowly, amid wave after wave of the bitterest strike battles, the near-starvation of multitudes in the richest country on earth, and the rise of imperialism leading to the carnage of 1914–18 and finally extinguishing the Liberal and Free Trade dream of peace and prosperity through the development of capitalist society.

In these decades the struggle for a democratic press entered a new dimension. They opened with *Justice* and *The Commonweal*, the little struggling periodicals of a revived Socialism basing itself in Britain as everywhere else on the teaching of Marx and Engels. They closed with the *Daily Herald*, born out of the strikes explosion of 1911–12, sustained by all the vital forces of trade unionism, recognised by all the adherents of the Cause as their own. No less new was the situation on the opposite side. In 1896 Harmsworth launched the *Daily Mail*, opening the era of newspapers conducted as an anti-labour and anti-union industry. By 1914 all the main features of the modern press scene existed, together with all the essential problems for democratic advance which they raise.

The Socialist journals were the first to appear in the labour press revival. By 1914 their influence, despite small circulations, had seeped into the wider movement's every corner. And their main business—explaining the need for basic social and economic change—brings them closer than any of their contemporaries pursuing more partial aims to the labour movement of a century later, confronted with the same need but magnified in urgency.

The event that opened the way for the ideas of *social* democracy of later Chartism to reappear was the Great Depression, beginning in 1874, which brought wide unemployment and struck hurricane blows at the proud craft unions. In 1879 the Engineers had 13.3 per cent of their members out of work, the London Compositors 14.3, the Iron-founders 22.3, the Boilermakers and Iron Shipbuilders 20.4. The Engineers regarded this year, in which they spent almost as much on strikes as in the previous twenty-six, as "the darkest in our life". It was the same with the rest of what was soon to be known as the "old Unionism"—the organisations of the skilled whose Liberal patrons now abandoned them to their fate. Between 1872 and 1885 no fewer than 320 societies were founded and disappeared: and the skilled workers' energies were increasingly dissipated in demarcation disputes stimulated by the scarcity of jobs.

It was not, however, from their organisations that the new start came, but from a broader basis—the Radical Clubs of largely working-class membership which had grown up in the seventies and come to serve as a kind of auxiliary arm of the Liberal Party. From them arose the first moves towards independence, as the workers tried to use the Liberal Party to advance their interests. From within this party, it seemed to many in the eighties, a saving arm was being extended to them by Joseph Chamberlain, first as mayor of Birmingham and later in the House of Commons. Operating from the same base that had given leaders to the Reform Bill agitation and to early Chartism, Chamberlain dangled social reforms before the workers, and linked workers and progressive middle-class democrats in many causes. Also at this popular end of Liberalism, Charles Bradlaugh provided a long-standing attraction that partly recreated the spirit of Carlile's earlier struggles for human rights. In addition to his fight against the blasphemy laws and other curbs on publication, he conducted a six-year battle to take his seat in the House of Commons without taking the oath, and his eventual success in 1886 was celebrated by working-class Radicalism as a great democratic victory.

Another of the old unifying causes—help for foreign nations fighting for their freedom—showed its strength when an uproar arose in the Radical Clubs over Tory Premier Disraeli's preparations to go to war against Russia, which was aiding Bulgaria's revolt against Turkey. It pushed the Liberal leader Gladstone into writing his pamphlet, *The Bulgarian Horrors*, denouncing the massacres by Turkey. And it was in this agitation that William Morris, who was to be the Cause's most influential teacher and prophet, first entered political life, when he joined the Eastern Association formed in 1876 to stop Disraeli's plan for war.

Neither the general unionism of the early thirties nor late Chartism had come within reach of effecting any basic social change. The Grand Consolidated of 1833–4 had owed something to earlier progress in organisation at the trade society level; it had owed more, however, to the political idea that the workers as a solid host could shoulder the new masters off their governing perches in the economy and in Parliament, paralyse them by the "sacred holiday" of a general strike, and proceed to remake society to suit the wealth-producers.

In the eighties the confidence again appeared that, in the words of Engels, "there is no power in the world which could for a day resist the British working class organised as a body". This evergreen fact of British life and society was reaffirmed in one of the eleven articles which Engels contributed in 1881 to the London Trades Council's *Labour Standard* (May 7, 1881–April 29, 1882). Writing amid the trials and tribulations of the old unionism, he warned that struggles on nothing but wages and hours were keeping the working-class in "a vicious circle out of which there is no issue". The fundamental evil was not the lowness of wages but the wages system itself. When this knowledge was extended among the workers "the position of the trade unions must change considerably. They will no longer enjoy the privilege of being the only organisation of the working-class. At the side of, or above, the Unions of the special trades there must spring up a general Union, a political organisation of the working-class as a whole."

The far-seeing conception terrified the Lib.-Lab. leaders of the Trades Council, as it terrifies their political descendants now. Engels broke his connection with the paper in protest against its "hotch-potch of every possible and impossible crochet" and its infatuation with Gladstone, grand chieftain of Liberalism. But in Radical club circles ideas were moving in the same direction. In June of the same year, H. M. Hyndman, a wealthy stockbroker who had read Marx's *Capital* in the French edition (an English translation was not published until sixteen years later) presented them with his book *England for All*, which summarised Marx's theories (without acknowledging their source and thus causing a breach between Marx and himself). Out of the discussions on the book arose the Democratic Federation. This campaigned at first on a Radical policy relating to foreign affairs, land nationalisation and Ireland, where the Liberal government formed in 1880 was intensifying repression. Three years later, at its annual conference, the Federation extended its programme of nationalisation of the land, railways and banks to cover all the means of production, distribution and exchange and restyled itself the Social Democratic Federation. In the same year another convert from the upper class,

F

H. H. Champion, started *Today*, a monthly magazine, and the weekly *Justice* as the Federation's weekly organ.

These launchings marked the start of an immense propaganda for Socialist ideas, without which the later advances toward the "political organisation of the working class as a whole" of which Engels had spoken could not have been made. Many of the trade unionist members of the SDF played an especially active and crucial part in the twenty years of struggles that prepared the way for such an organisation. Two of them, Tom Mann and John Burns, led the London dock strike of 1889—one of the labour movement's great turning points—and founded the mass dockers' organisation which became the Transport and General Workers Union. Another was Will Thorne, the London gasworker who was helped to improve his reading and writing by a fellow-member, Marx's daughter Eleanor, and who founded the union from which the National Union of General and Municipal Workers later grew.

No real workers' party, however, ever developed out of the SDF or out of the Socialist League formed at the end of 1884 when the majority of the SDF council broke with Hyndman over his intrigues and dictatorial procedures. In the 1885 general election the SDF accepted Tory money to put up candidates against the Liberals. In an extremity of reaction against this kind of opportunism—which had dogged progress toward independent working-class politics ever since the first Reform Bill installed the hated Whigs in power—the League came to hold that it had better keep out of the mock fighting among the established parties. A Socialist organisation had "no function but to educate the people and to organise such as it could get hold of to take their due place when the crisis shall come which will force action upon us", as the League's journal, the *Commonweal* declared. Neither the SDF nor the League, however, proved able as organisations to "fasten on to the real needs of the people", in a phrase used by Engels in his attempt to persuade the Socialist sects to broaden their outlook and programme.

The two Socialist journals each reflected this limitation in different ways and this made their existence always precarious. The *Commonweal*, started with £300 as the organ of the Socialist League, was kept going by gifts from Morris and "everybody I think good for a guinea" throughout its four years. The paper, of eight two-column 15 by 10 inch pages, appeared monthly with occasional supplements from February 1885 to May 1, 1886, and thereafter weekly. Its first number sold 5,000 copies but the sale soon fell to between 2,000 and 3,000 copies, most of which were sold at meetings. As the League declined in 1889, Morris was putting in £500 a year to cover debts and his "salary guarantee". The journal ended shortly after the League's "pure" attitude towards the industrial and political struggles of the day had laid it wide open to takeover by members of the Anarchist movement whose Europe-wide challenge to the revolutionary Socialism of Marx and Engels reached its height in the late eighties.

The *Commonweal* declared in its first issue that it had "one aim—the propagation of Socialism" and would try to "awaken the sluggish, to strengthen the waverers, to instruct the seekers after the truth". It said it would only deal with political matters when they "directly affect progress of the Cause" and would "organise discontent into Socialism". And it appealed to the workers who did not yet "know much of the cause that rests upon them" to help the journal to spread its principles.

This was written four years before the dock strike of 1889 triggered off an explosive spread of organisation among the unskilled workers. The old unionism was in advanced crisis when the paper began, and few Socialists foresaw the trade union regeneration that was to come so dramatically and so soon. John Burns, one of the leaders of the strike and a creator of the new unionism, had written two years before the strike that "constituted as it is, unionism carried within itself the source of its own dissolution" (*Justice*, September 1887). The unions were so crippled by their friendly society liabilities, he said, that they often submitted to the masters without protest, and had all "degenerated into mere middle and upper-class rate reducing institutions".

Articles by *Commonweal*'s main writer on trade union questions, its compositor Thomas Binning, reflect the mixed attitude of the League's propagandists for Socialism towards the body economic of the working class. In the paper's May Supplement in 1885, Binning said that "only by lifting up our poorer brethren can we hope permanently to better our own condition" and it was time to see "every worker as a comrade and to close up our ranks". However, he opposed "strikes for a few pence" and thought that there must either be a general strike or nothing.

"Fellow-unionists, our proper place is shoulder to shoulder with those who are educating, agitating and organising, not to obtain some trifling concession from the monopolists, but to utterly destroy the capitalistic vampire, the sole cause of the poverty, degradation and misery of the workers."

Although narrow approaches such as this prevented the League and its paper from "fastening on" to the needs of either the organised workers or the Radical-minded multitude, they exercised an influence, in particular after the dock strike, out of all proportion to their size and circulation. It would be wrong, too, to see either *Commonweal* or *Justice* as mere doctrinaire organs. Both were involved, despite their overall prepare-for-the-revolution approach, in key struggles. Practical aid for the unemployed, whose marches *Justice* helped to organise, and a prolonged battle for freedom of speech and meeting were among them. In the mid-eighties one of the aims of the authorities was to deny the streets to Socialists and prevent their open communication with the workers. Both papers fought hard in 1885 and 1886 to maintain open-air pitches and start new ones. There were big joint struggles —despite their doctrinal warfare—on this question, culminating in clashes at Dod Street in Limehouse, and later in Trafalgar Square (Bloody Sunday, when the unemployed worker Alfred Linnell died from injuries at the hands of the police). These battles established rights that were to prove of the utmost value over the following century. On all the many demonstrations of unemployed in 1886 and 1887 the Socialists were present, selling their papers. They also took a considerable part in the election campaign that won a Liberal–Radical–Socialist majority on the new London County Council in 1888. A thousand copies of *Commonweal* were sold at a Hyde Park demonstration in April 1887 against Tory coercive measures in Ireland, at which Morris was one of the speakers.

Justice faced financial troubles as severe as those of the *Commonweal*. Its problems were eased, however, after 1891 when it became associated with the profitable Twentieth Century Press which poured out pamphlets in a stream. Harry Quelch, the firm's managing director, also edited *Justice*. Volunteer SDF compositors handled the printing of the paper. Hyndman wrote later:

"We distributed bills, took collections, bawled ourselves hoarse at street-corners and sold *Justice* down Fleet Street and the Strand. This last was really a most extraordinary scene. Morris in his soft hat and blue suit, Champion, Frost and Joynes in the morning garments of the well-to-do, several working men comrades, and I myself wearing the new frock-coat in which Shaw said I was born, with a tall hat and good gloves, all earnestly engaged in selling a penny Socialist paper in London's busiest thoroughfare. Outside of the Salvation Army nothing of that sort had been done up to that time. There could be no doubt as to the earnestness of the men who thus made themselves ridiculous to all those who had never felt disposed to run any risk of that kind for any reason whatever."

It is also evident, however, that Hyndman with his built-in bent for manœuvres in the higher social reaches and what today would be called his conspiratorial view of politics, had little understanding for the SDF journal. He lamented in 1911 that the trouble had always been circulation because the paper was "a purely propaganda sheet—dealing with questions that the mass of mankind did not wish to have thrust upon them". He said that although the paper had done invaluable service "we should have done far better to have expended our money and enthusiasm in other directions. It was one of those fatal mistakes that cannot be remedied and which engender a sort of mania of obstinacy. . . ."

Today it is not the persevering with *Justice* that appears as a fatal mistake so much as Hyndman's failure of vision, caused by his notion that the "inevitable" breakdown of capitalism—once he fixed it for 1889, the centenary of the French Revolution—would come of itself, and that a Socialist party's business was to make Socialists rather than to lead workers. One effect of this approach was that it left more room for the third group styling itself Socialist—the Fabian Society founded in 1884, almost entirely from middle-class intellectuals in London—to establish itself in labour politics.

Not only the Fabians stepped into the gap left by the sectarianism of the Socialists and their too narrowly educative journals. Even before the storm burst in 1889, some of the first steps toward a link-up with the trade unions had taken place. In 1888 Champion, who had left the SDF over Hyndman's cash-from-Tories escapade, launched together with Tom Mann and John Burns the *Labour Elector*. It campaigned in particular for the eight-hour day, denounced "black" employers, exposed the futile performances in Parliament of the handful of Lib.- Lab. MPs, and prepared the way for the practical efforts beginning in the late eighties to strengthen and extend trade unionism and to form a working-class political party.

A year earlier, in January 1887, James Keir Hardie, a young miner who had built the Ayrshire Miners' Union and the Scottish Miners Federation and sought to break the long-standing support for Liberalism of the community in which he lived, had started a monthly paper, *The Miner*, after a meeting with the London Socialist leaders including Engels. Standing as a Labour candidate in the Mid-Lanark by-election in April 1888 he polled only a few hundred votes; but he had shown that an election could be fought without the help of the Liberal machine and the demonstration prompted the formation soon afterwards of the Scottish Labour Party. His journal prepared the way for this development.

"A Democratic Labour Party", Hardie wrote (August 1887), "is now one of the certainties of the near future. There are one million strong able-bodied men out of work today, for whom the passing of an Eight-Hour Bill would find employment. There are ten million working men, with their wives and children, whose lives are a weary round of toil and misery. These two classes cry aloud for help. Where is it to come from? Not from the Tories, not from the Whigs, nor from any other party now in existence, but from the Democratic Labour Party of the future, composed of men in earnest, men who have suffered, and who having a heart to feel and a brain to plan, will go to Parliament, not to ape the manners of the classes but to bring relief to the suffering masses."

It was this approach, described by Max Beer as "a religion of humanity rather than a question of the political capture of power"* that was to characterise the mainstream labour movement press from this time onward; the basically doctrinaire attitude of both *Justice* and the *Commonweal*—which scarcely referred to the Mid-Lanark election—handicapped British social democracy in its opposition to such trends. "Marxists", of whom Engels wrote to Marx in 1891 that they had "turned our movement into a fixed dogma to be learnt by heart", proved unable to develop and use the press as a weapon to combat the opportunism—both on the left and on the right of the labour movement—that was to flourish in Britain like the green bay tree. Morris often spoke of the need for a Socialist newspaper that would serve all the sections of the movement, but saw it as something to be achieved in the future, after the understanding of Socialism had been sufficiently propagated.

The Socialist failure remained failure despite the fact that working men members of the SDF like Mann and Burns played outstanding personal parts in the great battles. These began in the year 1888, which

* *History of British Socialism*, p. 324.

saw the start of that surge upwards from the lower depths of working life in Victorian Britain on the crest of which both the trade union movement in roughly its modern shape and independent labour politics were launched. Its opening episode was the strike by the 700 bitterly exploited Bryant and May match girls. This celebrated happening was unplanned: the girls simply walked out of the factory after reading an exposure of their conditions of work by the Socialist Annie Besant in her magazine *The Link*. After their success, events moved fast. Early in the next year, Will Thorne formed a union which rapidly won the eight-hour day for the Gas Light and Coke Company's stokers, whose shifts were of twelve and eighteen hours. The victory of the London dockers followed. And in the following three or four years millions of workers from the submerged 40 per cent of the population for whom membership of a union had been a scarcely possible dream joined the ranks of the organised.

Of the dockers' strike, the *Northern Star*'s old editor George Julian Harney (home in his old age from a long exile in America) declared: "All strikes, turnouts and lock-outs of the past must pale their ineffectual fires in the presence of the great revolt in the East End of London. Not since the high and palmy days of Chartism have I witnessed any movement corresponding in importance and interest." His article on the revolt, published in the *Newcastle Weekly Chronicle* on September 26, was reprinted in the *Labour Elector* two days later.

And Harney's early friend and admirer Engels, celebrating the same success and the new unions that grew out of it wrote:

"The new unions were founded at a time when the faith in the eternity of the wages system was severely shaken; their founders and promoters were Socialists, either consciously or by feeling; the masses, whose adhesion gave them strength, were rough, neglected, looked down upon by the working-class aristocracy; but they had this immense advantage, that their minds were virgin soil, entirely free from the inherited respectable bourgeois prejudices which hampered the brains of the better situated 'old' unionists. And thus we see these unions taking the lead of the working class generally, and more and more taking in tow the rich and proud 'old' unions. . . . The people look on their immediate demands only as provisional although they themselves do not yet know towards what goal they are working. But this vague idea has sunk in sufficiently deeply to make them elect as leaders only known Socialists."*

* Engels to Sorge, December 7, 1889, quoted by Allen Hutt, *This Final Crisis*.

At the TUC the "Old Gang", led by stonemason Henry Broad-hurst, was swept out in 1890 and the Legal Eight-Hour Day demand was adopted. Four years later the TUC declared for the nationalisation of industry, on the proposal of Keir Hardie.

But the old "aristocratic" habits of mind and middle-class allegi-ances died hard. Their influence was strongest in London, and the centre of activity now shifted somewhat from the capital to the north, as in the Chartist early forties. It is in events here that the origins of the *Clarion*, the most important of the papers pioneering an inde-pendent labour movement, are to be found. Out of one of the big strike battles of these years—at Manningham Mills in Bradford—there emerged the Bradford Labour Union headed by the leader of the strike, W. H. Drew. Its influence spread primarily through the medium of the *Yorkshire Factory Times*, founded in the year of the dock strike and edited by a Lancashire cotton piecer, Joseph Burgess. Ben Turner of the General Union of Textile Workers, who worked for the journal, wrote later that it was the establishment of this paper that "made our union prosper". Its success encouraged its owner to start a weekly aiming at a wider public, the *Workman's Times*, to which Burgess moved. Late in 1891 both papers were running Socialist articles by Robert Blatchford, a Manchester professional journalist who had parted company with his Hulton Press employers on the *Sunday Chronicle* because of his advanced views.

In this year a whole crop of weeklies appeared in response to the mood for change and the trade union advances, most of them surviving only a few months. They included the *Workers' Cry*, edited by Frank Smith, to promote a "Labour Army" organised on Salvation Army lines, the *Labour Leader*, with which the former Socialist Leaguer Fred Henderson was associated, the *North London Press* (later *People's Press*), edited by the Scottish Fabian, Shaw Maxwell, and the *Trade Unionist* edited by Tom Mann and aiming at the co-ordination of trade union activities and the reform of the London Trades Council. But the rapid failure of these London-based journals reflected the lukewarm support among the Londoners for the idea of an independent Labour party.

The northern papers fared better. On April 30, 1892, Burgess invited those of his readers who wished to join an independent Labour party to send him their names and addresses. Two thousand names were collected by his newspaper in the next four and a half months and by June several local independent Labour parties had been formed.

Burgess, who moved to London as O'Connor had done before him, to edit his paper from there, presided over the formation of the "National Independent Labour Party (London District)" on June 13, with the idea that it would join up with a national organisation when one could be formed. However, the refusal of the SDF conference in August to co-operate with the moves to form such a party—it voted for "benevolent neutrality"—frustrated this attempt. In the following year, under Hardie's presidency, the Independent Labour Party was founded in Bradford, with an overwhelming majority of the 120 delegates coming from the north and Scotland. Its programme: the eight-hour day, various economic and social reforms, and the "collective ownership of the means of production, distribution and exchange". The new party was loosely organised and the supporting papers and the public meetings held by Hardie and other speakers touring the branches formed its main links. The *Labour Leader*, which succeeded the *Miner*, became the ILP's paper. Until 1904, when it was transferred to the Labour Representation Committee, Hardie edited and largely wrote the journal as well as tiding it over financial troubles out of his own pocket. (Once he mortgaged his life insurance to keep it going.) The paper was almost entirely written in trains and hotel rooms and in odd intervals during his speaking tours, and ILP branches covered their expenses partly from its sale.

One of the best known of the dozens of local leaders who fought in these years to combine militant trade unionism and Socialist agitation was the devoted Tom Maguire who edited the *Labour Champion* in Leeds during the winter of 1893. He died of pneumonia, without food or fuel in the house, at the age of twenty-nine after several years of self-sacrifice on behalf of the unemployed. The people lined the streets for two miles when his funeral procession, a thousand strong, went by.

The Bradford conference had rejected a proposal to call the new party the Socialist Labour Party and the two streams that had gone to create it—Socialist aspirations and the labour representation movement—were not to combine formally for many years. But amid the rising militancy of the early nineties, after the big victories, the vague but potent and widespread idea that the day of justice was coming at last came to be strongly held. The *Clarion* was the journal that ministered to this mood, with its confused Socialism and latter-day Utopian hopefulness.

The paper first appeared on the streets of Manchester on December 2, 1891, announcing that it would follow "a policy of humanity; a policy not of party, sect or creed; but of justice, of reason and mercy". The circumstances of its launching—and indeed of most of its long life—were as haphazard as this definition. Blatchford's partner Alexander W. Thompson thought they should print 30,000 copies. Blatchford blindly doubled it. Thompson's son later related the upshot of this wild swipe of a press launching: "Although there was printing trouble and parts of the first number were almost illegible, although their Manchester posters were stripped from the hoardings by a storm, they sold nearly 40,000 copies. It did not quite eclipse the *Sunday Chronicle*; but it served."*

The circulation settled down at about 30,000, with a loss of £53 on the first quarter. Later, the paper began to pay its way and the three partners received £4 a week each, for which they had to write some 10,000 words apiece. The *Clarion* advertised itself as "an illustrated weekly Journal of Literature, Politics, Fiction, Philosophy, Theatrical Pastimes, Criticism and everything else". It never set out to be a Socialist or Labour organ, and sometimes distressed the dour Hardie by its "spirit of irresponsible levity".

It was the publication of Blatchford's *Merrie England*, first in the *Clarion* and then in 1893 as a penny book which sold three-quarters of a million copies, that made the paper something of a national institution. With an optimistic spirit that was in inverse proportion to its knowledge of how to proceed, the paper promoted an unprecedented expectation of what Socialism could bring. Blatchford wrote:

"I would make all land, mines, factories, works, shops and railways the property of the people. . . . I would institute public dining halls, public baths, public wash houses on the best plans and so set free the hands of those slaves—our English women. I would have all children fed and clothed and educated at the cost of the State. I would have them all taught to play and sing. I would have them all trained to athletics and to arms. I would have public halls of science. I would have the people become their own artists, actors, musicians, soldiers and police. Then, by degrees I would make all these things free."

* Lawrence Thompson, *Portrait of an Englishman*, p. 82.

As to means, the *Clarion* held:

"Let us once get the people to understand and desire Socialism and I am sure we may very safely leave it to them to secure it. . . . Socialism will not come by means of a sudden *coup*. It will grow naturally out of our surroundings and will develop naturally and by degrees."

The paper became a movement in itself. Around its missionary vans, cycling clubs, Cinderella clubs to entertain children from the slums, Clarion choirs, handicraft guilds, and holiday camps, a nation-wide society of hopeful people came together in the name of human fellowship.

The paper's yellow adhesive labels, visible at fifty yards distance, were plastered all over the land; among some favourite spots for them were the sides of grazing cows, the backs of tramps and publicans and huntsmen riding to a meet, railway carriage doors, hotel lookingglasses and graveyard tombstones. All men of good will were welcome to the movement. By the end of 1894 the *Clarion* was trying to unite the ILP and the SDF and Blatchford advised readers who desired their union to join both bodies as he had done and work within both for unity. Most of the *Clarion* organisations "canvassed for candidates of both bodies, sold the literature of both, and acted as if they were in fact united",* Lawrence Thompson recalled.

Blatchford boasted that he could "convert England to Socialism in seven years". But as the nineties drew to an end he concluded that "the British working classes are not fit for Socialism yet" and he himself was already on the path that led him to support the Boer War and then emerge as a leading anti-German jingo of the pre-1914 years.†

The Clarion movement was always bigger and better than its admired but vain and immature leader. In the enthusiasm aroused by the formation at last in 1900 of the Labour Representation Committee, which formally became the Labour Party in 1905, the *Clarion* recovered for a time from the disgrace into which it had fallen over its support for the war against the Boers. Blatchford bought a printing works, increased the paper's size, took on new contributors including the Fabian George Bernard Shaw, and conducted the paper with much

---

* Lawrence Thompson, op. cit., p. 137.

† A month after the outbreak of war in 1914 Lord Northcliffe gave Blatchford a full page in the *Weekly Despatch* at a salary of £40 a week. The articles he wrote were said to have put 50,000 on the paper's circulation.

freedom for all the current views. After the 1906 general election had returned twenty-nine Labour MPs the paper's sales rose from about 50,000 to 74,000 and—rarity for any labour journal—there was for a time even a rush to advertise in its columns.

It carried about it the aura of *Merrie England* and fellowship for long afterwards and survived even its creator's complete desertion to jingoism during the 1914–18 war. It lingered on until 1935, when Odhams Press took it over, to kill it shortly afterwards as a non-paying activity.

As the *Clarion* readers lived their dream, a full-scale counter-attack by the employers was raging. The London gas workers had lost their eight-hour day before 1889 was out. In the wake of a slump in 1892–3, lockouts smashed many unions, including the dockers. In 1897 the great engineering lockout and the five-month Welsh miners' strike ended in serious defeats. Four years later came Taff Vale—the legal decision making unions liable to damages due to strikes. And in 1909, a Tory working man, W. V. Osborne of the Amalgamated Society of Railway Servants, won a House of Lords judgment allowing him to prevent his union from levying its members or using its funds to support the Labour Party or maintain Members of Parliament.

Labour clung to its alliance with the Liberals in hopes of obtaining their help against this offensive, and helped them to their landslide election victory of 1906, which ended twenty years of Tory government. But not until 1913, in the Trade Union Act, did the unions partly recover rights which had been theirs from 1876 to the Osborne decision; the Act allowed them to set up political funds by special resolution but specified that objectors could contract out. Some other benefits were granted by Labour's Liberal overlords, including the eight-hour day and a State contributory insurance scheme. But the ground lost after the early nineties was fully retaken only by the 1910–13 strike wave which involved seamen, dockers, transport workers and many others in what one contemporary observer called "a general spirit of revolt". "The arrangements of society . . . seemed to have lost well-nigh all stability. Ferment and unrest spread throughout all ranks. . . . Educated and refined women had recourse to terroristic and conspiratory deeds. And masses of workmen, organised and unorganised, used the weapon of strike on an unprecedented scale.

Capital and labour moved in phalanxes against each other. The whole nation was in movement, as if driven by elemental forces".*

This was the clash out of which arose the *Daily Herald*, the first working-class daily newspaper, whose career pointed a new way forward. If no daily newspaper had appeared in Britain earlier on the labour side this was not because such a paper would have been financially or technically impossible in the previous quarter of a century. On the Continent, working-class daily newspapers had been launched many years before the *Herald*. They included *Humanité* in France (1904), *Vorwärts* in Germany (1891), *Volksrecht* in Switzerland in the nineties, and the *Arbeiter Zeitung* in Austria (1889). The British slowness in this respect arose principally from the paralysing tutelage in which the official movement stood to the Liberal Party. There were other reasons too: the disunity in the Labour ranks, as well as the ingrained bent of Socialists of every shade toward agitation and instruction and the pamphleteer trade. Powerfully at work, too, was the still great strength and prestige of the free press in its Liberal middle-class definition, affording a fairly high degree of public access to its columns. Indeed, little or no discussion in the labour and trade union movement even of the possibility of producing a daily newspaper appears to have taken place at all before January 25, 1911.

This was the red-letter day in the democratic press story when the London compositors, after they had been locked out in retaliation for their demand for a 48-hour week, produced the *Herald* as a strike sheet and sold 13,000 copies of the first issue. It even took a little time to realise what had happened. The compositors' aims did not go beyond winning support for their resistance to the lockout. Raymond Postgate, son-in-law of George Lansbury and later foreign editor of the *Daily Herald*, recalled that the compositor-journalists "stuck very closely to their trade interest; when a correspondent suggested that Trade Unions should take only papers like the *Daily Herald*, they were shocked, saying 'Our contemporaries serve the very useful purpose of keeping large numbers of printers in employment'."†

But the deed which had been out of reach from Hetherington to Blatchford had been done. A committee was left behind after the lockout, including T. E. Naylor of the London Society of Compositors and Ben Tillett of the Dockers, to work on the magic possibilities

* Max Beer, *History of British Socialism*, p. 345.
† Raymond Postgate, *The Life of George Lansbury*, p. 136.

revealed. Some cool support came initially from the parliamentary committee of the TUC. Official Labour and TUC support was withheld, however, because an attempt was being made concurrently, backed by Labour Party secretary Ramsay MacDonald to collect money for a rival newspaper to be called the *Daily Citizen*. And when the *Herald* rapidly showed its revolutionary character, the official leaders did everything they could to destroy it.

The paper's early life was a daily drama. Sales, which curiosity inflated in the first few days to about 230,000, soon fell sharply and the most acute troubles beset the paper. Ben Tillett's appeal for money on May 6 was headed: "AT ONCE!! AT ONCE!!!" On October 23 the paper said that it might come out again, and might not; it survived that crisis because a clergyman reader and his wife came in with their savings of £150. On another night the staff shared out equally what was in the cash box as wages. On a third, after the paper firm had refused supplies until its bills were paid, the machine-minders produced an edition with accumulated odds and ends of newsprint reels of varying size and colour. And once when the bailiffs were actually in the building, some of the directors "stood in the doorway orating about the workers' struggle and preventing them moving the furniture until help came".

Among them were Ben Tillett, the Transport Workers' secretary Robert Williams, and George Lansbury, who was to become the key figure in the paper's struggle to survive. Lansbury, whose career had begun with work in the SDF for the unemployed and the right to speak in Trafalgar Square, and who had later worked in the Labour Representation Committee and the votes-for-women movement, befriended and protected most of the rebel trends of the day. The strongest link between these was their rejection of Lib.-Lab. politics and of the preoccupation of the Labour Party leaders with manœuvres in Parliament.

The feeling that Labour politics had failed the workers and that its leading figures were "all the same" helped also to promote in these years the last major reappearance of the idea that the workers, by using their massed industrial strength could bypass Parliament and its shadow-boxing. The belief that the bosses and their State could be overcome chiefly by powerful unions commanding the field in entire industries inspired the world-wide Syndicalist movement, of which Tom Mann was the leading British exponent. In 1912, the *Herald* gave much prominence to this movement's activities and ideas, which helped in the pre-war decade to bring large and strong unions into being out of a multiplicity of small unions immersed in endless civil war.

The paper cannot be said, however, to have been the property of any single trend, and one must go back to the *Northern Star* to find a journal opening its arms so wide to all the dissident ideas of its day. In a leader for the second issue Lansbury promised that there would be no censorship of views. Invitations to write for the new daily went to personalities of the most widely differing views in the industrial, social and cultural fields.* Women's suffrage news and views got a whole page. The Irish national struggle was given sympathetic treatment. Parliament was reported under the heading "The House of Pretence". But every strike had the paper's unconditional support and industrial news appeared under the general heading "THE WAR THAT REALLY MATTERS".

The leaders of the TUC and the more firmly established unions mostly opposed the Syndicalist ideas; they saw their jobs threatened by the demands that the hundreds of sectional trade unions should be merged into a dozen or so industrial unions. In October 1912 the conference of the TUC resolved to support the *Daily Citizen*, which would express official policies, and the paper was entrusted to Clifford Allen, a Fabian protégé of Ramsay MacDonald. Two years later it was ailing badly and a special joint conference of the TUC and the Labour Party called to consider its plight unanimously recommended a voluntary levy of a shilling per member per year to put the paper on a safe footing. But very few unions collected the shilling and the paper folded a few weeks after the outbreak of the war in 1914, which it supported. (The *Clarion*'s sales slumped from a pre-war peak of 90,000 to 10,000 at the same time and for the same reason.)

The ownership of the *Daily Herald* was vested in the Limit Publishing Company,† with Lansbury as chairman. In December 1913 Lansbury replaced the Syndicalist editor, Charles Lapworth, after Lapworth had roused the ire of some of Lansbury's middle-class and business friends who were giving financial support to the paper, by

---

* Bernard Shaw sent Lansbury a postcard refusing to write and opining that "neither you nor anybody else can keep a daily labour paper going".

† The name was a bit of raillery reminiscent of Unstamped days. The Liberal leader Lloyd George had said in answer to a question on the *Herald*: "That paper is the limit."

declaring that Philip Snowden was a potential traitor to be watched
—a judgement vindicated over twenty years later when Snowden
joined the Tories in the National Government of 1931.

Syndicalism was toned down after Lapworth's removal, and early
in 1914 some wealthy personal admirers of Lansbury contributed
heavily to a subscription fund that reached £11,000. As a daily newspaper, however, the *Herald* was an almost immediate casualty of the
outbreak of war; it could not hold its sales in competition with newspapers selling war news and fomenting militarist feeling. But unlike
the *Daily Citizen*, which was sunk without trace, the *Herald* survived,
by becoming a weekly for the duration of the war.

Its three pre-war years, as a forum of labour movement debate and
an organiser in the struggles of dockers, railwaymen, builders and
miners, provided one of the main schools for the massive challenge,
on the widest scale since Chartism, that was to follow the war. To
objections made that it supported strikes indiscriminately, the paper
replied in May 1912:

> "We have considered the matter. We have considered every phase of it
> and we say: 'Prepare your organisation and then strike'. STRIKE AND STRIKE
> HARD."

The angry men involved in the 1911–14 battles, Postgate recalled,
"needed some means of communication and some way of co-ordinating
their actions; what their unions could not and would not give them
they found in the *Daily Herald*. Its columns are full of reports, resolutions and articles which are effectively the rebels' communications
with each other. The records of these years show many instances in
which union executives adjure their members not to come out on
strike, or to refrain from helping their fellows by refusing to handle
'black' goods, and in which the *Daily Herald* urges them to do the
opposite and they often follow the paper's advice and not that of their
leaders."*

While the paper encouraged all the rebellious trends—and many
wordy battles took place among the Syndicalists and Socialists,
Suffragists and Suffragettes, and various "rogue" recruits to the Cause
from the middle class, like G. K. Chesterton and Hilaire Belloc—this
never prevented it from taking up daily cudgels for the poor against
the rich, and not now in weekly commentary but in competitive daily

* Postgate, op. cit., p. 143.

news-story terms. The first big story it had to deal with was the sinking of the *Titanic*.

"Other papers recorded well enough the shock of the loss of the fastest, most richly equipped and safest ship in the world and the hundreds who went down with it. The *Herald* analysed the figures: 121 steerage women and children passengers were saved, 134 drowned; 246 first- and second-class women and children were saved and only twenty drowned; fifty-eight of the 173 first-class men were saved. 'They have paid', it said of the White Star Line, '30 per cent to their shareholders and they have sacrificed 51 per cent of the steerage children. They have gone to sea criminally under-equipped with the means of life saving, they have neglected boat drill, they have filled their boat with cooks and valets, with pleasure gardens and luxurious saloons; they have done all this to get big profits and please the first-class passengers. And when the catastrophe came they hastened to get their first-class passengers and their chairman safely away. Fifty-three children remained to die. They were steerage passengers! One hundred and thirty-four women and children slain. They were steerage passengers!"*

Remembered for many years was its coverage of the Dublin lockout of 1913. Over 100,000 men had been refused work because they would not sign a document abjuring the Irish Transport and General Workers' Union of James Connolly and James Larkin. The *Daily Herald* in column after column of exposure of the appalling conditions of the Dublin workers, and at meetings held by the Herald League of its supporters, arranged help in money, sent foodships and tried to persuade British workers to strike in solidarity. Hunger in Dublin and the aloof attitude of most of the British trade unions defeated this effort. Equally celebrated was the paper's defence of the London building workers when they were locked out early in 1914 after they, too, had refused to sign the document—which required them on pain of a £1 fine to agree to work with non-unionists.

The *Daily Herald* was swamped by the flag-wagging hysteria of 1914 amid which the labour movement's pledge to resist war collapsed in Britain as in most of the belligerent countries. In this hysteria and this collapse the most influential part was played by a press which the rise of imperialism since the nineties had profoundly changed, turning it into a mass medium of communication in the full modern sense. These changes must be examined here because they founded the baronial newspaper system which today obstructs and endangers

* Postgate, op. cit., p. 114.

democracy and forms a major barrier to social and political progress.

The forms of press organisation of Victorian Britain reflected the social apartheid of that age. For some four decades after Chartism, culture and education, the communication of ideas and the making of decisions, were reserved to a wide league of forces that extended from the still potent landed aristocracy through all the many shades of Liberalism, to the tamed officialdom of the trade unions. Below this self-confident upper sphere lay the multitudinous lower orders, kept in position by a powerful array of legal, social, religious and other ideological disciplines. A majority of the people bought weekly newspapers, usually of a Liberal-Radical tinge, if they took a newspaper at all, and the upper and middle ranks took in one of the national daily newspapers, whose circulations remained low in the hundred thousands, or more commonly took one of the provincial daily newspapers which appeared and thrived in all the main cities after the repeal of the newspaper stamp duty in 1855.

It was the decline of Britain's world monopoly and the revival of Socialism, starting roughly at the same time in the eighties, that began to change this pattern of segregation. The first break had come earlier, with the passing of the 1870 Education Act inaugurating systematic primary school education for all. The Act was itself an outcome of new competitive pressures on the British economy, both from foreign rivals and the increasing demands for literate labour for administration and business. The widening of the franchise, creating millions of working-class voters whose minds it became desirable for capitalism to directly influence, worked in the same direction.*

Press readerships with new interests and demands appeared. Significantly, it was in the field of the weekly journals and periodical magazines that what was to be called the "new journalism" had its first trials. The change coincided in time almost exactly with the "new unionism" that brought the unskilled millions into organised existence; in the year before the dock strike, Alfred Harmsworth started his weekly *Answers*, shortly after George Newnes had shown the extent of the potential market with his collection of easy-to-read snippets from every published source called *Titbits*, which rocketed to

---

* The 1884 Reform Act increased the electorate (excluding Ireland) from under three million to nearly five million. In 1911 out of a population of some 40 millions, 7,200,000 had the right to vote.

the then fabulous circulation of 900,000 within months of its first appearance, helped by competitions offering glittering prizes. Harmsworth exploited this commercial discovery and created a field of similar magazines and a quick fortune from nothing within three years. Nobody had ever started so many magazines before, or struck ore so rich. From this base in 1896 he launched the *Daily Mail*, which rose quickly to a sale of half a million and went over the million during the Boer war. With this paper, the first to be floated as a public company appealing to investors, the Klondyke Gold Rush of the newspaper industry began, in which new foundations, the *Daily Express*, *Daily Sketch*, and *Daily Mirror* and others soon joined.

Francis Williams, an editor of the *Daily Herald* in its later days, has written:

"The *Daily Mail* looked for profits even more from advertising than from sales. The slogan 'A Penny Newspaper for one half-penny' was not just a slogan, it was a statement of economic intent. A method of selling advertising space was employed that has since come to dominate the industry. This was the net sales certificates, the regular issue of a chartered accountant's certificate of circulation on which advertising rates were based at a charge of so much per column inch per thousand readers."

This account says that Harmsworth—speedily ennobled as Lord Northcliffe—gave people living hard and dreary lives "the biggest show on earth every morning: a non-stop vaudeville act studded with 'muck raking' campaigns, political exposures, sex, drama and stunts. In the process of doing so, he demonstrated just how great a power to lead (or more often mislead) mass opinion could be secured by the ownership of newspapers of vast circulation."

The new press did its utmost in the critical early years of the century to prevent the emergence of a party of the working class conducting an all-round struggle. The *Daily Mail* and the *Daily Express*, when the movement held its annual conferences, regularly trotted forth the red bogey to influence the trade unionist wing of the Labour Party—when affiliations were being made at a great rate—to reject Socialism. The sectarianism of the SDF and its failure to develop a participatory type of press in these years helped to prevent the large potential support for such a party from bearing fruit.

While the underlying aim of the new press was from the start to sway the millions entering the trade union and labour movement, the days of Tory newspapers with large working-class readerships did not arrive immediately. The *Daily Mail*, in particular, aroused the workers' bitter hostility. On the other flank, it caused not only the type of aristocratic contempt expressed in Lord Robert Cecil's remark that it was a paper "written by office boys for office boys"; it also outraged the whole Victorian free press tradition which regarded newspapers as responsible institutions. A. G. Gardiner, the sternly Liberal and anti-Socialist editor of the *Daily News* from 1902 to 1921, said of the new press lords that they ran their empires "with the same material outlook as that with which a brewer runs a brewery", coerced small independent-minded journals into syndicates with "multitudinous voices echoing one masterful will", and aimed to "reduce Downing Street to the position of an annexe of Fleet Street".

In a celebrated onslaught on Northcliffe, Gardner protested in 1914 against the spy mania that the *Mail* was working up as a circulation-spinner, including attacks on people whose sole offence was that they had German or German-sounding names. He reminded Northcliffe, in an open letter, that in his *Evening News* of October 17, 1913, he had called the Kaiser a "very gallant gentleman whose word is better than many another's bond". He told him he was "the most sinister influence that has ever corrupted the soul of English journalism. . . . It has always been your part to prophesy war and cultivate hate." He accused Northcliffe of spending his life "in an infamous servitude to the changing passions of the hour . . ."

"You have preached war and exploited international hatreds as a trade . . . attacked every country in turn . . . and attacked it for the basest reasons . . . you have made journalism a byword for sensationalism, and a thing of reproach to those who are engaged in it. Do you deny it? There is hardly a man in Fleet Street who does not know it and deplore it. There is not an audience in the country, of any party whatsoever, that does not receive your name or the name of the 'DM' with a shout of derisive laughter. The people read you; but they despise you."

The press that the people "read but despise"—in a widespread schizophrenic servitude that has been frequently commented on since Gardiner—had begun its irresistible march, however. It arose at about the same time in all the main imperialist countries, to serve their preparations for war and to foment "international hatred as a trade", using it to divide the growing world forces for Socialism and peace. Born in the same year as the *Daily Mail*, the *New York Journal* plied the same trade; its crazed proprietor William Randolph Hearst, as the United States turned toward military conquests, cabled his man in Cuba: "You furnish the pictures, and I'll furnish the war."

In all the countries that were soon to be at war on a total scale, the new total communication medium was ready to hand. In Britain it took a particularly intensive form, with daily newspapers commanding immense nationwide circulations: the country's small size and the denseness of the "web of iron roads" of which Harney had spoken in 1848 helped the national newspapers, with their huge advertisement revenues, to force the hitherto sturdy weekly and daily provincial press products into a secondary place. Technical developments in lino-type machinery for composing text and in rotary printing machines, and the production of newsprint strong enough to be printed on both sides in a continuous web or roll, had been steadily raising the cost of newspaper production since the eighties. The completion of a world electric telegraph network, increasing the extent and cost of competi-tive news-gathering services, presented a further growing advantage to the big circulation national papers.

Competition for the expanded mass market for newspapers led to changes, too, in their editorial style and appearance. Slowly the slab-like columns of type gave way to all the main innovations that brought the daily papers down from the middle-class breakfast tables to the market-place: news on the front page, started by the *Daily Express* in 1901, headlines extending across several columns, tabloid presentations relying heavily on pictures, displayed feature articles in which the *Daily Mail* was the first to specialise, and amid the excitements and agonies of world war the "streamer" splash headline across the page which became general after 1914. To complete the new showmanship came changed sub-editorial techniques, again pioneered by North-cliffe, designed to project the news with built-in angling, emotive and thought-conditioning skills of whose employment the reader was often entirely unconscious. The newspaper press that had hardly changed in appearance for a century—because first the stamp duties and then the greed for advertisements made every inch of space seem too precious to waste on display or other enticements—now appeared in a garb tailored to its new part as a mass persuader.

Holyoake's "wilful little printing press" had become big technology and big communication. The rest of this record deals with labour's fight against these odds and efforts to create in new conditions a real freedom of the press.

9

Battles for Independence

We have not got a press which fulfils the ideals of the early democrats who thought that once the legal restrictions were gone the one object of a newspaper would be to educate the public and provide the citizen with the most impartial account possible of events, so that he may exercise his right as a voter in the most intelligent way. The press has become a vast industry with big business in the saddle.

New Statesman Editor KINGSLEY MARTIN, December, 1938

IN THE NEW EPOCH that opened with the Socialist revolution in Russia, the associated movement in Britain that led to the 1926 general strike brought battles over the freedom of the press which were partly fought on old ground and partly on new. The revived conflict was over restraints and persecutions by government and the law. But this no longer involved only valiant individual publishers at grips with legal and financial difficulties but the labour movement, as an organised force, confronting in addition to all the old problems the claim of big business to command over the heart, soul and thinking of the people.

Most people in 1914 would have regarded the freedom of the press as a secure achievement and a settled matter. But from the emergency regulations of 1914–21 continuously to the Industrial Relations Act of 1972 this freedom faced all its once defeated persecutors again, as courts, police and government renewed their assault.

The main focus of the contest shifted, however. The question passed beyond the old battlegrounds on which the *right* to publish was the chief prize. It burst the bonds of *institution* within which the classical bourgeois definition by *The Times* in 1852 sought to confine it. And the need for direct *representation* of the people through the ownership and control of newspapers stood again revealed as the real core of the question.

More closely than ever before, the press story in the years between Lloyd George's "Khaki Election" of 1919 and the 1945 election was interwoven with all the political and social changes. Time and again, newspapers appeared on the scene as direct participants in the action, and a complete account of press developments would require a full history of these years. This survey will look at four major episodes which raised the basic democratic issue most sharply. They were the post-war career of the *Daily Herald*, the general strike, Munich, and the struggle of the *Daily Worker* after its suppression in 1941.

The weekly *Herald* had opposed the war mainly from a pacifist point of view. It was already taking a canvass early in 1915 of readers' opinions on what the peace terms should be and this theme grew stronger after conscription was introduced in 1916. By the end of this year the Cabinet was discussing its suppression. After President Wilson of the United States had asked each side in the war to state its peace terms Northcliffe's *Evening News* in January 1917 placarded the street with the single word "NO". The *Herald* riposted with placards reading "YES". Its policy of a "peace without victory" was rejected, however, by the Labour Party conference held later in the same month.

The movement of which the paper was to become the voice did not come from anywhere at the top, but from a rank-and-file workers' revolt against the war. It was this movement—to which the Socialists of the competing sects gave the lead as they had done in the revolutionary revival of the eighties—that did the groundwork for the *Herald*'s great postwar days. Its main centre was the Clyde, with the first big inspiration coming not through the written word but the ceaseless denunciations of the war by John McLean of the British Socialist Party.*

Out of the temper that he fashioned, and the bitter struggles to defend trade union rights—both against the employers and government and the "truce" unilaterally declared by the official union leaders at the start of the war—arose the Clyde Workers Committee, with its own journal *The Worker*, in 1915. The suppression of this paper and of the Glasgow *Forward* marked the resumption of a *direct* government action against the press of a kind unknown since the aftermath of the Napoleonic wars. Socialist Labour Party† member J. W.

* Formed in 1911 by the Social-Democratic Party (former Social Democratic Federation) and some left members of the ILP.

† Founded in 1903, with *The Socialist* as its organ. Strongly influenced by the American doctrinaire Socialist Daniel de Leon, but a force among the militants in the Scottish engineering shops and shipyards. It bought a printing machine on the instalment system, soon after its formation, and its members in the Edinburgh printing trade did all the setting and composing. It claimed a circulation of 8,000 in January 1920.

Muir, and William Gallacher the committee's chairman, were sentenced to twelve months' imprisonment, and the printer, Walter Bell, to three. *Forward* was forbidden after it had printed a true account of a meeting between the Clyde shop stewards, Lloyd George, and Arthur Henderson, the chief Labour representative in the Cabinet, at which the Prime Minister was greeted with jeers and heckling and the singing of the Red Flag before the meeting ended in disorder. This was the year, too, in which people were jailed solely for having anti-conscription leaflets in their pockets.

The setting up of the National Shop Stewards' and Workers' Committee Movement in the same year created an anti-war basis on which pacifists and Socialists began to link up more closely on a national scale. The key event was the victory of the internationalist and anti-war trend within the British Socialist Party. After gathering strength around a fortnightly magazine, *The Call*, its supporters were able at the party's conference in Salford later to break with Hyndman and twenty-one others of his jingo group, who withdrew after they had been defeated on the question of whether the conference should debate policy on the war in private or in public (i.e. muted by the war frenzy).

It was in this paper, on the eve of the Russian Revolution, that the BSP drew up a declaration to be made at a Paris conference (which was never held) of Socialists in the Allied countries. It exposed the imperialist origins of the war, demanded the withdrawal of Labour and Socialist parties from all the warring governments, reminded the parties of their pre-war pledges to take action in war conditions to "bring about the downfall of capitalism" and called for a negotiated peace without annexations.

The overthrow of Tsarism that came in the same week, followed by the Soviet revolution in November, moulded the entire British labour movement in the early twenties. It stirred hopes and energies that threw the official leaders on to the defensive and discredited the profound opportunism and many-sided corruption to which they had fallen victim in the Lib.-Lab. era founded on the enormous wealth of a ruling class drawing tribute from the ends of the earth.

Of the November revolution, *The Call* wrote that "Socialists—genuine and not make-believe Socialists—have seized the reins of power" and asked: "Are we going to help them?" It was in the revived *Daily Herald* that the question was given its most effective answer. Before the paper resumed daily publication, it had held on March 31, 1918, the first of a series of huge meetings in the Albert Hall to welcome the Revolution and demand in general terms that all governments follow the Russian example in restoring freedom. Twelve thousand people filled every seat and five thousand were turned away. The Albert Hall management cancelled Lansbury's booking for the meeting at which the daily publication decision was to be announced. Prime Minister Lloyd George declared that he had no power to intervene. Then the Electrical Trades Union removed the fuses from the hall and warned that they would plunge the whole of Kensington in darkness if the Albert Hall manager tried to reconnect the supply; the government, with a great Victory Ball planned in the borough, surrendered. The meeting was held, the announcement made, and on March 31, 1918, the first issue appeared.

Lansbury, who had considered that £400,000 was necessary to re-float the paper properly, had managed to collect less than half of that sum—mainly from trade unions and Co-operative societies. The financial short-fall, however, was not the most pressing worry at the start. The paper-makers refused to supply newsprint. The ban was not relaxed until Robert Williams of the transport workers threatened the Newspaper Proprietors Association with a strike at the mills that would put them all out of business. Even then, the *Daily Herald* had for some time to buy newsprint supplies indirectly in various parts of the country. This trouble provided only a foretaste of stronger attacks to come.

Lansbury was accused in turn of accepting Egyptian, Indian and Russian money to keep the paper going. In May 1919 the paper took action of a kind that was still open to the press but was shortly to be stopped by the Official Secrets Acts. It published a secret War Office instruction to commanding officers, requiring them to find out whether their men would help in breaking strikes, parade for "draft to overseas, especially to Russia", and also whether there had been any growth of trade unionism among them. The government threatened to prosecute. But Winston Churchill had to admit in July that the document was genuine; he stated that troops would not be used for strike breaking but the war of intervention in Russia would go on. Another arbitrary act of the War Office which the paper exposed in the same month was an instruction to army officers to intercept bundles of the *Daily Herald* at railheads and burn them "with as little publicity as possible" to ensure that no copies reached the troops.

In the summer of this year a national "Hands Off Russia" committee was formed. By the following spring the danger of war with Russia reached a peak when the Poles with British and French help invaded the Russian Soviet Republic. On May 10 the Thames river workers, among whom the British Socialist Party, East London Workers Socialist Federation and the Shop Stewards Movement led by Harry Pollitt had been busily agitating, struck their historic blow: the dockers refused to load munitions for Poland on the *Jolly George* and the coalheavers refused to coal the vessel. The deed sparked an all-movement action from the working-class side showing a degree of unity never achieved before and only rarely paralleled since; it was in a special edition of the *Daily Herald* that the manifesto of the newly formed Communist Party calling for a general strike in the event of war against Soviet Russia was published on Sunday, August 8. Some 350 Councils of Action sprang up all over the country. The danger grew in July after the Poles had been thrown back from the Ukraine and Soviet troops were approaching Warsaw. The *Daily Herald* voiced the alarm and anger of British workers in issue after issue. August 8 brought its celebrated special Sunday edition with the streamer: "NOT A MAN, NOT A GUN, NOT A SOU."

An emergency meeting of the Parliamentary Labour Party, the party's national executive and the Trades Union Congress resolved that all action necessary, including a general stoppage, would be taken to prevent war and a Council of Action was set up to carry out the decision. British assistance to the Poles stopped dead, to the accompaniment of protests by Lloyd George that he had never intended war.

Ten days after its defeat the government charged that Lansbury was in Russian pay. Enormous derision was aroused throughout the labour movement by the grotesque charge, which contained a little elaboration by the Admiralty to the effect that the money was to be paid in "Chinese Bonds" whatever they were.* Lansbury at once published the complete list of the persons and organisations who had produced money for the paper. A little later, audited circulation figures of

---

* A *Herald* poet reacted with verses reading in part:

Chinese Bonds, Chinese Bonds
Smuggled by Peroxide Blondes
Tightly packed by Spiers and Ponds
Chinese Bonds, Chinese Bonds.

329,869—probably the highest circulation the paper reached in this phase of its existence—finished off the "Moscow Gold" fables.

The 1920s were elimination stake years for the press; newspapers that had thrived before the war on sales of a quarter of a million or less were shut down or merged, including many local newspapers with long reputations for a certain independence. To survive, the *Daily Herald*, hard-pressed by an advertisers' boycott, had to raise its price to twopence—twice the price of any daily paper of comparable size—on October 11, 1920. It explained in an article headed "Slaughter House Journalism—by a Newspaperman" that it could "dare" to go to twopence because of the financial support given by its readers. The bigger papers, it noted, were ready to stand heavy losses for a time because "they knew that they would be residuary legatees. What is a drain on them is, they hope, death to others. They can look forward to the time when they will have something like a monopoly of the market. Then they will be able to take it out of the advertisers and of the readers."

It was strange, this foreseeing newspaperman went on, that the papers that were prepared to go on selling below cost were so bitterly opposed to coal being sold below cost (through a government subsidy given to the miners in 1921 while it completed its plans to force them to accept a drastic cut in wages). The *Herald* price increase coincided with a strike by the miners which opened the battle leading to 1926. The impoverishment of its steadiest readers and supporters, amid the strike and the depression which followed the quick postwar boom, worsened the paper's already grave financial troubles.

The movement that sustained the paper in 1919–21 made greater advances toward unity than had been made in the entire period since the great dock strike. First there were the great amalgamations that transformed the trade union movement, with the emergence of the Transport and General Workers Union as the largest in the country, sharing the general labour field with the National Union of General and Municipal Workers. Then in 1921 the body that was later to be called the National Council of Labour was formed, pooling the strength and counsels of the TUC, the national executive of the Labour Party, and the Parliamentary Labour Party. In these years, too, the Labour Party, while retaining its original character as a political federation of trade unions, adopted Socialism as its aim and with this and the opening of its doors to individual membership emerged as a definite political party with 2,350 divisional and local organisations covering the whole electoral field. The fourth great event that gave the labour movement its modern shape was the success achieved by the Socialist groups when, under the galvanic shock of the Russian revolution, they united as the Communist Part of Great Britain, which was established as a fusion of the BSP with the main part of the SLP and the South Wales Socialist Society in August 1920.*

Such were the main constituents of the movement which roused itself to meet the onset of what the *Daily Herald* called a "frontal attack on the whole working class by the capitalists and their government", after Lloyd George had locked out the miners at the end of March 1921 to enforce sweeping cuts in wages. The miners appealed to their associates in the Triple Alliance and called on April 8 for a general railway and transport strike. In page after page of messages the *Daily Herald* voiced solidarity from all the main industrial centres. The government's plans were well prepared. In the previous year, after the triumph scored by the Council of Action and a miners' strike in the previous October (settled inconclusively), the government had rushed its Emergency Powers Act through Parliament in five days. This was now invoked to call up reservists, post machine-guns at pitheads, send troops in full battle order to the main centres of industry and set up supply depots in public parks.

The pits closed in the most solid stoppage yet. But the Triple Alliance leaders, in a turn-round that stunned the movement, first postponed and then on April 15, Black Friday, called the strike off. The miners had to resume work at the end of June on the owners' terms. During the struggle the *Daily Herald* ran a national collection which brought in £20,000 for the miners' starving children.

The paper plagued the life out of the brasshats and interventionists, whose chief spokesman was Churchill. It reproduced on February 28, 1921, part of the front page of a bogus issue of *Pravda*, organ of the Soviet Communist Party, produced by the Whiteguard administration of Wrangel in Southern Russia. It revealed that the phoney

---

* Another tributary stream was Sylvia Pankhurst's Workers' Socialist Federation, in London's East End, which had developed out of the left wing of the pre-war women's suffrage movement and, first in the *Woman's Dreadnought* (1914–17) and then in its successor the *Workers' Dreadnought*, opposed the war, supported the Soviet revolution and spread revolutionary Socialist ideas with a left-sectarian bias.

Pravda had been printed in London and the printer's imprint—set deliberately at the extreme bottom edge of the page—guillotined off at a secret printing house in Scotland Yard under the supervision of Home Office officials.

In the summer of 1921, Lansbury and his paper were involved in a rebellion that marked one of the peaks of the postwar militancy. In this year when unemployment topped the million—not to fall below that figure until the Second World War—councils in working-class areas were groaning under the burden of very big rate increases for the relief of the unemployed. On March 22, 1921, the Poplar Council refused to levy the part of the rates due to the County Council and other outside authorities and decided to raise a rate only for its own expenses, and 30 councillors went to jail for contempt of court.

It was one of the most gallant challenges of the day, but it scarcely compensated for the troubles overtaking the *Daily Herald* in spite of the united working-class support which it enjoyed. Years later Lansbury recalled that at this time he "almost shouted for wet towels" when asked to write about "the Labour press". He had become convinced, he said, that it was useless "trying to compete for a huge circulation until the Movement is willing to spend at least £200,000 down on an entirely new kind of paper". In 1921 he rejected several private offers for the paper, declaring that the name of the *Daily Herald* was not for sale to any private capitalist. But after Black Friday, the financial burden proved too heavy to be met, in spite of the price increase and gifts from the embattled miners and railwaymen. Early in 1922 Lansbury asked the Labour Party and the TUC for aid; in September the paper was taken over by the TUC and Lansbury gave up the editorship. The *Daily Herald* became the official organ of the right-wing leadership, and one of Northcliffe's top journalists, Hamilton Fyfe, was appointed editor. It was not long before a stream of complaints began flowing from the General Council criticising the members for their "miserable failure", as the paper said (August 24, 1923), to respond to the many appeals for support from the council and the Labour Party executive.

The three basic elements that were to be involved in the 1926 tragedy were clearly apparent by the time the *Herald* had passed its high tide as a fighting newspaper. They were: a militant labour rank and file of advanced solidarity; government, employers and capitalist press out for the kill; and a compromising trade union leadership

scarcely daring to think of the total challenge to the established powers
necessary if the wages movement were to avoid defeat.

After the taming of the *Herald*, the front position in this challenge
was taken up by the periodical papers of the two-year-old Communist Party. *The Call*, organ of the BSP, had ceased when the party
was formed, and been immediately followed by a new weekly, *The
Communist*, which ran for 131 numbers. This was more a magazine of
Socialist theory and history than an agitating and organising journal,
but by February 1921 had reached a circulation of 25,000 which was
rising fast. March brought a boycott of the Communist press by the
newspaper wholesalers which was not to be broken for many years.
For the first time since Chartist days the rebel press was systematically
denied the normal channels and had to rely directly on sympathisers
and supporters for its distribution. They succeeded in raising sales to
40,000 during the 1921 miners lockout and 60,000 two months later.

After Black Friday, police raids, intimidation of the paper's printers,
and libel actions stacked the odds higher against it. *The Communist*'s
own failure, like that of *Justice* and the *Commonweal*, to involve itself
closely in the real life and struggles of the workers, combined with the
same difficult conditions after Black Friday which hit the *Daily Herald*,
helped to drive circulation down. The organisation commission set up
by the Communist Party's fifth congress in October 1922 established
that the real sale of *The Communist* in mid-1922 was about 8,000.

The *Workers' Weekly* which replaced it in February 1923 set out
with the aim to reflect "the daily struggles of the working class in
fields, mines, railroads, factories and workshop . . . it will stand for the
workers' interests against all the forces of capitalism". Developing this
new emphasis, the paper reported strike news in detail, received 2,500
letters from worker-correspondents in its first year—894 of them were
published—started a Maintenance Fund, and organised some 60 distribution committees. Edited and distributed country-wide by volunteers,
it yet managed to reach a sale of over 50,000 within two months.

The following year brought Labour's first government, a minority
administration formed in January by MacDonald, by the grace of the
working men's old patrons the Liberal Party, and with the cunning
complicity of the Tory Party which spied and seized its chance to
discredit the idea of Labour administration by staging its first weak,
powerless and confused practical exercise. On the left, too, the trap
was seen and opposition ran high to the decision to form a govern-

ment in such circumstances. It was very much the spirit of the post-war militancy, which the *Herald* had focused, that the *Workers' Weekly* carried forward when it published an Open Letter to the Fighting Forces on July 25. Striking a defiant tone reminiscent of the little papers of Peterloo days or Harney's writings in Chartism's first wave, it showed how successive governments had used the armed forces for strike breaking and urged serving men to let it be known that "neither in the class war nor in a military war will you turn your guns on your fellow workers but instead will line up with your fellow workers in an attack upon the exploiters and capitalists, and will use your arms on the side of your own class".

Pushed by the storm that followed in the Tory press and the Commons, the government had the acting editor, J. R. Campbell, arrested on August 5 and 2,000 copies of the weekly removed in a lorry, together with many documents and papers, by police who stated that they were "looking for evidence". It was what can be called the *Herald* generation in the labour movement that sprang to Campbell's defence when he was charged under the Incitement to Mutiny Act of 1793. Under pressure both from the Labour benches in the House and demonstrations in the country, the government dropped the prosecution, to be at once denounced frenziedly in the press for "truckling to Communism" and undermining respect for confidence in the law courts. The affair sealed the fate of the Labour government. When a Liberal MP moved for a Select Committee on the case, and MacDonald made the issue one of confidence, the government was defeated and fell on October 8. Its great crime, which made its removal essential, was the evidence the affair had provided that it "could be forced to retreat *under the mass pressure of the Labour movement* . . . this could not be tolerated".*

Other journals started by the new party in its first three years were the theoretical paper *Communist Review* (May 1921), the *Labour Monthly* which under the editorship of R. Palme Dutt established itself as the broad organ of the trade union and labour movement with a Marxist direction, and for a short while in connection with the 1922 general election a *Daily Communist*, published in London and Glasgow. In these years, however, the weight was still heavy of traditions and mental attitudes going back to the days of Hyndman and *Justice*. The progress made away from the literary-political review of the old kind

* James Klugmann, *History of the Communist Party of Great Britain*, Vol. 1, p. 346.

towards a journal reflecting and organising working-class struggles, in the sense stated earlier by Ernest Jones and restated with still greater force and clarity by Lenin, was slow and halting. In 1923 the fulfilment of this aim still lay seven complex years ahead in the future. However, a force of thousands of workers ready to support and distribute an independent newspaper of their own had come into being, and was preparing the new breakthrough, the launching of the *Daily Worker* in 1930.

The 1926 general strike, Britain's greatest social confrontation up to that time, also gave new proofs of the need for both an independent labour press and firmer guarantees of democratic press rights. In this year more people went to prison for sedition in print, and for more years altogether, than at any time since Cobbett, Carlile and Hetherington. The press lords' newspapers served *en bloc* as an engine of class war and later vengeance. Events highlighted as never before the vulnerability of the working class in face of this force and illustrated more sharply than any previous contest had done the truth of Ernest Jones' dictum that a labour movement without its own press "is but half a movement . . . a disenfranchised cause".

We may take as our starting point the editorial in the *Workers' Weekly* of November 21, 1924, warning that the employers were preparing "a devastating offensive against the labour movement" and that the wage offensive would be accompanied by an attack on this movement itself. In its New Year (January 2, 1925) issue, it said that 1926 would be a year of struggle and that there was "a noticeable difference between the preparation of the employing class and the working class". The first Labour government—a minority administration depending on Liberal support—had fallen in the previous year. The forged "Zinoviev Letter"* had formed the basis for a plot

---

* The letter purported to be signed by G. Zinoviev, the President, O. Kuusinen, the Finnish Secretary of the Comintern, and Arthur MacManus, a British member of its presidium. It advocated preparation for military insurrection. Nobody ever saw the original of the alleged letter. The Foreign Office took it as a pretext for a Note to the Soviet Ambassador declaring that the Anglo-Soviet Treaties currently being negotiated could not be ratified unless the Soviet Government stopped the activities of agencies "whose aim is to spread discontent or to foment rebellion in any part of the British Empire". The Note, presumed to have been sent on MacDonald's authority, "settled the fate of the Election, and made every Labour candidate feel and appear a fool", the Labour historian G. D. H. Cole wrote later in his *History of the Labour Party from 1914* (1948).

directly involving the *Daily Mail*, the Tory Party and the Foreign Office, and carried forward with the effective complicity of the Labour leader Ramsay MacDonald, which ensured a net loss of forty Labour seats in the 1924 General Election and gave the Tory Party an overwhelming majority. This cleared the decks for action by the employers and the government.

In April 1926 the long struggle of the miners came to a head when they were locked out after preparations of the utmost care and precision had been made by the Baldwin government for a showdown with the whole working class. To the last moment the Industrial Committee of the TUC tried to draw back from the conflict. It was while the committee was closeted in negotiations with Baldwin behind the miners' back that one of the most dramatic events in press history provided him with the pretext for which he had been waiting. The print workers on the *Daily Mail* stopped the paper because of an editorial branding the general stoppage to which the TUC was committed as a "revolutionary movement intended to inflict suffering upon the great mass of innocent persons in the community" and calling for it to be resisted "by every resource at the disposal of the community".

The government described this skirmish as "an overt act of war" and broke off negotiations with the TUC. Next day the stoppage was complete. It was the aim of the government from the start to break the morale of the mighty labour hosts—and the key was in the communications media. Baldwin commandeered the plant of the *Morning Post* to bring out the *British Gazette*, with Winston Churchill in command, as a strike-breaking daily paper. It declared on May 7 that an organised attempt was being made to "starve the people and wreck the State". It suppressed all mention of peace moves by the Archbishop of Canterbury involving temporary subsidies to the coal-owners; but it blazoned forth a declaration by Cardinal Bourne that the strike was a "sin against the obedience which we owe to God".

Not a single linotype operator could it get to set the paper; a mechanical superintendent loaned by Lord Beaverbrook was the government's sole typesetter. Newspaper workers were out solid throughout the stoppage. In retrospect, however, their standing idle during the momentous nine days has always raised misgivings. They were idle during a crisis in which the authorities treated every attempt by the workers to publicise their case—except in the TUC's *British*

G

Worker—as an illegal act. Many opportunities were neglected. Throughout the strike, Lansbury was helping to produce a local bulletin on a duplicator at the Bow Labour Party headquarters. His colleagues on *Lansbury's Labour Weekly* walked from the suburbs to their office daily, but did no work there as "the General Council wanted no assistance".* Allen Hutt has noted in a classic chapter on the strike† that "but for the strange formalism which impartially closed down the Labour and Socialist press with the capitalist Press the Government would not have been able to take the initiative with its strike sheet". (This attitude still held the field strongly in the seventies, with print unions commonly refusing to exempt the *Morning Star* and other labour movement journals during strike protest actions in defence of trade union rights.)

By the mid-twenties a new force had appeared in communications; and the first major use found for the wireless broadcasting service was to carry the Tory government's farrago of false news, suppression of news, anti-union incitement, and strike-breaking appeals and instructions. The *British Gazette* and the radio together spread the lie that the strike was breaking up. Throughout the struggle this was the opposite of the truth—as the *British Gazette* admitted when it said on May 12, the last day of the strike, that "there is as yet little sign of a general collapse". Hours later came the sudden, and to millions unexpected and bewildering, announcement by the TUC General Council that the strike had been called off.

However, when today one reads the issues of the TUC-run *British Worker*, the fact stares out from every page that the call-off was "in the script" from the outset so far as the leaders were concerned. The *British Worker* brought out its first issue on May 5. Its hasty production was both a reproach to leaders who had omitted to make obviously necessary preparations and a tribute to the print workers and editorial staff who got the paper out. When all was ready for printing there was a police raid. Large numbers of the Paper Workers' Union were ready outside the building with motor cycles and cars and took away many of the 320,000 copies printed.

The main line taken from this first issue onward was to deny the *British Gazette*'s charges that the strike was an attempt at revolution

---

* Postgate, op. cit., p. 240.

† *Postwar History of the British Working Class*, pp. 126–63 (Left Book Club edition).

and to stress that the strike was an industrial dispute. The paper suggested to its readers not any form of struggle but that they should organise sports and entertainments. It carried repeated pleas from the General Council to the government for understanding, and do-nothing appeals to the workers. On May 6: "No attack is being made on the constitution. We beg Mr. Baldwin to believe that." On May 8 (advice to workers): "Keep smiling. . . . Refuse to be provoked . . . look after the wife and kiddies. . . . Get into the country, there is no more heartful occupation than walking."

The *British Worker* refrained from reporting many of the early arrests and prison sentences so that the conflict, as it said, should not be embittered. A crowning example of this self-censorship by the TUC organ was its second edition on the day of surrender. Under the headline "Miners' Thanks to Their Allies" it failed to report the miners' decision to continue the strike, and later issues never reported a statement by miners' leader A. J. Cook on the afternoon of May 12 that the Miners' Federation was "no party in any shape or form" to the calling off of the strike.

In the sharpest contrast with this record stood the activities, before and after the strike, of the militant journals. Throughout 1925 these had worked to build support for the miners. After the Cabinet had bought time by giving the coal-owners a nine-month subsidy on July 30, the *Workers' Weekly*, *Lansbury's Labour Weekly*, the *Sunday Worker*, and the ILP's *New Leader* warned that only an armistice had been gained. On September 25 the strike-breaking OMS (Organisation for the Maintenance of Supplies) was set up. The press lords' papers raised a simultaneous clamour for action to crush trade unionism. The *Workers' Weekly* regularly carried a warning in a frame showing now many weeks were left in which to prepare; the one on August 24 was headlined "34 WEEKS TO GO" and read: "Thirty-four weeks to go to what? To the termination of the mining agreement and the opening of the greatest struggle in the history of the British working class . . . WE MUST PREPARE FOR THE STRUGGLE."

The *Sunday Worker*, a united-front journal of the left launched on March 15, 1925, denounced OMS as a fascist-type organisation, under the headlines "Boss class gets ready for big fight". So wide was the popularity won by this lively and highly professional journal* that at

---

* The paper took bold steps into the field of popular Sunday journalism. Picking up the scandal-cum-politics tradition of the Hetherington and Cleave

the Liverpool conference of the Labour Party in 1925 a resolution supporting it obtained 1,143,000 votes to 2,036,000—the biggest "rebel" vote recorded at the conference. The other journal working to unify the left was *Lansbury's Labour Weekly*, started a fortnight before the *Sunday Worker*, after the leading figure of the years in which working-class unity had reached its peak had despaired of any good coming from the *Daily Herald* in its official phase. *Lansbury's* rapidly reached a sale of 172,000, about seven times that of the sixpenny *New Statesman*. Several times it offered the General Council plans for the organisation of the coming struggle and these are still to be found in the files of the paper.

The militant tide that supported all these papers reached its height at the 57th conference of the TUC at Scarborough in 1925, but nothing was done in the way of practical preparation. In this connection the big event of this year was a powerfully backed move at the Liverpool conference of the Labour Party to rescind an earlier decision to reject the affiliation of the Communist Party. High and mighty indignation poured from the millionaires' papers. *The Times* (September 25) declared that the only way to maintain the Labour Party's unity and credit was "the ostracism and condemnation of Communism". After the move to end the ban had been defeated the *Daily Telegraph* announced that there was now a "much better tendency in the Stock Exchange". And J. H. Thomas, who was later to go over to the Tories and become possibly the best hated of all the movement's renegades after Ramsay MacDonald, said in an interview in the *Weekly Despatch* on October 11: "Smash the Reds or they will smash us."

A fortnight later twelve leaders of the Communist Party were under

---

gazettes of the 1830s, it represented a real attempt to combine news reporting and Socialist agitation. Its second number on March 22, 1925 carried the main headline "STENCH FROM LAW CASES GROWING THICKER", with a secondary title reading "Military men, Titled Ladies and Rich Idlers Mixed up in Trials that Smell to Heaven". This was followed by a clutch of seamy court stories preluded with the comment that "corruption, crookedness, multiple adultery, lechery and trickery are the reigning elements of social life among the Upper Classes of the present day". The state of capitalist society, "matched anything in Rome before its fall or in St. Petersburg before the Russian Workers rose and cleaned out the stables". The tone may have been a trifle puritanical but the judgement has stood the test of time, and this robust "intro" could be slapped appropriately across the front page of any *News of the World* or *Sunday People* in the scandal-ridden seventies.

arrest, and they were jailed in November for six months. One of the three charges was "conspiracy to seduce persons in His Majesty's forces, to whom might come certain books and Pamphlets, to wit, the *Workers' Weekly* and certain other publications mentioned in the indictment and to incite them to mutiny".

On the eve of the strike the Communist Party produced a printed *Workers' Daily* in 40,000 copies. It reprinted a manifesto published in the previous day's *Sunday Worker* ending with the slogans: "A Council of action in every Town", and "Every Man behind the Miners". Thereafter the duplicated *Worker's Bulletin* appeared for ten consecutive days, with a total circulation of about 100,000, counting the numerous duplicated local bulletins which reproduced its leading articles. The distribution and even the possession of the *Workers' Bulletin* was an offence under the Emergency Powers Act. Hundreds of bulletins issued locally by the Councils of Action on duplicators or typewriters in trade union branch offices, in Labour Party, ILP or Communist Party premises or in the homes of their members fell under the same outlawry. In London these bulletins included the *Westminster Worker* and the *St. Pancras Bulletin*, in the west of Scotland the *Worker*, the *Workers' Weekly* and the *Workers' Press*, in Liverpool the *Workers' Gazette*; and there were many more with circulations ranging from a few hundred to 10,000. The Young Communist League produced *The Young Striker* in 4,000 copies a day.

Of the 2,500 arrests made during the strike a great number were for publishing, distributing or possessing such papers, and the sentences imposed ranged from two to six months. *Lansbury's Labour Weekly* said after the strike: "The Special Department at Scotland Yard was in full cry after Communists in particular. To be in possession of one of their multi-graphed bulletins was as good as a sentence without the option."

The first Communist executive meeting after the betrayal of the strike estimated that 1,000 of its members had been arrested. The London district committee's organiser, R. W. Robson, got six weeks merely for carrying a copy of the *Workers' Bulletin*. Marjorie, wife of Harry Pollitt, was fined £50 and costs—or three months—on a similar charge. A striker was jailed for chalking a pavement. Reports of jail sentences filled two and a half columns of the *Sunday Worker*'s first post-strike number.

A forty-year-old miner named Edward Wilson was jailed for three months and fined £100 for distributing the *Northern Light*, the bulletin of the Chopwell Council of Action. The police prosecutor asked the court to "stamp out" those associated with the council. The bench told Wilson: "We cannot have Chopwell and the neighbourhood governed by a set of men like you. The inhabitants . . . are not to be governed by a set of laws which you and your colleagues and hooligans of your description choose to draw up." This brutally offensive tone from the magistracy is one that the doughty hawker of the Unstamped, Joseph Swann, would have recognised. And it is also quite the old Chartist note of mockery that sounds again in this comment by the Kensington strike bulletin on the government's incessantly repeated claim that the entire strike was illegal: "Sir John Simon says that the General Strike is illegal under an Act passed by William the Conqueror in 1066. All strikers are likely to be interned in Wormwood Scrubs. The three million strikers are advised to keep in hiding, preferably in the Park behind Bangor Street where they will not be discovered."

The illegality of the strike was pronounced by a number of judges and lawyers. The wireless repeated their words as if they had the force of law. But the question was never tested in court and in the absence of such a decision many of the government's own actions were clearly illegal. G. D. H. Cole, who himself wrote for *Lansbury's* recalled later that the TUC General Council, in its determination to insist that the strike was a "purely industrial movement" was "flurried by the charges that it was engaged in a quasi-revolutionary conspiracy against the constitution and the law". The strikers, however, were not flurried, he added. "With hardly any exceptions they stood solid from the beginning to the end of the affair".*

A new kind of press came out of this background during the strike —the factory papers produced by shopfloor militants. At the peak of this Communist-led movement they numbered over a hundred and ranged in format from duplicated sheets to six-page printed papers. Not since the days of *Hog's Wash*, the *Black Dwarf* and *The Theological Comet* had so colourful an array of titles appeared. They included the *Black Squad* (Gowan), the *Cambrian Xray*, the *Feltham Tatler* (Feltham Repair Depot), the *Idris Ginger* and *Courage* (run by the workers at the Idris beverages plants), *The Live Rail* (Holloway Tram Depot) the *Cymmer Searchlight*, issued by the Cymmer group of the Communist

* *History of the Labour Party from 1914*, p. 166.

Party), and the *Red Observer*, a printed four-pager issued by Communists at the Tylerstown No. 4 pit.* They put into workshop idiom ideas expressed often in doctrinaire garb in the Communist journals.

These the government persecuted before all others, but could not stop their circulation from rising. The *Workers' Weekly* increased from its pre-strike 50,000 to about 80,000. The *Sunday Worker*, whose shareholders included Labour Party and ILP branches, Co-operative Guilds, and many trade union branches especially in the mining areas, had a sale of 100,000 before and during the strike and held it for some time after. Amid the post-1926 reaction and labour movement disarray, however, the Communist and other left journals proved unable to hold their increases. The general strike, during which the valour of this press had been proved, had also shown its limitations in combat with the press resources of the Tory and capitalist side. The question of starting a daily working-class newspaper, in conditions more difficult than those which had faced Lansbury's paper either before or after the war, was gradually brought to the front in these years, amid very sharp debates over both the possibility and the necessity of the project, to become finally a top priority for the Communist and militant trade unionist left.

Out of the aftermath of the general strike came the failure of the second Labour government and its replacement by the National Government of 1931, which took the renegades MacDonald, Snowden and Thomas in tow. Fascism took power in Germany two years later, amid the worst-yet world economic crisis in which the unemployment figures in Britain rose to three million. Admirers and accomplices of fascism in Britain launched the country on a six-year road to national shame and its darkest peril, along which efforts were made to install fascism here and Neville Chamberlain's appeasement policy built up Hitler's power to a height which made war inevitable.

The press story after 1931 has two sides. Most of the millionaire-owned newspapers justified or condoned each step in Chamberlain's betrayal and sometimes took a hand in it themselves. On the other side, a recovery from the trough of 1931 took place, producing in the Popular Front days a press that both reflected and inspired the people's resistance to fascism.

* James Klugmann, *History of the Communist Party of Great Britain:* "The General Strike", gives a full list of these papers.

The story begins with a capture by the Tory side—the Odhams Press takeover of the *Daily Herald*. This large newspaper and magazine producing group wanted to find a more profitable use for presses that were exclusively occupied in printing its *Sunday People*. Odhams received 51 per cent of the *Daily Herald* controlling shares and undertook to continue the paper as an official Labour journal. It then gave the paper the most costly circulation build-up that Fleet Street had yet known; various promotional schemes and competitions raised sales from 400,000 to nearly two million, by an expenditure of £1,325,000, or about £1 per reader. The sordid transaction revolved around a man and a policy. The policy was right-wing Labour collaboration with capitalism. The man was J. S. Elias (later Lord Southwood), a poor East End button-maker's son, whose great wealth had been founded at the dirtiest end of "popular" journalism when he took on a lucrative contract to print *John Bull*, started in 1906 by the evil Horatio Bottomley. This weekly organ of blackmail and hate campaigns—first against the French and after 1914 against the German people—reached a circulation of nearly two million. In 1922, Bottomley's Victory Bonds swindle earned him seven years' penal servitude and Elias narrowly escaped financial ruin in the sales slump that overtook *John Bull* in consequence.

Three months before the Odhams takeover eight men had met in an old warehouse in Tabernacle Street, London EC1, to produce the first number of the *Daily Worker*, which was printed on an old German rotary machine that had once printed the *Clarion*. The launching came nine years after Lenin, in a letter to the British Communist Tom Bell, had urged the Communists to start a daily newspaper "not as a business . . . but as an economic and political tool of the masses in their struggle", warning at the same time that the British government would "apply the shrewdest measures to suppress every beginning of this kind". The call for such measures came immediately, and first in *The Times*, the pompous old glorifier of press freedom and independence. The paper said editorially on January 2 that because the new paper had published a message from the Communist International "the Government must act, and with a directness that will prevent all misunderstanding in Moscow".*

The press lord pack took up the cry and on January 22, Arthur Henderson, the Foreign Secretary, announced that he had informed

*William Rust, *The Story of the Daily Worker*, p. 11.

the Soviet Ambassador that the message of the International was "calculated to impede relations between the two countries". The *Morning Post* (May 22, 1930) accused the Labour government of pitiable weakness and demanded to know what effects its failure to act would have in India, even if the new paper's "incitements to mutiny in the Army were ineffective". (The *Daily Worker* had urged workers not to handle munitions for India and soldiers to stand by their class.) Later the *Morning Post* sent a special messenger to ask if William Rust, the editor, had been arrested yet. Within six months a national boycott by the newspaper wholesalers had begun and was to continue until 1942. Libel cases also strewed the paper's path throughout the period.

So it was as a very *extraordinary* business that the paper survived. Tens of thousands of workers were its agents, distributors and lifeline. With the wholesalers' boycott came prosecutions. In July 1930, three staff members were jailed for periods of five, six and nine months for comtempt of court. On September 17, after the Invergordon naval mutiny provoked by cuts ordered by the National Government, the paper headlined its report of the affair, "Sailors Join the No Cuts Fight", and published a manifesto of the sailors declaring themselves resolved "to remain as one unit refusing to sail under the new rates of pay". After a raid by the police the issue of September 25 appeared with spaces containing only the words "Censored by Printer". When the printer, Mr. W. T. Wilkinson, appeared before the Bow Street magistrate, he was given bail on condition that no matter appeared in the paper "in any way touching or concerning the armed forces of His Majesty". Suppression in plenty had been visited on the press before, but this was the first time that *pre*-censorship of newspapers had been applied in Britain since 1695 when the licensing regulations were allowed to lapse.

William Rust recounted in his history of the paper, published in 1948: "I was informed by the detective inspector in charge of the raid that all material for the paper would have to pass through the hands of his men, who, he said, 'will pass anything that is not inflammatory'." At the press, police officers examined page-proofs, struck out a reader's letter, changed the headlines on the report of a speech by Tom Mann and also deleted paragraphs. The police admitted that they had no search warrant, but ransacked every cupboard and table and then carried off their spoil in two vans. Questioned in the Commons on these incidents, the Hon. Oliver Stanley, Under-Secretary at the Home Office, denied that any police censorship had been applied.

Not until March 1935 was the *Daily Worker* able to announce that Special Branch detectives had ceased to hang about its offices. By this time the paper, after a period in which it was best known as an organ for the struggles of the unemployed, had considerably broadened its coverage and character as a newspaper; the lead which it gave in opposing the onrush of fascism after the black year of 1933 was the decisive factor in this change. After the coming to power of Hitler, the paper became the heart and soul of a united front campaign against the danger of fascism and war. The press lords reacted differently. Lord Rothermere wrote in his *Daily Mail* (July 10) that the Nazi führer had "converted a despondent and embittered nation into one radiant with hope and enthusiasm". The *Daily Herald*, in what the *Worker* described as "a friendly handshake", said it was important to realise that the National Socialists called themselves "Socialists" as well as "National", that their creed was in many ways "anathema to the big landlords, the big industrialists and the big financiers", and that their leaders were "bound to go forward with the 'Socialist' side of their programme".

As the menace grew, the *Daily Worker* came, as the thirties advanced, to hold the central position in a broadening popular alliance to resist and defeat it. Above all its part in the defence of democracy in Spain against fascist intervention and the lethal "non-intervention" of the British and French governments earned the paper this position. It was the prime mover, too, in the tremendous popular mobilisation in East End streets that stopped Oswald Mosley's home-grown fascists in 1936 and 1937. And it helped to bring about important realignments in the wider labour movement.

One of these was the Unity Campaign of 1937, linking members of the ILP, the Communist Party and Sir Stafford Cripps' Socialist League, and another the Gollancz Left Book Club movement which won anti-fascist sympathisers among the middle class. But it was not until late in 1937 that the *Daily Herald*, which had persisted in crediting Hitler with good intentions, took up a half-hearted posture of opposition to the non-intervention policy.

"During these vital years the hysteria created by the Press made it practically impossible to obtain a dispassionate hearing for the proposal that Britain and the Soviet Union should consider the question of joint action against Hitler," wrote William Rust. "In these years the Press Lords were very fond of the Nazis primarily because they regarded them as a means of crushing Communism, which Fleet Street hated much more than it did Fascism."

In preparation of the Munich disaster many British newspapers established close relations with the Nazis and played Hitler's game. Former *Times* editor Wickham Steed revealed in his book *The Press*, published in 1938, that Hitler, "fortified by the Munich Agreement and by the scrap of paper which he and the British Prime Minister had signed . . . placed his veto on the return to office of three prominent British public men [Eden, Churchill and Duff Cooper]. When this news was broadcast on the evening of Sunday, October 9, the whole nation was moved to wrath. Of the depth of this wrath hardly a hint was given the next morning in the leading British newspapers, some of which were almost apologetic. Inquiry into this humiliating behaviour on the part of our 'free press' elicited the information that certain large advertising agents had warned journals for which they provided much revenue that advertisements would be withheld from them should they play up the international crisis and cause an alarm that was bad for trade."*

The "There will be no war" optimism—expressed in the *Daily Express* banner headline—was carefully orchestrated by the Foreign Secretary Sir Samuel Hoare (later Lord Templewood). In his book *Press, Parliament and People*, former *Daily Herald* editor Francis Williams has described how Hoare arranged confidential meetings with proprietors and editors, and the mild reception given by the Cabinet to the German demand that no news or opinions unwelcome to Hitler should appear in the British press. Francis Williams resigned the editorship after his leading articles had been cut by the chairman of the commercial board of editors without consultation because he felt they might "drive away some advertising support".

The German Ambassador in London, Von Dirksen, wrote to the editor of the *Daily Mail*, on May 6, 1938, thanking him very sincerely for "his courtesy" in submitting before publication an article by Lord Rothermere which said among other things that "Czechoslovakia is not of the remotest concern to us". Lord Kemsley offered, when he visited Hitler in the summer of 1939, to give space to the Nazi viewpoint

* Steed, op. cit., p. 249.

in his newspapers and Von Dirksen reported him to have spoken "with pleasure of his conversations with Reichsleiter Rosenberg. He was strongly impressed by the personality of Reichminister Goebbels, whom he thought a clever and broadly educated man."

Press lords and their editors were prominent in the pro-Nazi Cliveden Set of aristocrats, politicians and financiers, and it was under its influence that *The Times* opened the way to the betrayal of Czechoslovakia with its "suggestion" that the country's so-called Sudeten areas should be ceded to Germany. The Cliveden Set had been given its name and thrust into the limelight through its exposure in the bold privateer journal *The Week*, run by *Daily Worker* foreign editor and former *Times* man Claud Cockburn. Visitors to Cliveden House, Lady Astor's Buckinghamshire residence, included the Hon. J. J. Astor, chairman of *The Times*, his editor Geoffrey Dawson, the editor of Lord Astor's newspaper the *Observer*, Mr. J. L. Garvin, as well as four or five Ministers. Public opinion at large, however, would not quickly or easily accept that a government elected in the "peace through collective security" general election of 1935, was deliberately swinging away from this policy towards co-operation with fascist Germany and Italy.

When Chamberlain flew to Berchtesgarden, Hitler's mountain retreat, and talked with him for three hours, the Tory newspapers proclaimed that the Nazi army was ready to strike (long proved conclusively to have been the opposite of the truth) and that only the concession of Hitler's demands could stave off war and give Britain time to complete its defences. "Good luck, Chamberlain", said the *Daily Herald*—taking a position well to the right of the Liberal *News Chronicle*, which warned of the possible fatal consequences of Chamberlain's visit, as did Winston Churchill leading a small Tory group which thought the Chamberlain gamble too risky. On September 22, Chamberlain flew to see Hitler again, met him at Godesberg, and four days later, on the day before Parliament was recalled, made his paralysing speech to the nation about "a quarrel in a faraway country, between people of whom we know nothing". The National Council of Labour put out strong verbal condemnations of Chamberlain, and some 2,500 protest meetings were held all over the country in the following weekend. But at the crunch, when the Tory Premier announced in the Commons on September 28 his decision to fly to Munich to conclude an agreement with Hitler, Mussolini and Daladier over the dismembered body of Czechoslovakia, not one protest came from Conservative, Labour, Liberal, or ILP members, only William Gallacher, the Communist MP, rising to denounce the sellout.

Francis Williams, writing of the government's press-nobbling activities, recalled later that several ministers "made contacts with newspaper proprietors at various times to persuade them that outspoken criticism of Hitler's policy or of the Nazi atrocities against the Jews would be against the national interest. Many of these approaches were, unfortunately, successful." Editors who spoke out forthrightly in their leading articles, were apt "to find themselves involved in long arguments with their proprietors, who had just received the most confidential information from an important member of the Cabinet that such words just at this moment would do the gravest harm to negotiations then proceeding, as a result of which things would shortly take a turn for the better".

The various parts played in the Munich affair by *The Times* under Dawson and his associate editor Barrington Ward, by the *Observer* under Garvin, and by the mass circulation dailies have been well probed and established. Another responsibility, however, has emerged less clearly from the postwar histories and biographies. This was the failure by the left as a whole to mobilise and unite at an early enough stage forces that were potentially strong enough to have averted the disaster. To a very large extent, it was the sheer fog generated and cast over events by a poisoned press that prevented a practical anti-war coalition emerging out of the many-sided anti-fascism of the later thirties.

Press assets on the Labour side included, in addition to the *Daily Worker*, the Sunday *Reynolds News* which the Co-operative movement had acquired and was developing into a lively journal, advocating unity on a broad democratic basis, the left Labour weekly *Tribune* launched on January 1, 1937, to speak for the Socialist League headed by Sir Stafford Cripps, and some vigorously anti-fascist trade union journals.

In addition, as misgivings about appeasement mounted also in ruling-class circles, before its deadly climax at Munich, the Liberal *News Chronicle* and *Manchester Guardian* opened their columns wider to the opposition views. And in the Munich days, papers ranging from the Tory *Daily Telegraph* and *Yorkshire Post* to the *Daily Mirror* filled many columns with letters expressing readers' protest and indignation.

The United Front movement initiated by the Communist Party and the *Daily Worker* in March 1933 gained steadily growing support for joint action to remove Chamberlain and oppose the fascist dictators. It was stimulated further by the resignation of Foreign Secretary Eden in February 1938. It took its broadest shape in the United Peace Alliance movement launched by *Reynolds News*; the alliance was to include Liberals, Tory critics of Chamberlain, and supporters of the League of Nations. The *News Chronicle* took up the campaign, in which a number of local organisations were formed, mainly of Labour lefts of middle-class background, Liberals, and supporters of the League of Nations Union and the pacifist National Peace Council.

At Easter the conference of the Co-operative Party voted for the peace alliance. The national executive of the Labour Party, however, put pressure on its local parties to "liquidate the new organisation", arguing that Labour should concentrate its efforts on winning a majority at the next election.

The annual Co-operative Congress threw out the plan in June. The 4,492,000 votes cast against it (to 2,382,000 in favour) were made up partly by Co-operative members traditionally opposed to any political action by the movement and partly by Co-operative supporters of the official Labour line. The National Union of Railwaymen voted against it at its conference in the same month. The *Reynolds* scheme petered out just before Munich.

That autumn there was no Labour Party conference at which Labour reactions to the Munich betrayal could be expressed. The TUC met in September, before the decisive days of the crisis. But the large majority by which it supported the demand of the National Council of Labour that Britain stand firmly by Czechoslovakia showed the power that could have been rallied to stop Chamberlain's final act of treachery.

When the Popular Front idea was revived *after* Munich it was in a considerably less popular aspect, dominated by the idiosyncratic personality of Sir Stafford Cripps. He presented the scheme primarily as an electoral manœuvre in which a large part of the Labour Programme would have to be put on one side temporarily. This laid him wide open to arguments—always powerful with a movement that had spent most of its life first escaping from the embrace of Liberalism and then piecing itself together after the apostasy of MacDonald and Co—that he was "surrendering Socialism". Cripps and three other Labour MPs were expelled and some local parties were disaffiliated for disloyalty. After the Whitsun conference of the party had rejected Cripps' appeal, and the Co-operative Party in April had reversed its vote of the previous year, this largely barren affair of personalities in the leading ranks came to nothing.

It is a story of great possibilities never realised and for this failure the big-circulation press which for a decade camouflaged the vital issues facing Britain was the main instrument. Significantly, it was in the Munich year that there arose the widest general debate on freedom of the press and democratic rights which had been held since the previous century.

After many cases in which the Official Secrets Act of 1920 had been employed to harass opponents of the government, over 800 delegates attended a conference called by the National Union of Journalists and the National Council of Civil Liberties. In a message, H. G. Wells said that interference with free discussion had "tainted British news with a flavour of untrustworthiness far more detrimental to our reputation abroad than the stark lying and falsification of the German propaganda". A Bill was unsuccessfully introduced (by Dr. Dingle Foot) to curb the use of the Act for any purpose other than anti-espionage, after several Tory MPs had demanded increased government powers to deal with "press licence".

Munich and its aftermath exposed the extreme vulnerability of the press at law more clearly than did any other episode before or since in this century. Legal freedom of the press at the best of times has remained in this century the most dubiously established of all the democratic rights. It was defined by the eminent constitutional lawyer, Blackstone, as solely consisting in "laying no previous restraint upon publication and not in freedom from censure for criminal matters when published". In normal circumstances the principal operative curbs are the civil law of libel and the law on contempt of court. But prosecutors still have available to them the unrepealed laws of criminal and seditious libel, and even the blasphemy laws. Numerous statutes provide endless scope for striking at anyone judged by a court to be acting in such a way as to stir up class against class, cause a breach of the peace, or bring Her Majesty's Government into contempt.*

* The 1797 Incitement to Mutiny Act was used in 1912 to convict Tom Mann and the printers and publishers of *The Syndicalist* for urging soldiers to disobey their officers if they were ordered to fire on strikers.

In the Cliveden programme, an assault on liberties at home was the reverse side of the Munich policy. One of the covers it used was the alleged need for "national service" in the crisis; calls came in 1938 and 1939 for sacrifices from the trade unions and the unemployed, and applicants for national assistance were pressured to enter government training camps. *Reynolds News* revealed in October 1938 that Chamberlain's close adviser Horace Wilson was to supervise government plans for a National Register and the creation of a strict and all-embracing press censorship. The Newspaper Proprietors Association drew up the plans for its self-regimentation in the event of war and the government prepared in secret the establishment of a Ministry of Information. News-reels featuring Nazi aggression were censored, as were statements made in them by Wickham Steed and the *News Chronicle* commentator A. J. Cummings. In France and other European countries, governments, whose leading figures were many of them soon to serve as Nazi quislings, were carrying out similar measures against the press, before and after Munich.

In Britain this anti-democratic turn led directly to the suppression of the *Daily Worker* in 1941 and to a struggle that will always rank among the top engagements in the battle for press freedom by any definition.

By the outbreak of war the *Daily Worker* had taken large strides forward in its nine years; at first a journal of comment mainly on day-late news and of propaganda blasts against the National Government, it had won wide acceptance by 1939 as a real newspaper and became the recognised pacemaker for the left and anti-fascism. By the time of its seventh birthday celebration held amid the struggle to defend democracy in Spain, dismissive attitudes towards the paper that were common in its early days were vanishing, as its ceaseless challenging and campaigning—for the unemployed, for the defence of Dimitrov in the Reichstag Fire Trial frame-up, and above all for Spain—brought it new friends. Sales in pre-war years never rose above 50,000, except on Saturday when they often reached 100,000. But the paper increased its size and developed a features coverage and some of the services provided by the big dailies; it also acquired its own printing machine bought with contributions to the Fighting Fund on which its continued existence came to depend totally.

To the last, the paper, with its "Chamberlain Must Go" slogan sprouting on walls and hoardings all over the country, fought to avert war. In March 1939 it caused a sensation with its call for the formation of a new government headed by the Labour leader Clement Attlee, the Liberal Lord Sinclair and Winston Churchill. "Every day's delay in removing Chamberlain is dangerous and criminal," it wrote. "The house is burning, the Fire Brigades are in league with the fire-raisers who are only interested in drawing the insurance—which for them means the establishment of Fascism in Britain."

All summer the government conducted its feint of negotiating for an Anglo-Soviet military pact. But in August Chamberlain's chickens came home to roost when the Soviet Union and Germany signed their non-aggression pact; on September 1, Hitler invaded Poland and two days later Britain and France were at war with Germany. The phoney war with fascism succeeded the phoney negotiations with the Kremlin.

In the spring the phoney war turned real. At Dunkirk Britain faced its gravest-ever political and military crisis. New defence regulations—2D for suppressing newspapers and 18B providing for imprisonment without trial—were hurriedly approved by Parliament. Chamberlain went, but Tory anti-Soviet diehards filled the new coalition Cabinet headed by Churchill. On July 10 the Home Secretary threatened to suppress the *Daily Worker* unless it stopped its "systematic publication of matter calculated to foment opposition to the war". Action was threatened under 2D which empowered the suppression of newspapers not, as under the initial 2C, after trial, but without trial. Luftwaffe attacks which began in August found Britain without proper air-raid shelters and the 2,000 dead and seriously injured in the mass raid on London on Saturday, September 7, showed up the miserable inadequacy of the protection provided. Herbert Morrison, who succeeded Tory Sir John Anderson as Home Secretary, denounced as fifth columnists all those who like the *Daily Worker* advocated the construction of deep shelters. Blitzed itself, the paper got out its Saturday, September 21, issue with linotypes turned by hand and pocket torches as the sole working light.

Next month the paper was excluded from the press table at the Southport TUC on the ground of a successful libel action which TUC chairman Sir Walter Citrine had taken against it earlier. Daily front-page news in the paper as the year ended amid devastating air attacks was the growth of the movement for a People's Convention which would secure a "peace neither of conquest nor capitulation". An enormous London rally held by this movement on January 12 was attended by 2,234 delegates representing 1,284,000 workers. The event sealed the paper's fate. On January 21, the Newspaper Proprietors' Association and the editors of all the national newspapers were called together by Morrison and told that the *Daily Worker* was being suppressed later in the day. The deed was carried out by a large cohort of police in the afternoon and the paper's Glasgow-printed Scottish edition suffered the same fate.

The suppression was the thin end of a broad wedge; a wider attack on press freedom now developed. The threat of action against them under 2D hovered over all editors. Persistently, unofficial proposals were mooted for the closing down of all newspapers except *The Times*, the *Daily Herald* and the *Daily Express*. In a Commons debate on the suppression of the *Worker*, Aneurin Bevan said that the *Daily Mirror* and the *Sunday Pictorial* had both been threatened on account of their "subversive" attitude. All they had really done, he said, was to demand the removal from the Cabinet of some of the ministers most compromised by their part in Munich. Bevan attacked in particular the government's cowardly action in securing the connivance of the other newspapers in suppressing the paper that "represented almost the sole opposition". Defending his action, Morrison said that the paper had not succeeded in undermining morale, but he was apprehensive that it might. He never explained why, if that were so, he had suppressed it at a moment's notice, instead of resorting to the slower but more just machinery of trial and proof required by Regulation 2C. A supporter of the suppression, Labour MP G. R. Strauss, who only disapproved of the method by which it had been carried out, wrote later that the action "may or may not have weakened the influence of the Communist Party, but it certainly had a most serious effect on the independence of the Press as a whole". In a pamphlet issued in this year, the Press Freedom Committee of the National Council for Civil Liberties warned that "if Britain is to remain free, the Press, too, must remain free—restrictions upon the freedom of expression are a prelude to national disaster".

For the next nineteen months, William Rust's history relates, the paper, "temporarily disembodied though it might be, grew in potency and influence with every week that passed". The fight against the ban made the *Daily Worker* a household word throughout the labour movement, and far outside it. The second period of the ban—that after the Nazi invasion of the Soviet Union on June 22, 1941—was longer than the first. For fourteen months after the character of the war had been transformed, the ban was obdurately maintained. *Reynolds News* contrasted Morrison's swift action with the government's slowness in measures to "prevent the heart being burned out of London . . . and in applying compulsory powers to property". Morrison's wish to intimidate the press as a whole was his chief motive, it said. There was much talk at government levels in these months of the desirability of a drastic reduction in the number of national newspapers, even of the merging of all papers in a single sheet. On February 1941, questions were put in the House, and not answered, about Cabinet threats privately to the *Daily Mirror* and the *Sunday Pictorial*, which were strongly criticising the conduct of the war. The *Mirror* had been the only newspaper represented at Morrison's meeting with editors to criticise the suppression of the *Worker* as a dangerous precedent.

This was the year in which uncertainty and confusion about the future were at their height. The news blackout made all newspapers particularly suspect to their readers and the public even started to turn to the German radio for news. In April the *Daily Worker*'s offices in Cayton Street were destroyed in an air raid, together with its new rotary press, irreplaceable in wartime. The outlook for its reappearance had never been blacker. A campaign had already been begun, however, that was to grow into the biggest and most socially extensive press freedom battle fought since the grand engagements of a century earlier. Already by the big turn in the war in June 1941 with Hitler's attack on the Soviet Union the movement against the ban embraced over a million trade union members. This figure rose to two million when the engineers, shock force of war production, added their million by a 43–4 vote at their national committee.

Powerful forces, having got their chief opponent in the press down, were determined not to let it rise again. There were old scores to pay off—and the Tory leaders were already looking ahead to the postwar when their basic line of organising an anti-Soviet and anti-Socialism front in Europe could be resumed. So the struggle for reappearance proved most bitter and protracted; the question became a top item on all the issues for which the war was being fought. In August, as the support mounted, Rust announced that the editorial board was so confident that the raising of the ban could not be long avoided that the necessary arrangements had been made for printing the paper. Formerly hostile newspapers, led by the *News Chronicle* and the *Manchester Guardian*, now supported the campaign, and the question of the *Daily Worker* began to merge with all the fundamental questions of the war—production, national unity, the Second Front, and the kind of Britain that must follow the war.

It was over the Second Front that all the dark forces concentrated their powers of sabotage, aided by the ignorance and prejudices created by two decades of misinformation in the media about the Soviet ally,* Lord Halifax, the man of Munich who was now British ambassador in Washington declared categorically that there would be no Second Front in 1941, giving Nazis the green light for their drive on Moscow. Stupendous shocks came in the following year: Pearl Harbour, Malaya, Singapore.

The *Daily Mirror* was warned that it might be suppressed under 2D —ostensibly because of a bitter cartoon on shipping losses, but in reality because the paper and its stable companion, the *Sunday Pictorial*, were employing their mammoth circulations to put over a generally left critical line and sharply campaigning for the Second Front.

On March 21, the lift-the-ban campaign held its greatest rally, with 1,903 delegates from 645 London organisations and 177 factories packing the Central Hall. A message sent by the elder statesman of Liberalism, Lloyd George, said the continued suppression was "an act of stupid and wanton partisan spite and of sheer despotism. No wonder there still remains a trace of suspicion in Russia as to the wholehearted genuineness of our co-operation." On May 28 the Labour Party conference, in the teeth of an executive recommendation, voted for the ending of the ban by 1,244,000 to 1,231,000 votes.

Still the battle was not won. In the summer the Nazis mounted their offensive carrying them to the Volga and the Caucasus after Rommel had forged ahead in North Africa, Tobruk falling to his army in June. Not until this gravest moment of the war was the movement against Morrison's ban able to break through. After a large demonstration in

---

* One of the thirty-two numbers of a *Commentary on Current Political Events* produced by *Daily Worker* staff during the period of the ban asked: "What is a military expert? Answer: a man who, having predicted that the Maginot Line was invincible and that the Red Army would collapse in two weeks, now expects you to take his word that a Second Front in Europe is impossible" (No. 18, December 3, 1941).

London on Sunday, July 26 to demand the opening of the Second Front, 1,500 delegates from 350 constituencies went to the Commons in one of the most remarkable mass lobbyings ever seen there. They took copies of the *Daily* ——, a four-page specimen newspaper showing what the *Daily Worker* would have been like if it had appeared on the previous day. The leading article, entitled "Stalingrad", asked: "How long will it take until both people and Government fully realise that the fate of Britain is being decided upon the banks of the Don and the Volga?"

There was not now much hope for Mr. Morrison. The Co-operative Congress, with its 8,700,000 membership, had condemned the use of 2D and demanded its annulment. Trade union support for the lifting of the ban now embraced over fifty national unions, with a membership approaching three million. Out of the five big unions, Morrison could now only count on two, the general labour unions. The Scottish Trades Union Congress had passed a resolution against the ban. And the TUC itself, due to meet at Blackpool in the second half of September was certain to carry a lift-the-ban resolution by a much greater majority than the Labour Party conference. The ban was lifted on Wednesday, August 26, and the paper appeared again a fortnight later.

The rest of its wartime history belongs to the struggle to turn the tide of the war that was linked everywhere with the Stalingrad defeat of the Nazis in the winter of 1942–3. The paper worked by common admission more effectively than any other to raise production, miners' leader Will Lawther summing up this situation in the often quoted words "the redder the pit the greater the output". In these years, too, the paper's fight against suppression could take aid and comfort in a certain spread of grass-roots journalism arising out of the anti-fascist spirit and made possible by the special wartime conditions. Newsprint rationing and the reduction in advertising partially reduced the normal advantage held by the big papers. After the establishment in 1936 of the progressive monthly *Leiston Leader*★ in Suffolk, several independent journals, mostly duplicated but some printed, sprang up in many centres throughout East Anglia and the south Midlands. Noteworthy among them was also the *Peterborough Leader*, which began as a mimeographed local bulletin of the Communist Party in 1939 and grew into an effective organiser of political struggle, filling a

★ Still appearing regularly in 1973—an all-time record for a local duplicated paper.

particularly important role during the banning of the *Daily Worker*. By the end of the war it was a brightly produced printed journal with a healthy advertisement revenue, a circulation of 3,500, and a profit to show.*

Such healthy developments in the localities were paralleled in the workshops by the growth and popularity enjoyed by a number of rank-and-file workers' papers such as the *Metalworker* and the *New Propeller*. This chapter in press history demonstrated the abiding strength of a do-it-yourself newspaper tradition that went back to the Radical penny papers and showed its capacity to reassert itself under favourable conditions.

All the built-up frustrations over the conduct of the war, all the distrust for politicians who had never repented Munich, all the memories of disappointment and betrayal suffered since 1926 vented themselves in the general election held eleven weeks after the end of the war. It was a soldier who, catching the mood of the hour, gave the *Daily Worker* its celebrated eve-of-poll slogan: "Vote as Red as You Can." Churchill did not get his confidently expected repetition of the Khaki Election of 1919—but was engulfed together with Toryism in a new 1906. The Labour Party swept to power with an absolute majority, gaining 390 seats to the Tories' 211, with Liberals and Independents falling to ten each, and the Communists increasing their representation to two. Typical of the euphoria of the hour were the first words spoken by Mr. Attlee as premier-elect, after the declaration of the poll: "We are facing a new era . . . we are on the eve of a great advance of the human race."

The *Daily Worker* was ready with plans to become a large-circulation paper of the labour movement—aiming at sales of half a million—which every year since Lansbury's time had proved to be indispensable to the advance of which Mr. Attlee spoke. The plans were endorsed by a meeting at which twelve national trade union executives were represented on May 12 just after VE-Day. They included the transfer of the ownership to a Co-operative Society, the People's Press Printing Society,† which formally took over at the paper's

* The driving force behind the paper was the remarkable Will Granger, schoolteacher and amateur astronomer of note, who took advantage of a regulation allocating a supply of newsprint to any proprietor who could prove publication in or before 1940.

†Within six months the society reached a membership of over 14,000, including 266 trade union and 45 co-operative organisations and raised over £100,000 of its initial £150,000 share capital target.

sixteenth birthday celebration on January 6 in the Albert Hall in the following year.

The circulation rose as preparations went ahead to publish in a larger building in Farringdon Road on an advanced rotary machine capable of the much larger daily print that was now envisaged. But building difficulties and the great freeze-up of the winter of 1947 caused delays and it was not until November 1, 1948, that the enlarged paper (four broadsheet pages, six on Saturdays) could appear. By then the cold war was well under way. Also, the costs stranglehold on all newspaper production which is unsupported by big advertisement revenues was closing in on the paper's ambitious plans. It was announced that the new paper would cost 1½d. instead of 1d. and a special fund-raising effort had to be made in the summer of 1948 to bring capital resources up to the needed £250,000. Weekly revenue from advertisements had fallen by two-thirds in two years as the pre-war pattern of boycott, partially broken in wartime, set in strongly again.

The first copies from the new press were handed out to a welcoming demonstration of 20,000 people in nearby Clerkenwell Green, to be auctioned for £45 apiece in this famed old rallying place of Radicals and Chartists. The next day a telegram arrived at the paper from Tolpuddle, signed by George Loveless, a descendant of one of the Martyrs of 1834. It read: "Today is a proud day for us all. This is what our ancestors fought for. Long live the People's Paper."

The larger paper achieved in its first year daily sales of between 100,000 and 110,000. This fell short of the sales of the *Daily Herald* in 1919–22. Yet it marked for three reasons the highest point reached by working-class journalism. The popular struggles that had built up the paper, rescued it from suppression and launched it as a fully-fledged national newspaper after the war, had been on a scale without precedent since Chartism. It had become the first and only daily paper owned by its readers and owing nothing to wealthy subscribers. And it was the first all-round newspaper projection of the linked three causes of trade unionism, Socialist ideas, and defence of peace and internationalism.

IO

Monopoly or Democracy?

"Look how the whole capitalist world is stretching out long arms towards the barbarous world and grabbing and clutching in eager competition at countries whose inhabitants don't want them. . . . It is for the opening of fresh markets to take in all the fresh profit-producing wealth which is growing greater and greater every day . . . and I say this is an irresistible instinct on the part of the capitalists, an impulse like hunger, and I believe that it can only be met by another hunger, the hunger for freedom and fair play for all, both people and peoples. Anything less than that the capitalist power will brush aside."

WILLIAM MORRIS, in the May Day Special of *Justice, 1896*

"The reorganisation of the press and mass media, and the dissolution of the press monopolies would ensure the expression of a variety of views, and the transmission of news without distortion for commercial ends. Newspapers and periodicals would be owned and controlled by political parties and social groups, trade unions, co-operatives and professional associations, organisations for women, youth and those catering for particular fields of literature, art and sport. . . . "

The British Road to Socialism, 1968

ONCE AGAIN, fundamental questions of freedom are raised by the postwar press story, as they were at the start of this record. In three decades, monopoly ownership has strengthened its grip, despite the verdict furnished against it by its own record in the general strike, the rise of fascism, Tory reaction in the thirties, Munich and war. Today it is a matter, more urgent than before, not simply of reforming one undemocratic institution, but of the entire fate of traditional rights and liberties and of the further progress of the labour movement which principally won and sustained them.

The press monopolies have to be dissolved. A massive democratic access to all the media must replace their existing domination by big business, sweeping away the tight network of restrictions on genuine popular participation in debate and decision making.

Today's press empires lay claim to powers truly totalitarian, however much the claim is masked by talk of freedom and democracy. Yet if their hunger for dominion over people's minds has grown ravenous, so too, the other hunger for freedom and fair play for all, of which William Morris spoke in the last article from his pen, has also grown stronger and its manifestations more broad and varied.

In Britain, the struggle between the two nations, whose reflection in newspaper developments we have followed, proceeded after 1945 in conditions, domestic and world-wide, transformed by the defeat of fascism, by the advance of social and national liberation in Asia, Europe and Africa, by the changed balance of forces between the two world systems, and by the specific variety of the circumstances facing each people and country—a variety long envisaged in theory but only now revealing itself in all its manifold richness.

Simultaneously there began the era of truly mass communications, intensive in each country and extensive to the whole world, in which all events impinged on man's consciousness everywhere. In the conflict between the systems, the battle of ideas took on a newly crucial importance. Advances both in physical transport and in printing, radio, electronic and computer technology supplied the means for this transformation. The older media of newspapers and advertising, radio and cinema, joined after the war by television, together grew into the vast communications industry, which rests at one end on the tiny transistor and at the other on the giant space rockets that place its satellite relay-points in orbit round the earth.

All the media came more and more to feed each other as well as their immediate customers, and the industry in its totality to maintain a saturating stream of sights, sounds, ideas and emotions. The word communications, implying a two-way exchange, concealed the one-way nature of the traffic—from governors to governed—which the industry mainly carried.

In the advanced capitalist countries an explosive expansion of the media, dependent on high technology, large investments and state aid, occurred chiefly as part of the normal drive into new fields of profit. But the field worked by the media does not produce wheat or meat, minerals or oil; the "product" does not consist of tangible goods or services, but belongs to the realm of mental, emotional and spiritual activity. The media invade and partly subjugate this field. The *commodities* into which they translate the alienated thinking and affective energies of man are flawed in the process, and must always incurably remain so while this type of production continues.

In the press, the still reigning theory of freedom clung in the postwar more firmly to the conception of news and comment as commodities, that is, goods supplying consumer needs as determined by the laws of the market. The more the media were orchestrated to serve monopoly capitalism, the more insistently they sought to hide behind the commodity freedom camouflage. That was one contradiction. The other was the widening uncrossable gap between this conception of freedom and the Radical, Chartist and labour movement tradition of freedom as a form of representation. In the late sixties and seventies of the present century, the nineteenth-century *Times* view that the freedom of the press entirely resides in its dependence on commerce came under growing fire. Press lords, feeling the draught from public questioning of their despotic powers, tended to curb the new-rich boasting and megalomaniac utterance which had always been their mark, and to proclaim the entire independence allegedly allowed to their hired editors. New times, new disguises, at which we must look more closely.

First, we should look at the main changes that arose from the overall crisis of Britain as an imperialist centre, and the conflicts at home which this crisis conditioned, because these influenced the development of the news media profoundly. The postwar brought a gradual forced dismantling of the old political empire (on which, as Ernest Jones said, the sun never set and the blood never dried) and its replacement by neo-colonialism employing finance, fraud and corruption rather than military means. Labour and Tory governments in succession officered a complex struggle to do three things: preserve the imperialist substance, fight Socialism and the national liberation movements, and compete with American and other rival imperialist centres. By the nineteen-seventies all three efforts were increasingly breaking down and the attempt to push on with them merely deepened Britain's economic and social crisis. This attempt also proved to be the built-in self-destruction mechanism that brought down the Labour governments of 1945 and 1966, although these had initially enjoyed, in the one case overwhelming, and in the other fully adequate, electoral support.

By the seventies the various mini-ideologies of the welfare state, affluent state, classless Britain, mixed economy and "technological revolution", which had concealed the bankruptcy of Toryism and the betrayals of right-wing Labour, littered the ground with their corpses, and lingered mainly as bad smells. The ten million strong trade union movement had shifted toward militancy over pay and conditions, and steadily leftward in its political ideas. Some of the largest unions, representing mainly unskilled and semi-skilled workers, set the pace, as had happened after the class-peace slumbers of the eighteen-eighties. They faced a broad employers' offensive that took its drive from the big merger developments of the sixties and an ever-accelerating concentration of capital. Their resistance, together with a growing recognition throughout the movement of the need for a basic social change and sharpening debates on how it could be carried through, was reflected strongly at the 1973 TUC and Labour Party conferences. It motivated votes for extended nationalisation, and a rebellion against the Common Market membership into which the British people had been bulldozed two years earlier.

What happened in the media became in the postwar years increasingly important and sometimes decisive—in the controversy over nuclear weapons and policy, in the peace and liberation movements over Vietnam, the Middle East and Africa, in the fight against racism and apartheid, in the long effort to substitute détente in Europe for the cold war mania and delusion, and, most obviously, in each round of parliamentary and local elections and in every wage claim and industrial action. Moreover, all the great international conflicts of the postwar years bore a politico-military character—Berlin, Suez, Cuba, Vietnam, and the Middle East wars of 1967 and 1973—in which world-wide movements of opinion, reflecting the various interests involved, and formed by the media, mingled inextricably with the battlefield results or strategic military calculations.

In these years, too, profound changes within the world Socialist and working-class movement also enhanced the role of all the mass communications. The exposures, starting in the mid-fifties, of the distortions of Socialist practice and theory in the countries where the working class held power, opened floodgates to a painful, difficult and continuing new assessment of Socialist achievements and a rethinking of Marxism, and in particular of the relationship between Socialism, democracy and national liberation.

This could be no internal dispute on the revolutionary and

anti-imperialist side. The capitalist-controlled media joined hungrily in the fray, eager to profit by the differences and divisions in the vast array of forces opposing them. They sought to save the dying system of production for profit in its hideous last phase by fostering fear and hatred of the countries engaged in real social change. Crises and upheavals in Hungary, Poland and Czechoslovakia, and the differences between the leading parties and the governments of the Soviet Union and China all in different ways fed and heightened the battle of ideas between capitalism and Socialism, imperialism and human progress.

There was another tributary to this quickened tempo. The monopolist drive altered and partly radicalised the thinking of people well outside the old formations of the labour and working-class movement, creating the new lefts, new dissents, and new causes that were expressed in the "underground journalism" starting in the sixties with its guerilla sniping at all Establishment communications. The media in turn conducted an unending struggle to canalise these ideas and feelings into harmless courses, to confuse young people in particular, and to divert them away from positive action to end capitalism.

Around communications and their domination by Toryism and the City repeated squalls occurred. All blew themselves out and real public access to the media and participation in their control was less in 1974 than in 1945. For this the right-wing labour and trade union establishment must bear a great share of responsibility, since it failed to seize numerous openings for a democratic advance in this field.

The 1973 annual conference of the Labour Party, which set itself tasks that, if carried through, could not but lead to the biggest confrontation with Toryism and the money power since the 1926 general strike, took no decision for real action against commanding heights of the press.

The 75,000-word draft programme produced before the 1973 Labour Party conference merely recorded that the importance of the media was "curiously underplayed". It pointed to the growth of interlocking ownerships in fewer and fewer hands and said that it was important to prevent this. "Market distortions", it declared, "impose a form of censorship that is fundamentally no different from the government censorship that we all abhor." But it added that more work on the subject would be necessary "before we are in a position to propose any definite solutions to the problems in this complex field". On the press the document said that true independence could only come about "if there is freedom from government control and other forms of censorship; freedom from financial dependence upon limited interest groups and from the danger of takeover; and freedom of the editorial function from control by either owner or advertiser. Internal democracy, in fact, is one of the strongest possible guarantees of a democratic and responsive press". But in the "Priorities for Action" listed in the programme, the media were not mentioned.

Arguments still holding the field are that the condition of the press has not so far prevented Labour from winning elections and will not do so in the future; that the incontestable unfairness of the system to the labour and trade union movement can be surmounted; and that under no alternative arrangements could the press escape losing its freedom. This was basically the attitude taken by Labour leader Harold Wilson in a television interview with *Times* editor William Rees-Mogg on October 16, 1972. Mr. Wilson complained then that "the press is overwhelmingly anti-Labour and will go to almost any lengths to discredit Labour and discredit Labour's leader". This was in reply to a demand that *The Times* had made, in connection with the Labour leader's declared opposition to British entry into the Common Market on the negotiated terms, that Mr. Wilson must never be allowed to become Prime Minister again. Mr. Rees-Mogg defended this high-and-mighty intrusion by declaring that it had been "a painful and important judgement, but a judgement which has to be made by a newspaper which is trying to review events". Mr. Wilson, asked whether any specific action on the press could be expected from a future Labour government, replied that the matter was one not for governments but for "self-improvement within the press". Further questioned about people in the Labour Party who argue that "in a world where newspapers have become big business owned by big corporations it is naïve to expect them to be anything other than betraying an anti-Labour bias" he said merely that he would like to see more newspapers conducted on the basis of a trust, or jointly edited.

Yet the evaded question was not simply one of an isolated abuse that could be remedied by management changes or by calling the bold bad barons of Fleet Street to repentance. It concerned the command of daily print by a handful of ultra-wealthy men. They submit themselves to no election, acknowledge no control or responsibility, and stand completely outside British democracy. They can pillory shop stewards and militant workers with impunity, provide a platform for racist incitement, slander immigrants, students and council tenants, and under the cover of talk about the national interest systematically blacken active trade unionists on the one hand and glorify right-wing Labour leaders on the other, and suppress and distort the ideas and actions of the Communist movement. They have the absolute command of a press which—to the best of its ability—damages and corrupts hearts and minds to save the profit system.

The Times itself, in a centenary article many years earlier on the abolition of the newspaper stamp duty, had declared that the press had been turned into a predominantly business exercise, in a process that engendered forces greater than the journalists. Two years later Francis Williams wrote that "we are faced to a degree which would have appalled those who fought for Press freedom over the centuries, by monolithic structures that show every sign of becoming more, instead of less, tightly knit and restrictive".

The warning was fulfilled exactly. The kill-sheet of the press jungle battles contained newspaper names by the score. Between 1949 and 1966 seventeen long established daily and Sunday newspapers died and the number of weeklies fell by 88.* The sixties opened with a lengthy slugging match between Thomson, Odhams and the International Publishing Corporation (*Mirror* group) in which the main spoil was the magazine and periodical field in which Odhams held a lush near-monopoly of the mass-sale women's colour gravure magazines.

At the start of the Battle of Long Acre—so called after the site and printing establishment owned by Odhams in the centre of London —five main groups dominated the field. In the order of their capital assets they were the IPC, headed then by Northcliffe's nephew Cecil Harmsworth King, Odhams (*Daily Herald* and the *Sunday People*), Lord Rothermere's Associated Newspapers (*Daily Mail* and *Evening News*), Beaverbrook Newspapers (*Daily Express* and *Evening Standard*) and the *News of the World*. All these groups except Odhams had heavy investments in commercial television, whose inauguration in 1955 had

---

* The main casualties were: morning papers—*News Chronicle* (1960); *Nottingham Journal* (1953); *Daily Despatch* (1955); *Sussex Daily News* (1955); *Birmingham Gazette* (1956); *Daily Herald* (1964); *The Bulletin*, Glasgow (1960); Sundays—*Sunday Chronicle* (1955); *Sunday Graphic* (1960); *Empire News* (1960); *Sunday Dispatch* (1961).

sharpened the competition for advertising revenue and further under-mined any newspaper in the "popular" range with a sale of under two million copies.

At the elbows of the publishing magnates in each succeeding round of this battle sat accountancy wizards from City merchant banks, as the trafficking in papers and magazines now involved a wider range of big business than ever before. Flitting uneasily in the wings were Ministers anxious about possible harm to the democratic image; and in the case of the *Daily Herald*—still tenuously linked to the Labour Party—party leaders Hugh Gaitskell and later Harold Wilson were also active in the corridors of press power. The political correspondent of *The Times* said that the prime minister and other ministers were "gravely considering the implications not only for Britain and its press but for capitalism as a whole".

The *Mirror* group triumphed and the *Daily Herald*, ailing seriously despite a circulation of a million and a half, fell to it as the least welcome item in the victory. It became known as "King's Cross", which the IPC chief continued to shoulder for three years. Then in January 1964, King agreed with the TUC that the *Herald* should be wound up. Finally, the paper that had been sitting like a sickly crowned ghost on the ruins of its labour movement past was exorcised. King paid the TUC £75,000 for its 49 per cent holding of the shares and in the following September started a new paper, the *Sun*, in the printing vacancy created at the Odhams presses. Five years later, an apparently almost extinct newspaper property, after losses on *Herald* and *Sun* had totalled £13 million in eight years, it was acquired by the Australian press buccaneer Rupert Murdoch, on terms that Fleet Street was later to regard as a gift. A revamped tabloid *Sun*, employing a brash new sex, sport and scandal formula, took a 10 per cent bite out of the sales of the IPC's *Mirror* within a year, and quickly went on to the "safe" mark of a three million circulation.

All through the sixties the scale of combat escalated, together with the capital sums involved, in a lethal pattern of closures, amalgama-tions, and pressure on the trade unions which came to a head in the Fleet Street shutdown of September 1971. A dozen years after the carnage of the sixties began, Fleet Street's big circulation league had been reduced to four groups. This Division One of the press accounted for 85 per cent of all national newspaper sales. Its members were the IPC, Murdoch's News International, Beaverbrook Newspapers, and

Harmsworth Newspapers. Cautious expectations began to be expressed in the early seventies that stability might yet reign and further closures be avoided. The "Scottish clearances" of spring 1974, in which Beaverbrook axed its Glasgow printing operation, rapidly dashed such hopes. They showed that none of the conditions making for concentration were slackening, and the top magic circles of press ownership remained permanently at risk of being broken up and rationalised by new amalgamations and shutdowns, in which the value or potential value of city-centre property sites weighed more in the balance than circulations.

Outside these circles, the difficulties of labour movement newspaper publication had become mountainous. Two Royal Commissions examined and buried the problem. The first, in 1948–9, reported tamely that any further decrease in the number of national newspapers would be a matter for concern. The second commission followed the "Bouverie Street assassination" of October 1960, when Associated Newspapers merged the *News Chronicle* and the *Star* overnight with its *Daily Mail* and *Evening News* respectively. In addition to this unceremonious killing off of the last weak survivors of the great Liberal Mohicans, the commission had before it the IPC's absorption of Odhams and the *Herald*.

The first commission had been told to inquire into "finance, control, management and ownership". The second, which every development since the first required to be wider in scope, was in fact narrower; it was instructed to examine "the economic and financial factors affecting production and sale". Its report pronounced that press amalgamations were "in line with developments in other industries and no special exception can be taken to them merely from the economic point of view". It turned down a proposal by the *Daily Worker* that nobody should be allowed to own more than one newspaper and, indeed, opposed any such statutory limit on numbers as "unduly rigid". It proposed only the setting up of a press amalgamations court which would stop mergers if it was satisfied that they were against the public interest. It called for a new Press Council to "scrutinise changes in the ownership, control and growth of Press undertakings and to give wide publicity to information on these matters". No newspaper enterprise, it thought, should control a television company. Rejected by the commission were several schemes advanced to ease the monopolist grip; a national press corporation that would hire out printing time and facilities, a legal limit on the proportion of space that a newspaper might give to advertising, a proposal for a levy on newspapers, based on circulation, the proceeds from which would be returned in the shape of subsidy to help lower-circulation newspapers, and a plan to charge an Excise duty on advertisement revenues exceeding £2 million a year.

The commission said that it considered all these measures to be unpredictable in their results. Some of its members went out of their way to reaffirm the defence of the press as a business, saying that they regarded the above proposals as "divorced from the political realities of a free society". It was wrong to "employ statutory devices which, while nominally applicable to all newspapers, are, in fact, deliberately discriminating against those which are achieving commercial success in the hope of assisting those which are not". Not content with giving this green light for mergers, the commission attempted to turn the real force of the inquiry against the print unions. It said that in some newspapers "it would not be unreasonable to look for a reduction of about one-third in the wages bill" and it recommended measures that the proprietors might take.

These were years of growing financial difficulty and falling circulation for all papers serving the labour and trade union movement. The most widely felt shock was the closing of the *Sunday Citizen* (the renamed *Reynolds News*) in June 1967 by its Co-operative movement managers who saw no remedy in sight for increasing losses. The 28-page farewell issue of the paper that had begun 117 years earlier as *Reynolds Weekly Instructor—A Journal of Democratic Progress and General Intelligence* vividly recalled its own great days of support for working-class struggles, warned Premier Wilson that he was disillusioning Labour's lifelong supporters by his policies in government, and assailed in particular his failure to help the independent press. A message from the weekly *Tribune*, organ of a group of left labour MPs trying to change these policies—which led to disaster at the polls in 1970—called the death of the *Citizen* a sad and serious blow to every section of the movement. Two of the 28 pages were occupied—giving a wry note to all the valedictory tributes—with full-page advertisements for the *Sunday Mirror* ("speaks out for every citizen") and the *News of the World* ("16 million readers every Sunday"), as they competed for the disfranchised *Citizen* readers.

H

Two months earlier, at the height of labour movement anxieties about the newspaper scene, a Press Crisis Teach-in had been held jointly by the already doomed *Sunday Citizen*, the *Morning Star* (which had succeeded the *Daily Worker* in the previous year) and *Tribune*. A joint statement said that "the continuance of democracy depends on the freedom and ability to produce newspapers of varied political opinion and the freedom of the people to buy and read the newspapers of their choice". It proposed a subsidy on newsprint (which accounts for about one-third of newspaper production costs) to be financed within the industry "as a means of helping newspapers which, in present conditions, are likely to cease publication". It also urged that the heavy government spending on advertising should be more fairly distributed through the national press. After the disappearance of the *Citizen*, the *Morning Star* was left as the labour movement's sole representative in the national newspaper field.

In February 1960, when the Tories had been in power for nine years and were to hold it for another four, the *Daily Worker* held a discussion conference which powerfully rallied the left forces, and could take some credit for the left advance registered at that year's TUC and at the succeeding Labour Party conference in Scarborough. The paper campaigned for the implementation of the Scarborough decisions, at the opening of what was to prove a long, bitter—and in 1973, still inconclusively settled—fight involving the entire movement over the claim of the party's parliamentary leaders to a right of veto on conference decisions.

In the forties and fifties, the *Daily Worker* had fought a long defensive engagement on behalf of the whole of the left. It opposed the cold war and fought to avert the threatening nuclear war. It faced up to the anti-Communist onslaught that followed the revelations of the errors and distortions of the Stalin period in the Socialist countries and the Hungarian events of 1956 that cost the British Communist Party almost a quarter of its 32,000 members. It struggled against the tide of right-wing reformist ideas that reached its high-water mark, after Labour's third successive election defeat in 1959, in the efforts of the Gaitskell leadership to remove all vestiges of Socialism from Labour's programme by striking out the Socialist Clause 4 from the party's constitution.

It was in this struggle of a basic democratic character that the paper, whose circulation and financial reserves had been falling steadily, succeeded by tremendous efforts in raising its sales for the first time since the war. Backed by an over-fulfilled £10,000 appeal, it also increased its size. The challenge that it offered coincided with the opening of the greatest of the postwar commotions over freedom of the media. In 1961 the *Daily Worker* submitted evidence both to the Pilkington Committee on Broadcasting and the second Press Commission. It also campaigned with growing support against the refusal of the Independent Television Authority to accept advertisements for the paper, a ban which was still unbroken, however, in 1974. In the sixties the paper fought against the first big push by big business to take Britain into the Common Market, and helped promote the demand for a general election as the Tory government's policies raised unemployment to the highest level since the war. But circulation losses during 1962–3—caused partly by Arctic winter conditions, factory closures and spreading redundancies and short-time working—cancelled the earlier advance in circulation.

As the long night of Tory rule neared its end, the *Daily Worker*'s main emphasis in 1963 was on resistance to State freezing of wages and the struggle to force an election. It warned insistently at the same time that the dominant right-wing approach of the Labour opposition in Parliament was preventing it from offering an impelling alternative to the voters. In the same year it launched a major effort to broaden out its readership, using the opportunity presented by the sale of the *Daily Herald* to the IPC. The Labour government returned in 1964 inherited serious and deep-rooted problems from the thirteen years of Tory rule, including a balance of payments crisis, and like every previous Labour administration was subjected to heavy pressure from British and international financiers. The *Daily Worker* pledged to the country-wide meetings of its Co-operative shareholder owners in 1965 that it would oppose any kind of wage freeze and demanded effective measures to prevent the continuous rise in prices and the cost of living in all fields. The see-saw movement of its circulation, without any strong sustained upward trend, continued in the early sixties, as it contended with rising costs and implacable advertisement bans and boycotts, by government and business. This situation led to an increasingly direct Communist Party involvement in its struggle for sales. Associated with this was a decision in 1966 to employ accumulated reserves to produce a larger (6-page) paper with a wider all-round news and feature coverage—taking a calculated, but grave financial risk—and at the same time to recommend to the readers a change in the name of the paper.

The basic motive for this much discussed change of name was to enable the paper, while continuing to carry editorially the Communist policy, to serve as a forum and platform for all the growing left forces. The change replaced a title felt to have become unnecessarily restrictive, and signalled an intent to widen still further the basis for unity in action of all the left and forward-moving elements in the movement. That the reasoning was well founded was shown in the following years. A steadily wider range of Labour MPs, leading trade unionists, personalities of the peace movement, and leaders of anti-racist and anti-apartheid opinion contributed to its columns. Many trade unions gave the paper their blessing and contributed generously to its funds, the Transport and General Workers Union declaring in 1969 that it was "the only daily paper at present in circulation that fully represents working-class views and supports free trade unionism". By 1973 something like a trade union press freedom front had come into existence, with many annual conference resolutions expressing in this year their support for the *Morning Star*, *Tribune*, and *Labour Weekly*. They included the Engineers, Railmen, and Locomen and mostly they protested against the government refusal to place its informational advertisements in these journals. The Locomen expressed thanks for support given in publicising their union policies and said that the need to develop a newspaper that expressed the views and aspirations of the working class was paramount in a society where the national press was controlled by big business and served its interests. The Transport Workers and the Shopworkers passed similar resolutions.

The *Morning Star*'s first four years, from 1966 to 1970, in which it combined support for the Labour government with sharp criticism of its attempt to solve Britain's economic crisis by traditional capitalist and Tory methods, were hampered by refusal of any relief through government measures for the smaller papers. In 1967 and 1968 it did no better than hold its circulation, which was disadvantaged by a further increase in its price, in January 1968. In this year, with Labour candidates suffering heavy defeats at by-elections, and disillusioned Labour voters abstaining from the polls en masse, the *Morning Star* fought to resist this trend and to win support on the basis of alternative policies to those offered by Mr. Wilson. It warned in 1969 that the government planned to rush through a Bill limiting trade union rights. It carried the first appeal early in the following year for a recall of the TUC to deal with the emergency and for a one-day strike against the Bill—actions that helped to compel the Bill to be shelved.

At this time the *Morning Star* was also taking action to reduce its production costs by switching from production on the large letter-press rotary installed after the war, and never employed to capacity, to a smaller-scale, web-offset printing process of the kind to which many small and a few large newspapers began to turn over in the sixties. The change, leading to a small broadsheet paper of 6 pages, could not be carried out until August 1970. The *Star*'s first struggles to reach financial equilibrium on the new technical basis coincided with dejection in the labour movement following the Tory election victory of 1970 and with the full-scale offensive against living standards which followed. These were difficulties of the sort that every working-class journal had faced, from the 1926 General Srike onward, after political defeats. It was the *Morning Star* that to a great and recognised degree rallied the labour and trade union side, particularly in its support for the miners' victorious 1971 strike, which broke the first wave of the employers' offensive. The lesson which the paper forcefully drew and propagated from this success was that large-scale use of the workers' industrial power was essential to compel reaction to retreat. After two years in the thick of the confrontations that followed, particularly in the dockers' defiance of the Industrial Relations Act, and amid a welter of government, City and property speculator scandals, the paper again struck a rising circulation trend in 1973 and added 1,000 copies to its daily sales.

In this year, too, an enormous collection of over £55,000 in four months, equal to about £1 per head of its purchasing readership, and the largest and most impressive of a series of special appeals for money to help the paper to overcome critical difficulties, further reflected widening support. If the paper's support and prestige grew, so also, however, did all its difficulties of publication. New readers were gained in the late sixties and seventies principally in close-in work by its supporters, and the paper owed its continued existence, more even than any of its press ancestry, to a political movement directly sustaining its drive for circulation. This situation was recognised more explicitly than ever previously when the Communist Party's 1971 National Congress declared the struggle for *Star* circulation to be its No. 1 priority.

The growing support for the *Star*, earned by its campaigning on wide fronts and accompanied by the ending of many Labour and trade union political bans on participation in activities of the left and of its strongest organised force, the Communist Party, had shown by the seventies that cold-war obsessions and anti-Communist prejudices were losing much of the force—so harmful to the working class—which they had exercised for so long. Moreover, anger had built up against the denial of any independent voice in the press and other media to numerous other causes enjoying widening support: women's liberation and equal pay, a new deal for old people, social care and welfare in all its aspects, the immigrants struggling against second-class status and racist laws and attitudes, the defenders of the environment against anti-social development schemes, pollution and threats to public amenity. All these and many more movements could well echo in the early seventies the cry of *The Charter* newspaper of 1839 and ask why they had no newspapers of their own, why they alone were "destitute of this mighty auxiliary".

By the seventies the case for Parliament to act, and for the next Labour government to legislate, to enable parties and social groups to speak with their own voices in the press, had become stronger than ever. Irrefutable evidence existed, out of almost a century of clashes between democracy and the press lord system. The questions arise; what has shielded the system of press monopoly from effective reform and why have not even the smallest measures to curb the press barons' powers and help the financially weaker papers yet been won?

Two factors have already been indicated. One is the tighter links of newspaper proprietorship with a widening spread of interests—banking, property, mining, oil and other activities. Any assault on the press system also challenges this entire league of interests and the governments, Tory or reformist Labour, which do their bidding. The second is the conspiracy between all the main members of the media to help each to choke or divert democratic demands for popular control.

Yet the opposition of press and TV programme company proprietors could scarcely have beaten off change for so long without the wide currency and public credit still enjoyed by the basic commodity freedom legend. As the attacks on press monopoly grew—especially after the takeovers and closures of the sixties—the new doctrine of the independence of editors, which conceals the ownership question, became increasingly fashionable among press chain proprietors. It claimed that decisions taken by editors in line with their judgement of "news values" now determined newspapers' content and policy. Independent editors, through their competition for readers, were held to produce an overall diversity of coverage in which all or most of the chief trends of opinion and main social interests found expression. Associated with this defence there grew up a cult of "investigative", "campaigning" and "in depth" reporting. These were well established practices of competitive journalism. The adoption of the vogue words, however, was intended to brush up the image of the press as an impartial illuminator of every great event and controversy.

Some newspaper investigation of this kind undoubtedly did illuminate the scene. To a degree, the rival press groups in their battling for sales reflected change, mirrored new trends and helped to form them, as they faced the myriad new problems that the epoch of wars and revolutions ceaselessly throws up. Continually fresh leases of life were imparted to the commodity-values press and its legend in this process. Examples of this were the truths about the Vietnam war that forced their way into the papers and other media as the US aggression neared defeat, some exposures of racism and the share of British capital in the crimes of apartheid in South Africa, and various scandals ranging from property speculation and wretched housing to wickedness in the City and the thalidomide babies tragedy. Another example, and one which the "free press" of the capitalist world everywhere stuck as a feather in its cap in the seventies, was the role of some American newspapers in laying bare the Watergate scandals that produced a constitutional convulsion in the strongest of the capitalist countries. Obviously the free press of the advanced capitalist countries differs from the state-gazette organs of military and fascist dictatorships. As a reflector of changing opinion and new social and political currents it is evidently more free, or less unfree, than the controlled press of junta-type regimes, in the same way as bourgeois democracy offers better opportunities for progress and social change than the various forms of open dictatorship.

All the media also reflected ruling-class differences over tactics, often severe. The press was repeatedly seen to be striking out a line apparently independent of governments. This happened in Britain over Eden's Suez adventure in 1956. In America the media appeared to play a part of their own in the movement of opinion that led to

President Johnson's fall, and even more in the convulsion over Watergate in 1972–4. In Britain, again, the immense publicity given in 1973 to the revival of the Liberal Party—motivated basically by a desire to increase the political options open to capital in its struggle with labour —contributed to the "free" image of the media. Woven right into the commodity conception of newspaper freedom—because the efforts to establish it involved long and deep popular struggles—are historically formed attitudes of great force; press freedom is seen as a liberty of the same kind and order as freedom of meeting and association, freedom of religion, Habeas Corpus and the rule of law, the right to vote and all the other social gains based on individual right which are commonly held to make up the British constitution. So the press, conducted as a commerce, can appear, alone among big business enterprises, as a hallowed institution. Its controllers, motivated by money-getting and power mania in varying proportions, dig themselves deep into this bunker to ward off attacks. This special institution, this "fourth estate" occupying apparently a position apart from government, industry, parties and classes, holds a strong base. It has survived widespread awareness that it is owned and managed by very rich men in their own interests and those of their class and defends the private profit system of which most of its readers are victims, consistently opposes the labour and trade union movement to which most of its readers belong, is often caught redhanded in lies and dishonesty, acknowledges no responsibility to any social verification and neither admits nor corrects its errors.

The press declares no interests. Members of Parliament come under a legal obligation to declare any interest they have in matters under debate. Press owners, with powers vastly exceeding those of any lobbyist in Parliament, are under no such limitation. Yet their involvement in the profit system, in the interests of employers in conflict with organised labour, and on the side of imperialism in the global clash, is total.

Instead of any declaration of interest, Fleet Street deluges the public with sanctimonious drivel about its sacred role in democracy as a guardian of truth. A typical effusion was a *Times* leader (July 10, 1973) urging printworkers in dispute with the Newspaper Publishers Association not to stop the papers, since "the interruption of the press is the interruption of an essential part of our democratic system". It argued that a report which it carried on the same day in its news columns about Portuguese massacres in Mozambique illustrated this indispensable role of the press. "If Portugal had a free press, the first information might have been expected in a Portuguese rather than an English paper. If *The Times* did not get out, the people who did the killing in Mozambique would receive at least a temporary reprieve from world knowledge of what they had done. With all the faults of the newspapers —from ours to those of *The Sun*—a free press remains an essential part of the structure of liberty; frequent industrial disputes, as the United States has shown, are a threat to the variety as well as to the publication of a free press." It would be hard to decide whether impudence or hypocrisy were the more monumental in these words from the journal with the most consistent anti-union and colonialist record of any British newspaper down the years.

The distortion of thought and feeling by the media has been likened to the pollution of cities and the environment. Through a hundred channels flows a socially degenerating poison of mis-information, half-information and the manipulation of every human reaction. The democratic process, if it means anything at all, means that public decisions should be preluded by a clash of viewpoints in which every section and trend has its just chance to defend its interests and assert its solutions. Monopolised media stifle this dialectical, creative conflict.

The idea is ceaselessly insinuated that popular demonstrations, strikes, protests and assemblies are not the fulfilment of an accepted social right but a sinful departure from the norm—displays of arrogance, of will to violence, of anti-social behaviour. If these are pressed to the point where they threaten to gain a large or even a majority influence they are put down to the workings of agitators, freaks, foreign agents or, in the latest coinage for the February 1974 election, simply "militants" or "extremists". Newspapers which will make a noisy scene about the scandals constantly exposed will assiduously bury them as soon as the moment of public indignation has passed, to return to their normal business of slandering all the popular and progressive forces and, above all else, attempting to isolate the active part of the labour movement, always the most strongly flowing source of discontent and rebellion. The brainwashing never succeeds entirely; it has to be constantly raised in volume and increased in cunning. But though the money power's takeover of the spiritual realm can never win, it can and will fog every public issue, distort all decision making, and subvert democracy, until the enormous disparity between the

means at its command and those available on the side of progress is
challenged and remedied. More rigorously subjected than anything
else to processing by the media are Marxism and the Communist movement; the first is almost altogether interpreted either by anti-Marxists
or non-Communist professors of this teaching; the second is rarely
permitted to speak through its own spokesmen.

Radio and television began not directly within the market field, like
newspapers, but on the basis of government investment and various
forms of public control. Initially their freedom theory based itself on
statutory obligations allegedly aimed at securing impartiality of news
coverage and comment. In the sixties and seventies, however, when
private interests massively invaded this sphere with commercial
("independent") television and radio, depending as directly on advertising as the newspapers, the newer media were also infused with the
commodity freedom notion; this helped them to fend off democratic
demands for wider access and to weld the main media together under
ever more tightly knit big business ownership. This commercial invasion aimed partly at profit and partly to increase the direct control of
big business over television and radio. Backed by large campaign
funds and carrying on sustained lobbying and public relations drives,
it was represented to be an attempt to provide a healthy alternative to
the BBC monopoly and strengthen freedom of choice. In practice, it
strengthened monopoly and further reduced this freedom of choice.

The products of the communications network, although the system
itself enjoyed little respect, found eager consumers. They sought with
considerable success to wear the appearance of a greater variety, re-
sponsiveness to new ideas and situations, trendy controversialism and
sympathy with the permissive society (the pseudo-freedom of the
admen) than the media had shown in earlier days.

In what can be called normal conditions, the media's approach was
not to suppress—though whole areas of public interest were ignored—
but to process thought and feeling, to hold up a distorting mirror to
events and opinion changes. However, the cultivated appearance of
total freedom of communicators to cater for the market concealed a
quite other real relationship between the controllers of press, radio,
television and advertising, and the ruling establishment. "Commodity"
freedom masked a growing monopolist control and management of
all the media.

Apart from the direct power of veto by advertisers—mainly held in reserve since the scandals of the Munich period, but still decisive in the last resort—various means of direct and indirect state interference continued to form a built-in regulator of the "market" forces in the media. For the press, the Official Secrets Act (and the D notices warning editors off sensitive subjects), the easily manipulated law of libel, and a common law still providing a teeming arsenal of available weapons against freedom of publication, imposed the restrictions familiar to every editor and newspaper writer. A stream of briefings from official and big business sources flowed into every newspaper, radio and television editorial office. And the endless shifts and turns of policy by the millionaires' papers—most notoriously the overnight abandonment of opposition to the Common Market by the Beaverbrook press early in the seventies at a critical moment—were often dictated by no discernible sales-catching consideration but decided on political grounds by the press moguls and their City brethren.

Another of the defences rushed up by the undemocratic press was its denunciation of the press of the Socialist countries. Especially in the post-Stalin years, this press was held up as a warning example of perils alleged to be inescapable in any change from unlimited private enterprise in news.

The only available alternative to the commercial type of freedom, it was claimed, was a press controlled by the State, or by a single party in a one-party system, and giving a single account and interpretation of events. The press of the Socialist countries was portrayed as a mere sieve producing a single and highly selective and censored version of events, in contrast with the diversity and freedom from censorship of the Western press. Certainly many readers, beguiled by the discussive and controversial manners and appearance of British and other Western papers, readily accepted this hostile picture.

The press of the Socialist countries has its own problems. Its lateness in giving news and frequent shortcomings on the informational level, its heavy concentration on industrial production drives, its lack of the "human interest" coverage of the kind that has long spiced Western journalism, and the one-sided nature of the discussion which it carried on a range of social, cultural and artistic matters, have laid it open in various ways to attack in the West. Yet the millionaires' criticisms of this press remain basically dishonest and specious. Their caricatural picture exaggerates grossly the uniformity of the papers of the Socialist world and at the same time turns a blind eye to the real uniformity of their own newspapers. In their picture, one of the chief crimes of the press in the Socialist countries is its refusal to yield obeisance to either "news values" or the "free communications" myth. These, presented as absolute conceptions good for all mankind, serve in reality as vehicles for the social values that the profits system seeks to spread. It is vital to note here that the press of the socialist countries developed not out of triumphant liberalism speaking for capitalism in its ascendant phase, but from the revolutionary working-class movement; this created in its press one of the many means of organisation and production for Socialism, and for mass education and enlightenment on the largest and most rapid scale that history records.

The press of the Socialist countries from the first replaced, almost everywhere, a State-run press used by autocratic and fascist regimes to poison public opinion. The Socialist press, which was in its substance the most democratic the world had yet seen, carrying through a historic work of real popular representation and self-enlightenment of the working people which our own Chartists would have instantly recognised to correspond to their "knowledge is power" creed, ran into its own problems of growth, to which various answers were found. We should not, however, allow the Fleet Street moneybags to use the shortcomings and troubles of this press as a bogy against press democracy in Britain.

For the British people it is not a question, in any case, of making a choice between the two systems and their doctrines as exemplified in *Pravda* and *The Times*. The transplantation of the Soviet and Socialist countries' press traditions and methods would obviously neither work nor be acceptable. Indeed, the repeated claim that this is the nature of the choice facing Britain's labour and democratic movement is itself one of the principal means employed to confuse the issue and so protect the basic ownership and control of the press and other media by capital in its private or state, or combined, forms.

The real choice is between democratic control and monopoly control. In the newspaper field, this involves changes in ownership; these are as necessary to a properly functioning democracy as ownership changes are necessary to a properly functioning economy and industry. Socialist advance in Britain requires the social auditing of the press and other media and the reassertion of democracy, equally as it requires the national ownership and control of the major industries and of the banks, and the democratisation of the state apparatus and armed forces, which have been known for so long to be basic conditions for real social change.

The second half of this proposition is today widely understood and accepted. Too few people active in the labour and trade union movement yet recognise, however, that an authentic freedom of the media must rank now as an equal necessity, providing a main key to progress in electoral, wage-front and social welfare battles. Without it, these will be harder to win and well-nigh impossible to consolidate. "No communication without representation" might be the democratic watchword for the situation at which we have arrived.

One obstacle to an understanding of this necessity is the power of the "state press" bogy already discussed. Another is the constantly renewed illusion that there exists a wide consumer's choice among the products of the media. Readers rebelling against the muck-raking, sexationalism, reactionary prejudices and blatant absence of any principle except profit-making displayed by *Mirror* or *Sun* are free, it is argued, to console themselves with their "investigative" *Guardian*, their "quality" Sunday paper debating everything impartially, or the frequent critical examinations of press antics conducted on radio and television. Yet this freedom is a delusion, and more and more widely felt to be so, despite many individual achievements in the best traditions of journalism in revealing truth on particular questions. At the heart of this "freedom" is the flaw to which Marx drew attention when, almost at the dawn of the modern democratic press, in an article in the *Rheinische Zeitung* of May 19, 1842, he declared that "the first freedom of the press consists in its not being a trade".

Today's giant development of the media as commodity producers sprang from the commerce-based press of early capitalism. In the Victorian heyday, the full consequences could not appear. Newspapers were at first relatively small-scale production, and even after that stage had been passed journals serving minorities could still for a long time be produced independently with small means. Moreover, strong political and social interests—based not only on the labour movement but also on the warring factions within pre-monopoly capitalism—clung to newspaper publication as a hallmark of their identity and independence. The press as a universal caterer, as a branch of Communications Inc., grew up step by step in pace with the great consolidation of

big business interests and capitalist state power to resist the tide of
Socialism from its forward surge in the eighties and nineties of last
century. That was the basic impulse. The means through which it
worked was the steep increase in the cost of producing newspapers.
This elevated the always present subsidy element—coming mainly from
advertising but partly also from politically motivated expenditure—
into a prime condition of newspapers' existence. Newspapers have
become entirely dependent on subsidy, and on constantly selling, alone
among commodities, at well below their cost of production. The
commercial principle, once so devoutly held to be the sole real basis
for press freedom, has turned into its destroyer. This principle itself
has also become closely fused with direct state and Establishment practices of guidance and control—which always suspend commodity
freedom when it is judged necessary to do so in crises and emergencies.
State influence and big business ownership together mould the press
and all the media in their image. The packaging simply covers the
disagreeable faces of the social and human values that they purvey:
the relentless anti-labour and anti-union propaganda, the racist and
jingo sentiments, the false glamourising of royalty and the upper crust,
the trivialising of great issues, the acceptance of war and imperialism
as an inescapable part of man's lot, and all the greed and inhumanity
of what we today call the rat race and the Chartist papers in earlier
days knew as "the cannibal state of society".

The phoney package quickly wears thin. Hence the grand competitive to-and-fro busying with new brand marks, stunts and "campaigns"
designed to deck the shoddy product with shining armour, the growing shyness of press proprietors about being too visibly linked to
political party, and the swift succession of "new" policies. Yet the
decay of the freedom legend is irreparable, as even the defenders of the
system appear sometimes to recognise.

The problem was frankly put by Mr. E. J. B. Rose, editorial director
of the *Westminster Press*★ writing in *The Times* 1973 supplement on

---

★ A prime example of press-and-City unity. The paper is owned by Pearson
Longman, which also owns the *Financial Times*, *The Banker*, *History Today*,
Apollo, *The Economist*, *Professional Administration*, *Antiques Yearbook*, *Oil and
Petroleum Yearbook* and *Mining Yearbook*. And the parent company, S. Pearson
and Son Ltd. owns additionally an American and a Canadian oil company,
Lazard Brothers, the merchant bankers, an insurance company, and the Whitehall
Trust finance company.

the state of the Western press. He wrote:

> "In capitalist systems the forces of the market lead to concentrations of ownership, to mergers and the creation of monopolies which tend to eliminate independent editorial voices and may deprive the people of a real choice of views . . . in many free-press countries commercial pressures are more lethal to the health of the press than the hostility of governments or the constraints of the law."

This issue of *The Times*, while it continued to define press freedom exclusively in terms of independence from government controls, showed nevertheless how in country after country of the West the market conception of the press was leading to its growing unfreedom. It recorded gloomily that doubt was again in fashion about "the ability of individual freedom (of which press freedom is an essential component) to survive the pressures of the twentieth century". It noted in particular an alarming situation in Italy where the purchase earlier in the year of a 50 per cent share in *Il Messaggero* by a prominent industrialist "was universally seen as a political move to impose a right-wing line on what had hitherto been a courageously independent and critical paper". It added that the danger is not merely the economic concentration threat but that the few businessmen into whose hands the whole of the press could fall might be "deliberately seeking and using control of the press to promote right-wing policies and possibly even to encourage a neo-fascist revival".*

The same year brought a grim example and warning of the jeopardy in which monopoly press control places democracy. A major part in the preparation of the fascist coup in Chile was played by such journals as the mass circulation daily *El Mercurio*, which freely fomented the economic disruption and sabotage without which the murderous blow could not have been struck, and whose editor was rewarded with office in the military junta. *The Times*, which justified the Chile coup, was arguing a few months later that the trade unions' resistance to government wage-freezing raised the question of whether democracy could survive in Britain itself.

Clearly here is no marginal question involving freedom or democracy in the abstract, but a live-or-die matter for labour and Socialist

---

* Mr Rose added that "ironically enough, the main safeguard for variety of opinion and news coverage is the existence of an abundant party press, particularly that of the Italian Communist Party".

movements intent on real business. Right-wing elements controlled many newspapers and radio stations in Chile. For Britain the plans for commercial interest to run a public communications network of sixty radio stations the implementation of which began in 1973, raise sinister possibilities, and the Labour government formed after the February, 1974, election should be obliged to scrap these plans.

Public resistance to the communications brainwash gathered force after the press merger scandals of the early sixties. From diverse backgrounds, a hundred small Davids emerged to challenge—or simply to mock—the press Goliath. Technically, this dissident press ranged from professionally produced and printed journals to roneoed sheets, and in its contents mirrored a wide range of protest movements large and small. Its unifying cause was the rejection of the media themselves. In his book *The Trials of OZ*, Tony Palmer said that *OZ* arose because "it believed that proper newspapers either ignored what was happening or distorted it". Among editorial workers on the "proper newspapers", the Free Communications Group arose and effectively exposed the press lords' conduct of both their newspapers and their industrial relations. It sought a cure in increased editorial control of newspapers by the journalists employed on them, to enable the press to function as a true forum. Periodicals styling themselves "underground"—*Private Eye* and the *Black Dwarf*, *OZ* and *Time Out*—accompanied by a big expansion of student union journals at universities and numerous small neighbourhood, tenants' and squatters' papers—appeared for shorter or longer lives. Working the vein of "instant journalism" that is almost as old as print itself, they created new rebel followings.

The Free Communications Group and its journal approached the problem mainly from a professional journalistic viewpoint, seeking for answers within the existing structure and ownership. They expressed the bitter frustrations of Fleet Street communicators in revolt against what they felt to be their servile status. They showed how deeply disillusion with the media had penetrated the communicators themselves. However, their criticisms, corrosive and eloquent though they often were, by-passed the fundamental question of newspaper ownership and of democratic representation in their control.

The "undergound press" reflected the credibility crisis, and stimulated the discontent, especially among students, young workers, housewives, and many ranks of the socially deprived. Its links, how-

ever, with the organised working-class and trade union movement
were on the whole either non-existent or extremely tenuous.

In this movement, among the traditional creators and champions
of press freedom, resistance grew after the Tory election victory of
1970. Many trade union journals increased their commitment to
Socialism. Widely welcomed was the launching of *Labour Weekly* as
the organ of the National Executive of the Labour Party. Labour MPs
and print union leaders continued their campaign for legislation to help
the weaker papers. The general secretary of NATSOPA, Mr. Richard
Briginshaw, proposed late in 1973 the taking over of the Reed newsprint and newspaper (*Mirror* group) empire to form the basis for a
national printing corporation. He made clear that he was not proposing
a government press but "a process to compete with the existing one-
party press in Britain. It would be a large-scale operation allowing for
the widest democratic expression." Mr. Wilson and his colleagues
"should eschew the idea of some small-time operation of buying up a
small country printer", Mr. Briginshaw added, in the light of reports
that the Labour leader had some such project in mind as a sop to throw
to the press reformers.

Underpinning the revolt against the monopoly media, a number of
journals emerged or increased their influence in the seventies, particularly in the struggle to defend basic trade union rights. Ideas and moods
generated among workers new to active class struggles, and among
students looking for truthful answers and for exits from the social,
economic and cultural chaos, offered fertile ground for a wide range
of left and lefter-than-left groups each with its journal, which split
and reformed endlessly.

Among the Trotskyist journals early in 1974, only the *Workers Press*
(organ of the Workers Revolutionary Party, formerly the Socialist
Labour League) was published daily, and its circulation figure was not
given. Weekly journals included *Socialist Worker* (International Socialists) and *Red Weekly* (International Marxist Group).

While varying in their interpretation of Trotskyist doctrine, they
all had in common a divisive approach to the labour movement, expressed in sharp attacks on left trade union leaders and left Labour
MPs, and in criticism of the Communist Party and the *Morning Star*
for advocating left unity.

The mainstream struggle for a democratic press remains, as it has been since the launching of the *Daily Herald* in 1911, the effort to sustain a daily newspaper of the labour movement, one that will help to fight its battles on all fronts as well as to reflect the inescapable searching debate about the way forward.

The demand for measures at least to ease the Tory and big business grip on the media has won growing support. It had no place, however, in the programme with which Labour went into the 1974 election. Both the course run by this election and its aftermath provided the labour and trade union movement with warning signals louder and clearer than any previous event had given on the capacity of press, radio and television to nullify democratic choice. They abetted the basic Tory strategy of conducting the election as an anti-union and anti-Labour power game under cover of a classic red scare. The "moderation versus extremism" terms in which they presented the choice to the electors helped mainly the Tory Party, which had chosen this as its ground of combat. And the Labour leaders' decision to compete principally on this same ground, together with the Liberals' successful theft of some six million votes by their pose as the very princes of moderation opposed alike to both the Labour and the Tory "extremes" and records of failure, served essentially to strengthen the illusory and fraudulent terms on which the contest was conducted.

If the exercise by the media failed in its immediate aim—when the voters rejected the Tory demand for a mandate for "firmness"—its longer-term aims of promoting the emergence of an alternative non-Socialist main opposition in Parliament and preparing the way for a coalition government under "national" colours remained intact; they were pursued without an instant's pause after the result had been declared. The fundamental reason for the collapse of the Tory gamble was the earlier advances made by the labour movement left; this had installed significant demands (including measures of nationalisation, the re-negotiation of Common Market entry terms, action to check rising prices, and a number of social reforms) in the Labour election programme. These summoned forth grass-roots working-class energies sufficient to frustrate the three-pronged offensive of Tories, Liberals and the leagued powers of the media. But if the Tory defeat was conclusive, the Labour victory was not so: the offensive reduced Labour's share of the total vote—in the country with proportionately the largest working class in the world—to 37.2 per cent, its lowest level since 1931, and led to a minority Labour government which was confronted from its first day with an ultimatium requiring it to become the prisoner of big business or to give way to a Tory or Tory-dominated government.

More sharply than ever previously the choice for a Labour government emerged as one between unceremonious butchering off in the corridors of power and fighting in full view of the people for the policies on which it had been elected—and doing so above all in the field of the working-class and democratic struggle outside Parliament which now held the only key to its survival. After the momentous 1974 election, this field became decisive to a degree for which the 1926 general strike, the 1911–13 industrial struggles, Chartism and the two-year fight for the great Reform Bill of 1832, supply the only approximate precedents. This was the situation which projected the question of a real democracy in all the media to a top priority position for independent working-class politics and free trade unionism. The Committee on Communications set up by the Labour Party after its 1973 conference—it conducted its proceedings in much too leisurely and unpublicised a manner during the run-up to the election—faced after the election responsibilities as critical as any in the directly economic and social field confronting the new government.

The election experience proved all the seriousness and urgency of the problem for the Labour movement more clearly than any single event in its recent annals had done. The notorious abuse made by the media of opinion polls, their remorseless anti-Labour and anti-union bias, and their virtual suppression of voices of opposition from outside the charmed circle of the official Lab., Lib. and Tory approved paladins, stirred reactions ranging from anger and mistrust to the cynicism of "a plague on all their houses" among wide sections of the people. And their refusal of anything but minor and sporadic hearings to the publicly proscribed militants and red irresponsibles, whom they cast as scapegoats both for the economic crisis and the regrettable necessity for the election itself, helped to prevent the con-game from being sufficiently clearly exposed.

The media game failed, and to an extent the media shared in the Tory downfall. We have already seen, however, that they always contrive to live with their own defeats and failures, which are never admitted, and constantly rearrange their shopwindowfuls of phoney goods according to establishment requirements. Only true competition of news and views, only popular control, and democratic ownership in the case of the press, will end this shameful state of affairs.

Meanwhile the need grows more pressing for immediate curbs on the press lords' powers, as these become more arbitrary and irresponsible. The central concern here will remain the defence and promotion of the *Morning Star* as the only daily newspaper already actually serving the needs of the active movement. Only a *daily* journal, only a journal of *news*, can effectively answer the rich men's newspapers amid the fast-moving events which all the media mirror back to readers and viewers with such immediacy, instant interpretation and mind-conditioning skills. Only a paper owned by its readers and independent of the millionaires can keep alive the principle of *representation* in the press which inspired all the poor men's guardians of earlier days.

The labour movement will forget at its peril that the measure of press freedom won in two centuries of struggle has no guarantee in law or constitution and that, in the words of T. J. Wooler in the opening number of the *Black Dwarf* in the year of Peterloo, the real freedom of the people lies in their power and will to uphold their liberties. If the anti-union legislation of 1971 did not actually land any editors and publishers in court as illegal "strike inducers", that immunity owed nothing to the promises of the Solicitor General (that the legislation would never be used against the press) and everything to the success of the trade unions and their members in rendering the legislation largely inoperable.

The 1973 conference of the TUC deplored "the threat to the freedom of the press implicit in Section 96 of the Industrial Relations Act" and pledged itself to resist its use to "interfere with free reporting and comment". Section 96 is aimed at persons who "knowingly induce" another person to break a contract to which that other person is a party "unless the inducer does so within his authority on behalf of a union". The journalists' trade union leader Mr. Ken Morgan pointed out that his members, standing in the same jeopardy under the Act as all other trade unionists, ran an additional professional danger; Section 96 could "catch the journalist who reports or comments in any way sympathetically on the workers' case in an industrial dispute".

The Act, and the National Industrial Relations Court which it set up, threatened free trade unionism and press freedom alike. These causes, which we saw linked together in a common struggle at the start of this survey, depend still more inseparably on each other today.

It is time, and past time, to achieve the aim announced by the *Northern Star* in 1843, of "a press for the representation of the Labouring Classes, whose interests from time immemorial have been shamelessly neglected". The changing of the papers into democratic, socially conducted organs is now a necessity dictated by every requirement of the movement to bring about fundamental social and economic change. It will be no leap into the dark of a regimented press—as the regimenting masters of the media are never tired of claiming that it can only be—but a renewal of traditions which are deep-rooted in our democratic and labour movement story.

This record has explored these traditions and tried to set them in the perspective of today's working-class and progressive struggles, in the conviction that they bear lessons of inestimable value and provide every ground for confidence that these struggles will end in victory.

Sources

Main sources for this survey—in addition to newspaper files at the Bishopsgate Institute, Marx House Memorial Library, the London School of Economics and the British Museum—included the following:

PRESS

Aspinall, A., *Politics and the Press, 1780–1850*

Ayerst, D., *Guardian, Biography of a Newspaper*

Boston, R., *The Press we Deserve*

Cole, H., *Socialism and the Press*

Collet, C. D., *History of the Taxes on Knowledge*

Dutt, R. P., Requiem for the *Herald*, Press Freedom (*Labour Monthly*, March 1964 and February 1967)

Fox-Bourne, H. R., *English Newspapers*

Glenton, G. and Pattinson, W., *The Last Chronicle of Bouverie Street*

Grant, J., *The Newspaper Press; Its Origin, Progress and Present Position* (1870)

Halloran, J. D., Elliot, P. and Murdoch, G., *A Case Study*

Hutt, A., *The Changing Newspaper, 1622–1973*, The Passchendaele of the Press (*Marxism Today*, March 1961)

Hollis, P., *The Pauper Press; A Study in Working Class Radicalism of the 1830s*

Kidd, R. (NCCL), *The Fight for a Free Press*

Labour Research Department, *Who Owns the Press?*

Matthews, G., *Press Lords* v. *Press Freedom* (pamphlet)

Morison, S., *The English Newspaper*

Moonman, E. (ed.), *The Press, A Case for Commitment* (Fabian Tract 391)

Read, D., *People and Press (1790–1850), Opinion in Three English Cities*

Robertson Scott, J. W., *The Life and Death of a Newspaper*

Rust, W., *The Story of the Daily Worker*

Steed, H. W., *The Press*

Thompson, E. P., *The Struggle for a Free Press* (pamphlet)
Todd, J., *The Big Sell: The Structure and Strategy of the Mass Media*
Wickwar, W. H., *The Struggle for the Freedom of the Press (1819–1832*
Williams, J. B., *The History of English Journalism*
Wintour, C., *Pressures on the Press*

GENERAL

Altick, R. D., *The English Common Reader, 1800–1900*
Aspinall, A., *The Early English Trade Unions*
Beales, H. L., *The Early English Socialists*
Beer, M., *A History of British Socialism*
Brailsford, H. N., *The Levellers and the English Revolution*
Butler, J. R. M., *The Passing of the Great Reform Bill*
Cole, G. D. H. and Postgate, R., *The Common People, 1746–1946*
Cole, G. D. H., *A Short History of the British Working Class Movement,
    Chartists Portraits, The Life of William Cobbett*
Coltham, S., *Essays in Labour History* (Beehive)
Halevy, E., *A History of the English People in the 19th Century*
Hammond, J. L. and B., *The Town Labourer, The Village Labourer* and
    The Town Labourer, The Bleak Age
Harrison, R., *The English Defence of the Commune, before the Socialists*
Hobsbawm, E., *The Age of Revolution, Labour's Turning Point, Labouring
    Men, Captain Swing*
Hovell, M., *The Chartist Movement*
Hutt, A., *This Final Crisis, The Postwar History of the British Working
    Class, British Trade Unionism—A Short History*, Karl Marx as a
    Journalist (*Marxism Today*, May 1966)
Jackson, T. A., *Trials of British Freedom*
Jefferys, J. B., *The Story of the Engineers, Labour's Formative Years*
Klugmann, J., *History of the Communist Party of Great Britain*
Maccoby, S., *English Radicalism, 1832–1852*
Morton, A. L. and Tate, G., *The British Labour Movement 1770–1920*
Pelham, H., *The Origins of the Labour Party*
Pollard, S., *Essays in Labour History*
Postgate, R. W., *The Builders' History*
Rothstein, T. A., *From Chartism to Labourism*
Rude, G., *Wilkes and Liberty*
Thompson, E. P., *The Making of the English Working Class*
Webb, S. and B., *History of Trade Unionism*

BIOGRAPHICAL

Aldred, G. A., *Richard Carlile, Agitator; His Life and Times: Jail Journal and other writings by Richard Carlile*

Barker, A. G., *Henry Hetherington, 1792–1849*

Bamford, S., *Passages in the Life of a Radical*

Braddon, R. *Roy Thomson of Fleet Street*

Cudlipp, H., *Publish and Be Damned*

Fyfe, Hamilton, *Northcliffe, An Intimate Biography*

Holyoake, G. J., *Sixty Years of an Agitator's Life*

Hyndman, H. M., *Record of an Adventurous Life*

King, C., *Without Fear or Favour*

Koss, S. K., *Fleet Street Radical—A. G. Gardiner and the Daily News*

Lovett, W., *The Life and Struggles of William Lovett in Pursuit of Bread, Knowledge and Freedom*

McKombie, W., *Memoirs of Alexander Bethune*

Page Arnot, R., *William Morris, The Man and the Myth*

Pound, R. and Harmsworth, G., *Northcliffe*

Postgate, R., *The Life of George Lansbury*

Saville, J., *Ernest Jones, Chartist*

Schoyen, A. R., *The Chartist Challenge*

Thompson, E. P., *William Morris, Romantic to Revolutionary*

Thompson, L., *Portrait of an Englishman*

Torr, D., *Tom Mann and His Times*

Wrench, E., *Geoffrey Dawson and Our Times*

DOCUMENTS

Cole, G. D. H. and Filson, A. W., *British Working Class Movements: Select Documents, 1789–1875*

Cole, G. D. H. and Cole, M., *The Opinions of William Cobbett*

Hollis, P. (ed.), *The Poor Man's Guardian, Facsimile Edition, and Introduction*, Merlin Press

Kovalev, U. V., *Anthology of Chartist Literature*

Lenin On Britain, Marxist Leninist Library, Lawrence & Wishart

Lindsay, J. and Rickword, E., *A Handbook of Freedom*

Marx-Engels, *Selected Correspondence* (Lawrence & Wishart edition)

Morris, M., *From Cobbett to the Chartists*

Saville, J. (ed.), *The Red Republican and the Friend of the People, Facsimile Edition*, Merlin Press

Index of Papers

A selective list of papers mentioned in this record. In brackets are the principal editor or publisher and/or organisation with which the paper was associated.

Description: C—Chartist, Comm—Communist, L—Labour representation or Labour Party, O—Owenite, R—Radical, S—Socialist, T—Tory, TU—trade unionist, W—Whig/Liberal.

CHAPTERS 1–3

Moderate (Mabbott), 1648–9 (Leveller)
North Briton (Wilkes), 1762–3 (W)
Briton (Smollett), 1762–3 (T)
Hog's Wash, later *Politics for the People* (Eaton), 1793–5 (R)
Pig's Meat (Spence), 1793–6 (R)
Tribune (Thelwall, London Corresponding Society), 1795–6 (R)
Moral and Political Magazine (London Corresponding Society), 1796 (R)
Patriot, 1792–3 (R)
Cabinet 1794–5 (R)
Cambridge Intelligencer, 1793–1803 (R)
Political Register (Cobbett), 1802–35 (R)
Twopenny Register (Cobbett), 1816–20 (R)
Political Register (Sherwin), 1817–19 (R)
Black Dwarf (Wooler), 1817–24 (R)
Republican (Carlile), 1819–26 (R)
Anti-Cobbett (Canning), 1817 (T)
Shadgett's Weekly Review, 1818 (T)
White Dwarf (Merle and Shadgett), 1817–18 (T)
Reformists' Register (Hone), 1818–19 (R)
Gorgon (Wade), 1818–19 (R, TU)
Medusa (Davison), 1819–20 (R)

CHAPTER 6

Northern Star (O'Connor, Harney), 1837–52 (C)
Charter, (Lovell, London Trades), 1839–40 (C)
National, 1839 (C)
Operative, 1838–9 (C)
Southern Star (O'Brien), 1840 (C)
Champion (Cobbetts), 1840 (C)
London Democrat (Harney), 1839 (C)
Scottish Patriot, 1839–41 (C)
Red Republican (later *Friend of the People*) (Harney), 1850–1 (C)
People's Paper (Jones), 1852–8 (C)
Chartist Circular (Universal Suffrage Central Committee for Scotland),
    1839–2 (C)
Democratic Review (Harney), 1849–50 (C)
Labourer (O'Connor), 1847–8 (C)
United Irishman (Mitchel), 1848 (Irish Democrat)

CHAPTER 7

Beehive (Potter), 1861–75 (TU)
Notes to the People (Jones), 1851–2 (C)
Workingman, 1853–8 (TU)
British Miner (later *The Miner, Miner and Workman's Advocate, Workman's Advocate*, and *Commonwealth*), 1862–7 (TU)
Reynolds' Weekly Newspaper, 18 August 1850–14 September 1924 (R)
Lloyd's Weekly News (later *Sunday News*), 1842–1931 (R)

CHAPTER 8

Justice (Quelch), 1884–1925 (S)
Commonweal (Morris), 1885–94 (S)
Labour Standard (London Trades Council), 1881–2 (TU)
Labour Elector (Champion), 1888–94 (L)
Link (Besant), 1888 (S)
Clarion (Blatchford), 1891–1932 (S)
Yorkshire Factory Times (Burgess), 1889–1919 (TU, L)
Workman's Times, 1890–4 (TU, L)
Worker's Cry (Smith), 1891 (L)
Labour Leader (Hardie, ILP), 1889–1923 (L)
Daily Herald (Lansbury, Labour Party, TUC), 1911–64 (S, TU)

General Index